The Regulation of Transnational Mergers in International and European Law

Nijhoff International Trade Law Series

VOLUME 2

The Regulation of Transnational Mergers in International and European Law

By

Dimitris Liakopoulos and Armando Marsilia

MARTINUS
NIJHOFF
PUBLISHERS

LEIDEN • BOSTON
2010

This book is printed on acid-free paper.

Library of Congress Cataloging-in-Publication Data

Liakopoulos, Demetres I.
The regulation of transnational mergers in international and European law / by Dimitris Liakopoulos and Armando Marsilia.
p. cm. — (Nijhoff International trade ; 2)
Includes bibliographical references and index.
ISBN 978-90-04-17771-0 (hardback : alk. paper)
1. Consolidation and merger of corporations—Law and legislation—European Union countries. 2. Antitrust law—European Union countries. 3. International business enterprises—Law and legislation—European Union countries. 4. Consolidation and merger of corporations—Law and legislation—United States. 5. Antitrust law—United States. 6. International business enterprises—Law and legislation—United States. I. Romani, Mauro. II. Title.
K1362.L53 2010
346'.06626—dc22

2009041696

ISSN 1877-7392
ISBN 978 90 04 17771 0

PRINTED IN THE NETHERLANDS

Armando Marsilia:
To my parents

Dimitris Liakopoulos:
To my family

CONTENTS

PREFACE

This is a timely contribution to the scholarly literature on the regulation of transnational mergers. Professor Dimitris Liakopoulos and Professor Armando Marsilia are well qualified to undertake the study. Practitioners and scholars of merger law will benefit from going deeper into the chapters of this book.

Merger control tends to be problematic. Private parties often have close relationships with their national regulator. 'Capture' is a way of describing the relationship between major actors and their regulators. Both regulators and their political masters may be subject to capture in different and sometimes conflicting ways. They may wish to create national champions or to promote one company or industry over another, rarely with any sustainable political or economic rationale. It follows from this that there is much potential for conflicts between regulators. But even without such political problems, coordinating process and outcomes may create problems, also if one regards this as a matter of regulatory risk from the point of view of one of the companies or investors involved.

EU merger control in its modern form goes back some twenty years. It became subject to a regime with a central role for the European Commission with the 1989 Merger Regulation based on one-stop shop and strict deadlines. It was not pushed forward by industry, and national regulators opposed it. Notwithstanding its obvious advantages in terms of lowering regulatory cost and uncertainties, it was only after it was well into its implementation that it received any industry support.

US and EU cooperation also has an established history, with achievements and also continuing challenges. The political dimension, and the mere administrative and technical issues, still pose considerable problems. A fully rational system may lie some time ahead, and it may still not have found effective advocates.

In this book Professor Dimitris Liakopoulos and Professor Armando Marsilia analyse the problems, and they have considered different responses. The topic of this book is 'The regulation of transnational mergers in international and European law'. A pressing problem associated with the regulation of transnational mergers is allocation of jurisdiction. More than one country may wish to exert jurisdiction and apply its national competition law, and may have fully legitimate interests in regulating the anti-competitive effects a merger may have in its territory. This leads to a risk of inconsistent decisions on the legality of mergers. Competition laws and their application by regulating authorities may diverge. The authors argue for regulatory approaches sensitive to the transnational nature of mergers and extending cooperation between competition authorities. They are in favour of bilateral cooperation agreements so that countries can better coordinate the enforcement activities. However, their view is that this is not sufficient. Transnational mergers should also be regulated multilateral competition rules created through instruments of hard law.

Professor Dimitris Liakopoulos and Professor Armando Marsilia point out how every attempt to introduce legally binding multilateral competition rules has failed because of the opposition of countries which perceive this to constitute unacceptable limitations of sovereignty. So there is doubt as to the realism of the preferred hard law route. The alternate route is to introduce multilateral competition rules through instruments of soft law. National sovereignty is not threatened by these instruments to the same degree, and the reverse side is that countries may not implement soft law instruments.

Professor Dimitris Liakopoulos and Professor Armando Marsilia advocate the creation of an international merger control framework (IMCF) for the regulation of transnational mergers. The IMCF will rest on an informal and a formal pillar. The informal pillar includes non-legally binding competition principles. It would go some way in countering the risk of non-implementation if these principles are consistent with the concepts of legitimacy and efficiency, and in a regime of peer reviews and assistance programmes. The formal pillar includes bilateral cooperation agreements applying to mergers affecting the countries having concluded the agreements. The authors regard it to be an essential pre-condition for the effectiveness of bilateral agreements, is ensured by a regime of a high level of cooperation at least equal to that ensured by the informal pillar.

This is the second book in The Nijhoff International Trade Law Series. The Series is a forum for important and original research. It moves across the boundaries that have divided the law and include studies of trade law subjects that would fall within the fields of public and private international and comparative law. Comparative law is increasingly used as a tool in the making of law at national, regional and international levels. Private international law is now often affected by international conventions, and the issues faced by classical conflict rules are dealt with by substantive harmonization of law under international auspices. Mixed international arbitrations, especially those involving state economic activity, raise questions of public and private international law, while in many fields (such as the protection of human rights and democratic standards, investment guarantees) international and national systems interact. National constitutional arrangements relating to 'foreign affairs', and to the implementation of international norms, are a focus of attention. The focus is on scholarly monographs, with a particular emphasis on those which are interdisciplinary in nature, both in relation to legal disciplines and the humanities and social sciences. Edited collections of essays will also be included where they are appropriate. The series is wide in scope and aims to cover studies of particular areas of substantive and of institutional law, economic and historical works, theoretical studies, and analyses of current debates.

Mads Andenas
General Editor

INTRODUCTION

I. *The aim of the book*

This book is the result of many lessons which have taken place between 2004 to 2006 at various Universities in Great Britain and seminars in the United States. The first four chapters have been written by Prof. Armando Marsilia and the remaining chapters are from the hand of Prof. Dimitris Liakopoulos. The present version is updated until March to 2009.

The purpose of this book is to explore the possible strategies for the regulation of transnational mergers. It may be helpful to clarify at the outset that the meaning given to the term of transnational mergers in the present context includes those merger operations whose economic effects are felt in the territory of more than one country.[1] The globalisation of economic activities has greatly innovated the traditional structure and dimension of markets. The liberalisation of the international trade regime, which has removed the barriers hindering the flow of trade and investment across countries, has triggered the process of globalization.[2] Accordingly, economic activities have an increasingly international breadth and firms strive to expand their business by entering foreign markets. Mergers enable firms to acquire the control of the assets they need to establish or consolidate their market positions more rapidly than is provided by mere internal growth. Thus mergers are a useful medium through which firms can pursue expansionary strategies.

---

[1] See: G. Abbamonte, V. Rabassa, "Foreclosure and vertical mergers", (2001), ECLR, 214. D. Bailey, "Standard of proof in EC merger proceedings: A common law perspective", (2003), CMLR, 845. B. Bishop, C. Caffara, "Merger control in new markets", (2001), ECLR, 31. L. Colley, "From defence to attack? Quantifying efficiency arguments in mergers", (2004), ECLR, 355. J.B. Vesterdorf, "Certain reflection on recent judgments reviewing commission merger control decisions", in M. Hoskins and W. Robinson (eds.), A true European, Essays for judge David Edward, (2993), Hart publishing, 10. J. Vickers "Competition, economics and policy", (2003), ECLR, 95. M. Broberg, The European Commissioni's jurisdiction to scutinise mergers, (2003), Kluwer. J. Cook, C. Kerse, "EC Merger control", (2005), Sweet and Maxwell. A. Jones, B. Sufrin, EC competition law: Text, cases and materials, (2004), Oxford University Press, ch. 12. D. Stephen, "Mergers and merger remedies in the EU: Assesing the consequences for competition", (2007), Cheltenham, UK, Edward Elgar. J. Cook, C. Kerse, "EC merger control", (2005), Sweet and Maxwell. D.F. Broder, "A guide to US Antitrust law", (2005), Sweet and Maxwell. S. Mathijsen, "A guide to European Union law", (2007), Sweet and Maxwell.

[2] Maher Dabbah, The Internationalization of Antitrust Policy (Cambridge University Press, Cambridge 2003) 13. Joseph Wilson, Globalization and the Limits of National Merger Control Laws (Kluwer Law International, The Hague/London/New York 2003) 29. For an explanation of the reasons underlying the merger &acquisitions activities, see UNCTAD, Press Release, TAD/INF/PR055 03/10/00, Survival in Global Business Arena is Key Driver of Cross Border Merger and Acquisition Boom. Questions Mount in Developed and Developing Countries as Merger Activities Hits Record Levels, States New UNCTAD Report, 1996.

Statistics reveal that over the last decade the number and value of transnational merger operations have constantly increased-with the notable exception of the years affected by economic recession. In 1990 the value of transnational merger and acquisition deals was $151 billion. By 1999 this figure had soared to $720 billion. The annual growth rate in the number of transnational mergers and acquisitions between 1991 and 1995 was 23%. By 1998 this rate had more than tripled, reaching 76,4%.

II. *The problems regarding the regulation of trans-national mergers*

Ictu oculi, the basic question that competition law enforcers and practitioners have to address when dealing with transnational mergers is which national competition authorities can exert jurisdiction on a given transaction. The identification of the competent competition authorities in transnational mergers is complicated by two factors. Firstly, transnational mergers affect several national markets; but, on the other side, the scope of application of national competition laws and—of national merger control laws- is usually limited to the territory of the regulating countries. Secondly, the great number of countries that have adopted competition law in their national legal systems must be borne in mind. Some scholars have estimated that in 2002 about 90 countries have enacted competition law and many more are planning to do so.[3] As of March 2006, almost 100 competition authorities have joined the International Competition Network. Thus, if a merger affects several national markets, the competition authorities of the countries where such effects are felt may wish to regulate this operation with the aim of protecting their national economic interests.[4] Transnational mergers are

[3] Wolfgang von Meibom and Andreas Geiger, 'A World Competition Law as an Ultima Ratio', [2002] ECLR 445, 445.

[4] In to introduction to its first report on competition policy the Commission wrote: "(…) competition is the best stimulant of economic acivity since it guarantess the widest possible freedom of action to all. An active competition policy pursued in accordance with the provisions of the treaties establishing the communities makes it easier for the supply and demand structure continually to adjust to tenological development. Through the interplay of decentralized decision making machinery, competion enables enterpreses continuously to improve their efficiency, which is the sine qua non for a steady improvement in living standards and employment prospects within the countries of the Community. From this point of view, competition policy is na essential means for satisfying to a great etent the individual and collective needs of our society (…)". See a proactive competition policy for a competitive Europe, COM (2004) 293 final. See also: S. Ehlerman, "The contribution of EC competition policy to the single market" (1992) 29, CMLR, 257. In 2004 the Commission set out its ideas for a proactive competition policy characterised by: "(…) improvement of the regulatory framework for competition which facilitates vibrant business acivity, wide dissemination of knowledge, a better deal for consumers, and efficient restructuring throughout the internal market; and enforcement practice which actively removes barriers to entry and impediments to effective competition that most seriously harm competition in the internal market and imperil the competitiveness of European enterpreses (…)". Competition law and policy in the European

therefore likely to be subjected to the review of several national competition authorities, each applying their respective national competition laws. National laws, however, may regulate the various aspects of merger control regime differently,[5] such aspects ranging from procedural to substantive rules; from policy goals to the allocation of regulatory powers.

The multi-jurisdictional review of trans-national mergers can raise several problems which may be subsumed into three general categories:

A) Legal problems. The regulating competition authorities may take inconsistent decisions on the validity of mergers. For example, one authority may decide to approve an operation, another authority may decide to disallow it, while a third authority may decide to conditionally authorize the merger. The risk of inconsistency may be attributed to the different substantive standard tests adopted by national merger control laws. Inconsistency may be also created by diverging policy goals pursued by national competition laws and by the discretionary power of competition authorities in the evaluation of facts.
B) Business problems. The merging parties may have to notify the merger operation to many competition authorities and handle many merger control procedures. The parties and their counsels have therefore to examine the different national laws applicable to the merger control procedure. The application of different national laws may result in negative consequences for the merging parties: for example, they may be required to provide different data in the notification forms, which obliges the parties to collect different sets of data for each merger control procedure. Multi-jurisdictional review compels the merging parties to commit considerable financial and human resources to deal with the different merger control procedures, thus increasing compliance costs. Furthermore, the multi-jurisdictional review may decrease the legal certainty with respect to the outcome of the review of mergers.
C) Political problems. The divergent views of competition authorities about mergers may fuel diplomatic tensions between the countries concerned.

Union (OECD, 2005). This report was the basis for a peer review examination of the European commission in the OECD Competition Committee, October 2005. se also Report by EAGP, An economic approach to art. 82 (July 2005), Coordinator Patrick Rey.

[5] Ulrich Schawalbe, Daniel Zimmel, Law and economics in european merger control, Oxford University Press, (2009). A. G. Toth, The Oxford Encyclopaedia of European community law: volume III. Competition law and policy, Oxford University Press, (2008). Drauz Gotz, Bengtsson Claes, Jones Christopher, mergers and acquisitions, Leuven, Claeys and Casteels, (2006). Alison Jones, Smith Brenda, EC competition law: Text, cases and materials, Oxford University Press, (2007). Peter C. Carstensen, Susan B. Farmer, Competition policy and merger analusis in deregulated and newly competitive industries, Edward Elgar Publishing, (2008). Farrid Bektashi, Collective dominance in EC competition law: Role of structural links: Case law analysis under the EC merger regulation, VDM Verlag, (2008).

> This is all the more true when the merger operations affect important national interests. Inevitably, such frictions may complicate the execution of the proposed merger operation.

These problems will be labelled as the 'global competition problems' in the field of merger control. They emerge when a competition authority assesses the competitive effects of a transnational merger by focusing on the effects of the transaction on its domestic markets. The priority attached to national interests and policies seriously undermines the capacity of competition authorities to take into account the foreign economic interests that are equally affected by the transaction. The consequence is that competition authorities are unable to appreciate the overall economic effects of the merger on international markets. There exists a gap between the international scope of trans-national mergers and the scope of application of national competition laws. Such a gap weakens the viability of the application of national competition laws as an effective regulatory tool for trans-national mergers.

A new model for the governance of business activities which is attentive to their international nature can bridge this gap. This model should pursue the internationalisation of competition law and, more specifically, of merger control law. In this regard, the proposed internationalisation will not only touch on the contents of the merger control provisions but also on the way in which merger control is administered. Firstly, it implies the harmonisation of the procedural and substantive merger control rules. Secondly, it requires the establishment of mechanisms for cooperation and coordination between national competition authorities.

The internationalisation of merger control should be advantageous for both competition authorities and firms. The advantages for the former would consist in fostering mutual trust; providing efficient criteria for the allocation of merger cases; and in developing common methodologies for the purpose of the assessment of merger operations. The gains for firms would be increased legal certainty and less compliance costs.

The question now is which is the best approach to pursue the objective of internationalisation. Different options are theoretically open, which can be better presented in the form of the following questions: Should the internationalisation be pursued with instruments of soft law or with instruments of hard law? Should it cover only bilateral cooperation agreements or should it also include multilateral agreements? Should it require a full unification of national merger control laws or should it be limited to mere harmonisation through general competition law standards? Should it be based on a complex institutional framework or would establishing mechanism for cooperation and coordination be sufficient?

Before specifically addressing these questions, it is important to bear in mind that countries are not usually willing to cede their regulatory powers in the field of merger control as this would amount to an unacceptable curb of national sovereignty. In the light of the above observation, preference should be therefore given to those ideas which are less threatening to national sovereignty.

This book will review different ideas for the internationalisation of merger control, which may fall within two general categories: the bilateral strategy and the multilateral strategy. The former covers bilateral cooperation agreements, which normally are not serious menaces to national sovereignty. However, the benefits of bilateral cooperation are enjoyed only by the countries that are party to the agreements and by individuals and firms belonging to these countries. The multilateral strategy includes instruments of hard and soft law. The ideas that incorporate the instruments of hard law are normally sophisticated and complex and the key element of these ideas is the imposition of legally binding obligations on countries. However, their practicability is weakened by the restrictions they place on national sovereignty. The feasibility of the ideas that embody instruments of soft law may be, on the other hand, undermined by the lack of legally binding force.

In the view of this author, the proposed formula for internationalisation revolves around the creation of an international merger control framework (hereinafter IMCF), which will rest on a formal and an informal pillar. The latter includes instruments of soft law in the shape of international competition principles and has a general scope of application as it will apply to all transnational mergers affecting the participating countries. The formal pillar embraces bilateral cooperation agreements and its scope of application is limited to the mergers affecting the two countries that are party to a cooperation agreement.

III. *The structure of the book*

The structure of the present book is as follows. Chapter two examines the unilateral strategy, namely the extraterritorial application of competition law. Chapters three and four contain a comparative analysis of the procedural and substantive merger control rules enacted by the US and the EC. Chapter five compares the merger control laws adopted in different jurisdictions from the EC and US. Chapter six studies the bilateral strategy. This chapter not only discusses bilateral cooperation agreements, but it also examines the regional trade agreements that contain competition rules. Chapter seven focuses on multilateral instruments of hard law. Chapter eight concerns multilateral instruments of soft law. It includes a detailed analysis of the activities of the International Competition Network and suggests how the international framework for merger control should be created. Chapter nine draws conclusions.

CHAPTER ONE

THE UNILATERAL STRATEGY

I. *Introduction*

The main preoccupation of national competition authorities is to safeguard the competitive structure of their domestic markets from any possible distortions, included those brought about by the restrictive business practices carried out abroad. However, there do not exist either internationally applicable competition rules or supranational competition authorities on which it is possible to rely for the regulation of transnational restrictive business practices. Therefore a national competition authority which fears that a business practice may produce anti-competitive effects within its territory applies its own national competition laws to regulate such practice. When an alleged restrictive practice meets the statutory jurisdictional criteria of a given country, the competition authority of that country may be willing to exercise jurisdiction on such a practice, regardless of the place where it has been carried out. The application of national competition laws to transnational restrictive business practices will be labelled as the unilateral strategy.

This approach is not illegal per se, since it is a manifestation of national economic sovereignty, according to which countries have a legitimate interest as well as the right to regulate their economic interests and the structure of their home markets. However, recourse to the unilateral strategy may lead to some undesirable consequences. The regulating countries may apply their national competition laws beyond national borders and infringe the sovereignty of third countries.[1] Such exercise of 'extraterritorial' jurisdiction may not be permitted by public international law. Moreover, it is questionable whether the unilateral strategy is a suitable response to global competition problems.

This chapter will examine and critically review the unilateral strategy. The structure of the chapter is as follows. The second section introduces readers to the concept of extraterritoriality. The third section analyses the different grounds of extraterritoriality developed under public international law. The fourth section examines the inbound and the outbound extraterritorial application of competition law under the unilateral strategy. The fifth section deals with extraterritorial application of US and EC competition laws.

[1] Asif Qureshi, International Economic Law (Sweet & Maxwell, London 1999), chapter 3: 'Extraterritorial Jurisdiction in the Economic Sphere'.

The sixth section examines the issues of extraterritorial application of US and EC competition laws to merger cases. The seventh section explains why the unilateral strategy is unsuitable to effectively address global competition problems. The eighth section draws conclusions.

II. *The concept of extraterritorial jurisdiction*

The concept of extraterritorial jurisdiction was first developed at the end of the 19th century to address the problems created by the internationalisation of criminal activities. Extraterritoriality is still a valid instrument today to prosecute the authors of those activities which produce offensive effects in several countries. Equally, it can provide the legal basis for a country whose interests are harmed by a restrictive business practices carried out abroad to regulate that practice.

Extraterritoriality generally includes those situations where one of the stages of the process of the application of a legal rule takes place outside the territory of the enacting country. Legal scholars have attempted to further refine the concept of extraterritorial jurisdiction. The qualifying elements of extraterritoriality have variously been identified as "the exercise by a state of legislative and enforcement jurisdiction beyond its borders either over the citizens of other countries or over its own nationals", or as "prescribing conducts which is outside the territory" and finally as the fact that the authorities of the country that has enacted the rule apply that rule to conducts carried out beyond its national borders.[2]

It is possible to set out the noyau dur of extraterritoriality, which consists of the projection of the legal rules of one country upon situations that occur outside the territory of that country. Only laws which intend to regulate conducts performed abroad and which produce effects in the territory of the enacting country are likely to infringe national sovereignty. The principle of national sovereignty, one of the tenets of public international law, empowers countries to exercise exclusive and absolute rights over their territory, the so-called "reserved domain."[3] As, under public international law, all countries

[2] Alina Kaszorowska, 'International Competition Law in the Context of Global Competition Law' [2000] ECLR 117, 118. Brigitte Stern, 'Une tentative d'élucidation du concept d'application extraterritoriale' [1986] Revue Québécoise du Droit International 48, 51: "Il y a extraterritorialité de l'application d'une norme, si tout ou un partie du processus d'application se déroule en dehors du territoire de l'Etat qui l'a émise". André Nollkaemper, 'Rethinking States' Rights To Promote Extraterritorial Values in International Economic With a Human Face' in F. Weiss, E. Denters and P. de Waart (eds), International Economic with a Human Face (Kluwer Law International, The Hague 1998) 188.

[3] Ian Brownlie, Principles Of Public International Law (Clarendon Press edition, Oxford 1998) 291; Malcom Shaw, International Law (Cambridge University Press, Cambridge 1997) 454.

are equal, every country has to comply with a duty of non-interference with respect to the reserved domain of other countries.

Sovereignty may be exercised in the form of prescriptive jurisdiction, which includes the power to make decisions or rules and in the form of enforcement jurisdiction, which embraces the power to adopt exclusive measures in pursuance of the enforcement of decisions and rules. The geographical scope of the enforcement jurisdiction is restricted to the territory of the acting country. Accordingly, the principle of sovereignty is breached if a country carries out in the territory of a third country coercive acts with the aim of enforcing its legal rules or decisions without the consent of the third country concerned; or when it carries out such acts in its own territory and in doing so infringes or threaten to infringe the sovereignty of other countries.

The limits within which countries can exercise prescriptive jurisdiction are controversial. Several grounds to justify the assertion of prescriptive jurisdiction have been put forward, some of which still struggle to obtain sufficient recognition. It is agreed that the principle of nationality and the principle of territoriality are the general grounds upon which countries assert jurisdiction. The principle of territoriality confers jurisdiction upon the country in the territory of which the offence has been committed; while, according to the principle of nationality, a country asserts jurisdiction over all those who are connected to that country through the links of nationality, residence and other factors considered as evidence of allegiance. Another possible ground of jurisdiction is the protective principle, which states that a country has jurisdiction over foreign nationals who commit a conduct abroad if such a conduct harms the interests of that country, especially the national security interests. Under the universality principle, a country may try foreign nationals for certain types of offences committed abroad that are especially offensive under public international law. Finally, the principle of passive personality enables a country to try aliens for offences committed abroad that offend the interests of the nationals of that country.

The universality principle, the protective principle and the principle of passive personality derogate from the general rules laid down by the principle of territoriality and the principle of nationality. In fact these principles allow countries to apply their national laws beyond national boundaries, regardless of the place where the conduct has been carried out and regardless of the offender's nationality. Apart from the protective principle, such grounds of jurisdiction are rarely relevant in the field of competition law. The universality principle is not considered as an appropriate ground to establish jurisdiction in competition matters given the lack of consensus on the meaning of competition harm, as will be exposed in chapter five. As far as the protective principle is concerned, it is uncertain whether the injuries to competition can be regarded as threats to the national security of countries. Similarly, the nationality principle has not been often invoked since countries are not strongly motivated to intervene and regulate conducts which, though carried out by their nationals, are expected to cause anti-competitive effects only on foreign markets.[4]

III. *The grounds of extraterritorial jurisdiction*

A. *The principle of objective territoriality*

Some legal scholars illustrating the resilience of the principle of territoriality wrote "Territoriality, while accepted is a pot which may be filled with water or with wine". Indeed, this principle can be read according to two different interpretations: subjective and objective territoriality. Subjective territoriality allocates jurisdiction to the country where the conduct is commenced, even if it is completed or consummated abroad. However, the growing movement of persons and goods has rendered such an interpretation ineffective. A conduct may harm an interest located in the territory of one country, whereas its author may be in the territory of a second country. For example: X, who is in the territory of country A throws a bomb at Y, who is in the territory of country B. As a result of the conduct of X, Y dies. The question is: which country can legitimately claim jurisdiction over the conduct of X? A or B? According to the principle of subjective territoriality the jurisdiction is conferred upon A, although the effects of the conduct have been felt only within the territory of B. The terms of the problem remain unchanged if a restrictive business practice, instead of a physical criminal act, is taken into consideration. X and Y are two firms incorporated in country A. In that country they conclude a cartel that affects the interests of the consumers of country B. The principle of subjective territory confers upon country A jurisdiction over the cartel. B cannot apply its competition law to the cartel, even though the conduct of X and Y adversely affects its domestic markets.

Such inconveniences may be resolved with a broader interpretation of the principle of territoriality- objective territoriality. This confers jurisdiction upon the country in the territory of which a crime, though commenced abroad, is completed or consummated. In other words, it is necessary that the essential element of the offence is consummated on the territory of the country claiming jurisdiction.

The principle of objective territoriality was first applied during the Lotus case debated before the Permanent Court of International Justice. After a collision at high sea between a French steamer-The Lotus-and a Turkish collier, the latter sank and eight Turkish nationals died. When The Lotus moored at

[4] Andrè Fiebig, 'International Law Limits on the Extraterritorial Application of the European Merger Control Regulation' [1998] ECLR 323, 326.

a Turkish port the local authorities arrested the French officer of the watch and charged him with manslaughter. The Permanent Court first ruled that "international law prohibits a state from exercising jurisdiction in its own territory in respect of any case which relates to acts which have taken place abroad and in which it cannot rely on some permissive rule of international law." The decision recognised that countries enjoy a wide discretion regarding the territorial scope of application of their laws. They can apply their national laws extraterritorially unless their discretion is restricted by international prohibitive rules. The Court also held that "offences, the authors of which at the moment of the commission are in the territory of another state, are nevertheless to be regarded as having been committed in the national territory, if one of the constituent elements of the offence, and more especially its effects, have taken place here." From this excerpt of the judgment it can be concluded that Lotus enables, under certain circumstances, a country to assert jurisdiction over an offence where only a part of the criminal conduct takes place in that country.

B. *The doctrine of effects*

The language of Lotus is quite ambiguous since it refers to the place where the conduct is completed and to the place where the conduct produces its effects. So Lotus is also invoked as the basis for the doctrine of effects. This doctrine is a further attempt to extend the reach of the principle of territoriality and confers jurisdiction upon the country within whose territory the conduct produces its effects, even if that conduct has been entirely carried out abroad. Although it is strongly supported by American scholars and courts, the doctrine is far from being generally accepted. It is rejected by those who claim that public international law recognises only a limited range of grounds of jurisdiction, which does not include the doctrine of effects.[5] It is also feared that the doctrine may be incompatible with the constitutional principles of international trade law, such as the principle of multilateralism and the principle of non-discrimination, which are part of the legal system of the WTO. The Committee on the Extraterritorial Application of National

---

[5] John E. Ferry, 'Towards Completing the Charm: The Woodpulp Judgement' [1989] EIPR 19, 20. Aldo Frignani and Michel Waelbroeck, European Competition Law, (Transnational Publishers Inc. Ardsley NY 1998), 86. Paul Demaret, 'Extraterritorialité des lois et les relations transatlantique: Une question de droit ou de diplomatie ?' [1985] RTD Eur 1,31; R.Y. Jennings, 'Extraterritorial Jurisdiction and the United States Antitrust Law' [1957] BYBIL 146. Nicolas Ligneul, 'Droit International de la Concurrence: Plaidoyer pour une Approche Intégrée et Progressive' [1999] RMCLUE 458, 460. Paul Torremans, 'Extraterritorial Application of EC and US Competition Law' [1996] ELRev 280, 286. Demaret, above n. 29, 33; F.A. Mann, 'The Doctrine of Jurisdction in International Law' (1964) 3 Academie de Droit International. Recueil des Courses, 126, who argues that 'an inflexible territoriality principle is no longer suited to the modern world'. Bruno Nascimbene, 'Aspetti Internazionali della Politica di Concorrenza Comunitaria' [2002] Il Diritto del Commercio Internazionale 309, 312.

Law of the International Chamber of Commerce recommended that countries should refrain from an extensive extraterritorial application of their national laws; or they should exercise extraterritorial jurisdiction consistently with international law and with the rule of reasonableness.

The advocates of the doctrine of effects dismiss such criticism by observing that in international law there exist no clear-cut rules that prevent countries from asserting jurisdiction on the basis of the doctrine. Furthermore, the doctrine is a useful tool to deal with transnational economic activities and to regulate the offences caused by them. However, these scholars are aware of the need to set the precise limits within which countries can legitimately assert jurisdiction on the basis of the doctrine. In the absence of such limits the most influential countries may yield to "legal imperialistic" temptations and exert overtly extraterritorial jurisdiction with the consequence that the sovereignty of less strong countries is infringed. Justice Fitzmaurice in the Barcelona Traction case voiced such concern where he stated that countries should exercise jurisdiction with moderation and restrain in relation to situations in which a foreign element is involved.[6]

For these reasons legal scholars have proposed theories which should restrain the scope of application of the doctrine of effects within reasonable boundaries. A first possible option is the theory of primary effects, which confers jurisdiction upon those countries that have a legitimate interest in regulating a given conduct.[7] A country has such a legitimate interest when the primary effects of the conduct, defined as the direct and substantial effects, are felt within its territory. The necessity to establish direct and substantial effects as a pre-condition for exerting jurisdiction should prevent countries from exercising jurisdiction on those restrictive business practices that produce only indirect and insignificant effects in their territories. Other academics advocate the idea that jurisdiction should be assigned to the countries where the conduct to be regulated produces substantial, direct and reasonably foreseeable effects.[8] The first condition- the effects must be substantial- is fulfilled when the effects are appreciable and non negligible. Secondly, the effects must be direct: there must be exist a direct causal link between the conduct and the effects, which is not interrupted by other intermediary factors. The third condition, which requires that the effects must be reasonably

[6] Michael Akehurst, 'Jurisdiction in International Law: Antitrust Law' [1972–73] BYBIL 145, 198.

[7] Ex multis, Demaret above n. 29, 32; The Third Restatement Of Foreign Relations Law Of The United States recently published by the American Law Institute; Opinion of Darmon AG in Case 89, 104, 116, 177 and 125 to 129/ 95 A. Ahlstrom OY and others v. Commission, [1988] 4 CMLR 901, 930.

[8] Judgement of February 5th 1970, International Court of Justice, Reports of Judgements, opinions and orders, 1970, 4, 105.

foreseeable, refers to the intention of the parties to cause the effects in the country.[9]

IV. *The unilateral strategy and competition law*

The principle of objective territoriality, and especially the doctrine of effects, provides the legal basis for the unilateral extraterritorial application of national competition laws. Two different forms of extraterritorial application of competition laws may be examined: inbound and outbound extraterritoriality. Inbound extraterritoriality is where the competition law of a country applies to a restrictive business practice that distorts competition in the markets of that country, even though the practice has been carried abroad. As an example of inbound extraterritoriality, in Nippon Paper US competition law was applied to a price-fixing cartel agreement concluded in Japan, which intended and effectively produced restrictive effects in the US domestic markets.[10]

Outbound extraterritoriality concerns the application of one country's competition law to a conduct that is performed in the territory of another country which impedes or hinders the access of the firms of the first country to the market of the second country. In simpler terms, outbound extraterritoriality deals with the problem of market access. An example of outbound extraterritoriality may be found in Pilkington, where a US-based company complained that the pool of patent licence agreements set up by Pilkington, a British company, contained stringent territorial restrictions that prevented the plaintiff from exporting its products. As the conduct of Pilkington harmed the interests of a US firm, it was held to fall within the US jurisdiction, even though it was carried out abroad.

V. *The US and EC positions for extraterritorial application of competition law*

A. *The position of the US*

The US can be regarded as a strong advocate of extraterritoriality in competition law matters. Initially the US Supreme Court disapproved of the extraterritorial application of the Sherman Act and held that US law must be applied only within its own territory. Such a restrictive position was abandoned by

[9] Neale A.D. and Mel Stephens, International Business and National Jurisdiction, (Claredon Press Oxford, 1988) 167.

[10] United States v. Nippon Paper Industries Co. Ltd., 109 F. 3d 1. For a comment on the case, see Richard Reynolds, James Sicilian and Philip Wellmann, 'The Extraterritorial Application of the U.S. Antitrust Laws to Criminal Conspiracies' [1998] ECLR 151.

the US Supreme Court in Alcoa where it recognised the extraterritorial application of competition law and endorsed the doctrine of effects as the legal basis for extraterritoriality. Alcoa concerned an international cartel in the aluminum market, which was entered into, amongst many others, by a company incorporated in Canada, formerly owned by the US company Alcoa, and which was importing into the US. Learned Hand J. ruled that: "any state may impose liabilities, even upon persons not within its allegiance, for conduct outside its borders that has consequences within its borders which the state reprehends". Therefore, a conduct, carried out abroad, falls within US jurisdiction, provided that it is intended to affect, and does affect imports.[11] The Supreme Court confirmed this in Hartford Fire, which concerned a suit brought against London-based insurers who entered into a cartel which negatively affected the US domestic reinsurance market. The Court applied the doctrine of effects and found that the conduct put into practice by the British firms fell within US jurisdiction since it intended to produce and did produce relevant effects in the US markets.[12]

The US lower courts in some cases have attempted to attenuate the rigidity of the case law of the Supreme Court concerning the exercise of extraterritorial jurisdiction. Thus in Timberlane the court conditioned the application of the US law to a three-pronged test.[13] The first limb of the test mirrors the doctrine of effects spelt out in Alcoa. It requires that the effects of the conduct have to be so large as to amount to a cognisable injury to the plaintiff and to a civil breach of competition law. In addition, Timberlane calls for the evaluation of whether US domestic interests-and the links to the US-are strong enough, as opposed to the interests of foreign countries, to justify the extraterritorial exercise of US jurisdiction.[14] On the one hand, Timberlane confirmed the doctrine of effects as a criterion to establish jurisdiction. But, on the other hand, it put forward a rule of juridical reasonableness with the purpose of restraining the discretion of courts as to the exertion of US jurisdiction. Courts should therefore balance US interests with the foreign interests concerned and should close the proceedings before them if they are convinced that a third country has a stronger interest than the US in disciplining that conduct.[15]

---

[11] US v. Aluminium Co. of America et al., 148 F. 2d 416 (1945). After the Alcoa judgement the doctrine of effects has been also invoked in cases decided by lower courts, among which, US v. Watchmakers of Switzerland Information Center Inc. 1963, Trade Cases CCH, para. 70600 and Zenith Radio Corp. v. Hazeltine Research Inc. 1965, Trade Cases CCH 1965.

[12] Hartford Fire Insurance Co. v. California, 509 U.S. 764 (1993).

[13] Timberlane Lumber Co. v. Bank of America, 549 F. 2d 597 (1976) 608.

[14] Timberlane, ibid., para. 13. This test was also applied, though with some amendments, in Mannington Mills v. Congoleum Corporation 595 F. 2d, 1287 (1979).

[15] Jean Gabriel Gastel,'The Extraterritorial Effects of Antitrust Laws' (1983) I 21 Académie de Droit International Recueil des Cours 13. Marie Demetriou and Aidan Robertson, 'U.S. Extraterritorial Jurisdiction in Antitrust Matters: Recent Developments' [1994] ECLR 461,

The American Law Institute in its 1987 Restatement Third of Foreign Relations Law of the United States has codified this approach. It holds that, in order to assert jurisdiction, not only must courts apply the Alcoa test, but they should also apply a jurisdictional rule of reason, which can be regarded as an expression of international comity considerations. Thus, in case the conditions for the application of the doctrine of effects are met, a court should, nevertheless, refrain from exercising jurisdiction when it finds that a foreign country has a greater interest in regulating the situation.[16] The US Government has adopted a similar position in its Antitrust Enforcement Guidelines for International Operation in which it sets out various factors that need to be taken into account while assessing comity considerations.[17]

This balancing-interest test does not appear to be completely convincing. First, the comparison of the interests of foreign countries with the domestic interests implies evaluations that are typical of diplomatic functions, which do not fit well with the traditional functions of judiciary. Secondly, the courts may recognise the prevalence of the national interests of the country to which they belong to the detriment of foreign interests. The rule of reasonableness and the balancing-interests test of Timberlane make reference to the principle of international comity. However, after Hartford Fire, the principle of comity with regard to competition law matters seems rather unimportant as it has been held that comity is relevant only in case of a true conflict. Such a conflict occurs when a foreign party is forced to violate its national law in order to comply with obligations imposed by US law. Thus, the Timberlane test risks being meaningless, especially in the field of merger control where one of the constitutive elements of such conflict (the obligation imposed by

---

463. Antonio Bavasso, 'Gencor. A Judicial Review of the Commission Policy and Practice: Many Light and Some Shadows' (1999) 22 World Competition 4, 45; Richard Whish, Competition Law, (Oxford University Press, Oxford 2005) 395. Alison Jones and Brenda Sufrin, EC Competition Law: Text, Cases And Materials, (2nd ed., Oxford University Press, Oxford, 2004) 1238.

[16] Empagran SA v. F. Hoffmann-LaRoche Ltd., 315 F. 3d 338 (D.C. Cir. 2003).

[17] F. Schere, D. Ross, "Industrial market structure and eonomic performance", Houghton Mifflin, 1990. R. Lispey, K. Chrystal, "Economics", Oxford University Press, 2003. S. Bishop, M. Walker, "The economics of EC competition law. Concepts, application and measurement", Sweet and Maxwell, 2002. I. Maher, "Competition law and intelelctual property rights: Evolving formalism", in P. Craig and G. De Bùrga (eds.), "The evolution of EU law", Oxford University Press, 1999, ch. 16. C. Bellamy, G. Child, "European community law of competition", Oxford University Press, 2007. J. Faull, A. Nikpay (eds.), "The EC law of competition", Oxford University Press, 2007. M. Furse, "Competition law of the UK and EC", Oxford University Press, 2006. D. Goyder, "EC competition law", Oxford University Press, 2003. A. Jones, B. Sufrin, "EC Competition law: text, cases and materials", ultimate edition, Oxford University Press. C. Kerse, N. Khan, "EC antitrust procedure", Sweet and Maxwell, 2005. V. Korah, "EC Competition law and practice", Hart publishing, 2004. O. Odudu, "The boundaries of EC competition law: The scope pf article 81", Oxford University Press, 2006. R. Wesseling, "The modernisation of EC antitrust law", Hart publishing, 2000. R. Whish, "Competition law", Lexis Nexis, 2003.

one of the concurrent jurisdiction to carry out a conduct) will not occur because countries do not oblige firms to conclude merger agreements.

The position of the Congress is expressed in the 1982 Foreign Trade Antitrust Improvement Act56. It lays down that foreign commerce other than import commerce does not fall within the scope of application of the US competition law, unless the conduct has a direct substantial and reasonably foreseeable effect on the US commerce. In order to identify the export transactions that are exempted from the Sherman Act, the Foreign Trade Antitrust Improvement Act relies on a test, the wording of which is similar to the Alcoa judgment. The only difference is the added element of foreseeability and the exclusion of any reference to the interest-balancing test of Timberlane.[18]

The doctrine of effects has been further refined in Empagran by the US Supreme Court. In this case the Court has dealt with a previous decision of the DC Circuit Court of Appeals based on a broad interpretation of Section 6a of the FTAIA. The Circuit Court held that US courts have jurisdiction on damage claims brought by foreign plaintiffs against foreign defendants for injuries caused abroad by a price-fixing cartel, even if such injuries are not dependent on injuries felt within the US territory. The US Supreme Court disagreed with such an analysis and ruled that the appealed decision might have restrained the capability of a country to regulate independently its own commercial affairs, and thereby it might infringe the international law principle of non-interference. The Court reached the conclusion that US competition law cannot apply to a price-fixing cartel with domestic and foreign anti-competitive effects when the adverse foreign effect is not dependent on the domestic adverse effects. So, Empagran says that US courts can exert personal jurisdiction over foreign defendants provided that the foreign harms for which the plaintiff seeks compensation is dependent on US harm.[19]

Extraterritoriality raises even more serious concerns with respect to enforcement jurisdiction. Because of the limitation imposed by international law to the territorial scope of enforcement jurisdiction, countries are not allowed to carry out in the territory of another country any act of material coercion. Indeed, the regulating country has to have the consent of the foreign country concerned in order to carry out the exaction of sanctions, the servicing of summons and the gathering of evidence in the territory of the latter.

---

[18] Deepa Rishikesh, 'Extraterritorial Versus Sovereignty in International Antitrust Jurisdiction' (1995) 14 (3) World Competition 33, 40. Laurence Idot, 'Comment à Entreprise de Pâte de Bois c. Commission des Communautés Européennes' [1989] RTD Eur 341, 359.

[19] Opinion of A.G. Mayras in Case 48/69 et al. I.C.I. and others v. Commission, [1972] ECR 587, 604; Opinion of A.G. Darmon in Cases 89, 104, 114, 116, 117 and 125–129/85, above n. 37, 928.

Despite such restraints the US has opted for an aggressive exercise of enforcement jurisdiction by attempting to impose treble damages awards and disclosure orders of evidence on non-resident persons, alleged to be involved in restrictive business practices. To these intrusions the countries concerned respond with diplomatic and legal measures.[20] Legal responses have consisted of "blocking statutes", which prevent their nationals from complying with the orders issued by the US authorities.[21] These statutes prohibit disclosure, copying, inspections or removal of documents located in the territory of the legislating country when they are necessary to comply with orders issued by foreign authorities and also impedes the enforceability of certain foreign judgments. Moreover, some of these statutes, such as the UK Trading Interest Act of 1980 have provisions that specifically deal with treble damages. This piece of legislation prevents the recovery of treble damages from British nationals through a "claw back provision" that enables British citizens, companies or persons carrying business in the UK to bring an action before the UK courts to recover the non-compensatory part of any such damages they have paid. It should be noted that blocking statutes such as the UK Trading Interest Act of 1980 bring about some undesirable side effects. These laws statutorily rule out or at least attenuate the liabilities of nationals of enacting countries which can arise from the infringement of US competition law.

B. *The position of the EC*

The EC judicature has been traditionally more prudent on the extraterritorial application of competition law. Although the Commission and the Advocates General have often invited the European Court of Justice to apply the doctrine of effects, the Court has always rejected such proposals and has preferred to rely on the less controversial principle of territoriality.

In the Eleventh Report on Competition Policy the Commission expressed its preference for the extraterritorial application of the EC competition rules. It stated that Articles 81 and 82 EC Treaty should apply to the conducts performed by non-EC based firms, provided that these conducts have an appreciable impact on the Common Market. As legal base for the extraterritorial application of EC competition law, the Commission pointed to the principle of internal effects, which should have the same reach as the doctrine

[20] F. Hoffmann-LaRoche Ltd. v. Empagran SA, 542 US 155 (2004). Cedric Ryngaert, 'Foreign-to-Foreign Claims: the US Supreme Court's Decision (2004) v. The English High Court's Decision (2003) in the Vitamins Case [2004] ECLR 611. Peter Muchlinski, Multinational Enterprises and the Law, (Blackwell Oxford 1999) chapter 5, "The Jurisdictional Limits of Regulation through National or Regional Law", especially 146.

[21] For example, the French Act 19-07-1980, Journal Officielle de la République Française 17-07-1980 at 1799; the UK Trading Interest Act 1980.

of effects. The Commission considered extraterritoriality as an indispensable tool to protect the competitive structure of the EC markets from all the business practices that are alleged to cause anti-competitive effects within the EC, including those put in practice abroad.[22]

Dyestuffs is the first case in which the European Court of Justice examined the issue of extraterritoriality; it concerned a trans-national price-fixing cartel concluded by firms based outside the EC. In Dyestuffs the Court did not apply the doctrine of effects to establish EC jurisdiction, but it relied on the doctrine of single economic unit. According to this doctrine, the conduct of subsidiaries are imputable to the parent company provided that the subsidiaries lack autonomy to decide their market behaviour and put into practice directions issued by their parent companies. Since the firms that took part in the cartel had subsidiaries established within the EC and the conduct of the subsidiaries were held to be imputable to the parent companies, the Court decided that the contested cartel was caught by EC jurisdiction.

The European Court of Justice further clarified its views on extraterritorial jurisdiction in Wood Pulp.[23] The Commission instituted proceedings pursuant to Article 81 EC[24] Treaty against non-EC firms, which entered into an international cartel alleged to produce anti-competitive effects in the EC wood pulp market. The Commission exerted jurisdiction on the cartel because there were substantial direct and intended effects caused by the contested practice in the EC. Such effects were ascribed to the implementation of

[22] Ibid., para. 35. The Commission drew support from an obiter dicta in a judgment of the European Court of Justice. (Case 22/71 Beguelin Import Company. v. S.A. G.L. Import Export [1971] ECR 949). The Court said that article 81 (85) of the EC Treaty applies to an agreement entered into by some non-EC undertakings if the agreement is operative on the territory of the common market.

[23] Cases 89, 104, 114, 116, 117 and 125–129/85, above n. 68, 14.

[24] Article 81 (ex Article 85) is the principal weapon to control anti-competitive behaviour by cartels: "1. The following shall be prohibited as incompatible with the common market; all agreements between undertakings, decisions by assicurations of undertakings and concerted practices which may affect trade between Member States and which have as their object or effect the prervention, restriction or distortion of competition within the common market and in particular those which: a) directly or indirectly fix purchase or selling or any other trading conditions; b) limit or control production, markets, technical development or investment; c) share markets or sources of supply; d) apply dissimilar conditions to equivalent transaction with other trading parties, thereby plaining them at a competitive disadvantage; e) make the conclusion of contracts subject to acceptance by the other parties of supplementary obligation which, by their nature or according to commercial usage, have no connection with the subject of such contracts. 2. Any agreements or decision prohibited pursuant to this article shall be automatically avoid. 3. The provisions of paragraph 1 may, however, be declared inapplicable in the case of: a) any agreement or category of agreements between undertakings; b) any decision or category of decision by association of undertakings; c) any concerted practice or category of concerted practices which contributed to improving the production or distribution of goods or to promoting technical or economic progress, which allowing consumers a fair share of the resulting benefit and which does not: a) impose on the undertakings concerned restrictions which are not indispensable to the attainment of these objectives; b) afford such undertakings the possibility of eliminating competition in respect of a substantial part of the products in question".

the cartel within the EC.[25] Advocate General Darmon engaged in a thorough review of the current state of international law regarding extraterritorial jurisdiction and concluded that the principle of substantial, direct and foreseeable effects was the most appropriate criterion to establish EC jurisdiction.[26] The doctrine of effects had already been endorsed by Advocate General Mayras in Dyestuffs, where he stated that if the Commission had relied only on the principle of territoriality it would have been unable to prosecute the restrictive business practices carried out by non-EC firms despite their adverse impact on EC markets.

The Court took a different position from the Commission and the Advocate General ruling that the decisive factor to establish EC jurisdiction is not the place where the practice was formed; rather it is the place where the practice is implemented which is important, because anti-competitive effects are felt in the place of implementation. Given that the parties to the cartel had effectively implemented their pricing agreement within the EC the cartel was held to be within EC jurisdiction, regardless of whether the parties used subsidiaries, agents, sub-agents or branches established in the EC. Thus the Court did not subscribe to the doctrine of effects and developed a different criterion to ascertain whether the exercise of EC jurisdiction is consistent with international law: the doctrine of implementation.

This doctrine is considered by the Court as a manifestation of the principle of territoriality universally recognised in public international law, although commentators had been split on the meaning and scope of the doctrine of implementation. It has been argued that the requirement that a restrictive business practice is implemented within the EC is satisfied when the parties to the practice put it into effect by selling to EC purchasers either directly or through sales agents or sales offices.[27] According to this reading of Wood Pulp, the doctrine of implementation requires some form of presence of the firms in the EC markets.

It has also been argued that a consistent interpretation of the doctrine of implementation with international law would require a more qualified presence of firms in the EC markets. Since international law allows a country to assert jurisdiction on a given situation only if there exists a sufficiently close link between that country and the situation to be regulated, some scholars have argued that a restrictive business practice is implemented in the EC when a foreign firm sets up at its own risk a marketing organisation within the EC. Instead, the requirement of implementation is not met when the

---

[25] Re Wood Pulp, EC Commission Decision n. 85/201, [1984] CMLR 475, para 79.

[26] Opinion of AG Darmon in Cases 89, 104, 114, 116, 117 and 125–129/85, above n. 37, 920–932.

[27] Dieter Lange and John Byron Sandage, 'The Wood Pulp Decision and its Implications for the Scope of EC Competition' [1989] ECLR 137, 165; Torremans above, n. 32, 285. Yves Van Gerven and Lorelien Hoet, 'Gencor: Some Notes on Transnational Competition Law Issues' (2001) 28 (2) LIEI 195, 203.

non-EC firm sells directly to EC customers or through authorised independent dealers.

These theories appear to embrace quite a restrictive view on the scope of the doctrine of implementation. In the view of the proponents of these theories, the doctrine should only cover those restrictive business practices carried out through positive conducts. For example, if a group of firms enter into a cartel agreement to fix the selling prices of a particular product and then sells the products at the agreed prices in the EC, those firms can be subjected to EC jurisdiction upon the basis of the doctrine of implementation. On the other hand, the restrictive business practices carried out through negative conduct or inaction would not be caught by the doctrine of implementation. According to this interpretation of the doctrine, agreements by which parties undertake a non facere obligation to not sell in the EC or not to purchase from EC buyers should not fall within EC jurisdiction, even though such practices may produce anti-competitive effects in the EC.

In order to avoid such problems, legal scholars have developed ideas and theories that should extend the scope of application of the doctrine to negative conducts as well. It has been maintained that the doctrine applies to negative conducts when such conduct are the method by which anticompetitive effects are caused. A broad interpretation of the doctrine, according to which implementation includes the conduct performing the agreement and the effects caused by the conduct has been proposed. The conduct and the ensuing effects are a single undistinguishable entity and both of them have to be present in the EC territory in order to assert EC jurisdiction. This concept of implementation is so extensive that it can include restrictive business practices practiced carried out both in positive and negative form.[28] The theory of constituent effects, in the view of some scholars, should supplement the doctrine of implementation in order to regulate negative restrictive business practices. This theory indicates in the injury of the interests protected by the rule that has been infringed by the conduct the pre-condition for the application of that rule. A constituent effect consists of "an appreciable effect on

[28] Dieter Lange and John Byron Sandage, 'The Wood Pulp Decision and its Implications for the Scope of EC Competition' [1989] ECLR 137, 165; Torremans above, n. 32, 285. Yves Van Gerven and Lorelien Hoet, 'Gencor: Some Notes on Transnational Competition Law Issues' (2001) 28 (2) LIEI 195, 203. Theofinis Christoforou and David Rockwell, 'European Community Law: The Territorial Scope of Application of EEC Antitrust Law' (1989) 30 Harvard International Law Journal 195, 204. David Snyder, 'Mergers and Acquisitions in the European Community and the United States: A Movement Towards a Uniform Enforcement Body?' (1997–98) 29 Law & Policy in International Business 115, 121; Mark Friend, 'Competition and Industrial Policy: The Long Arm of Community Law' [1989] ELRev 169, 171. Todd Miller and Donald Baker, 'USA Merger Control Laws' in William Rowley and Donald Baker (eds.) International Mergers (Sweet and Maxwell, London 2000) 64–5. Joseph Griffin, 'Antitrust Aspects of Cross-Borders Mergers and Acquisitions' [1998] ECLR 11, 13.

the competitive market conditions". Jurisdiction is therefore conferred upon the country where not insignificant anti-competitive restrictive effects are produced by the conduct. Therefore, any conduct, regardless whether active or inactive, producing such effects within the EC markets should be within EC jurisdiction.

Negative restrictive business practices fall under EC jurisdiction should the EC exert jurisdiction on the basis of the doctrine of effects. Some scholars have embraced the idea that with Wood Pulp the EC has effectively adopted the doctrine of effects. First, they observe that, although the Court makes references to the doctrine of implementation, the judgment factually endorses the doctrine of effects in all but the name. Secondly, they outlined the difficulties of the distinction between the implementation of a conduct in the EC and the effects of a conduct on the EC, since these two concepts are inextricably linked. Finally, it seems improbable that the Court has introduced two different criteria for the assertion of jurisdiction: the doctrine of implementation as regards the application of the Articles 81 and 82 EC Treaty and the doctrine of effects as regards the application of merger control regulation.

VI. *Extraterritorial application of competition law to merger cases*

Apparently, the US and EC have adopted different criteria for the purpose of exerting jurisdiction on competition law matters. However the scope of application of the doctrine of effects and of the doctrine of implementation is analogous, with the only exception being that the former covers negative restrictive business practices while the latter does not. Now it is time to examine the approach adopted by the US and the EC in asserting jurisdiction over merger cases. Several scenarios concerning the possible extraterritorial application of merger control law may be illustrated:

- In the first scenario country A applies its merger control legislation to a merger which takes place between firms incorporated and trading in its own territory. In this case the merger review conducted by the competition authority of A cannot be considered as exerting extraterritorial jurisdiction as none of the merging parties have foreign elements with respect to A.
- In the second scenario the competition authority of country B assesses a merger, which has some foreign elements. The merging parties are not incorporated and do not have any relevant assets in B; but their volume of sales achieved in B meets the country's statutory jurisdictional thresholds. The exercise of jurisdiction of B over the merger can be regarded as an exertion of extraterritorial jurisdiction.
- In the third scenario the merging parties are incorporated in country D, but they have a stable market organization or production facilities in

country C. Because of the substantial presence of the parties in C the merger is likely to have relevant effects in the markets of this country. For this reason, the application of the merger control law of C to the merger should not be regarded as extraterritorial jurisdiction.

- The last hypothetical scenario deals with the problem of market access. Two firms incorporated and trading in country E decide to merge. The merged entity enjoys a great market power in the relevant market, which restricts the access of new entrants to this market. The competition authority of D, fearing that its national firms cannot enter the market of E, opens an investigation into the legality of the merger. This procedure can be considered as an extraterritorial exercise of jurisdiction, more precisely it is an expression of outbound extraterritoriality.

A. *The position of the US*

The US Clayton Act does not contain any rules with the specific purpose of delimiting US territorial jurisdiction on merger control. So the doctrine of effects, which is relied on for the assertion of jurisdiction with respect to Sherman Act, can be also applied to merger cases.[29] The doctrine enables the US competition authorities to subject to their regulatory review all mergers provided that they have direct substantial and reasonably foreseeable effects on US commerce, even if the merger involves foreign firms. However, where a merger agreement is entered into only by foreign firms the US competition authorities must demonstrate the existence of "minimum contacts" between US territory and foreign firms in order to assert US jurisdiction on that merger. The International Guidelines of 1995 shed some lights on the concept of "minimum contacts" by clarifying that such requirement is met when the foreign firms import their products into the US and collectively account for a substantial percentage of the US sales of the product. It is irrelevant whether the firms have production facilities in the US.

Further difficulties concern the enforcement of remedies adopted by the US competition authorities when such remedies concern assets located abroad. The execution of these remedies requires the cooperation of foreign competition authorities, as the Institut Merieux case revealed. Institut Merieux,—a French company—which was the sole supplier of rabies vaccines in the US market, decided to buy Connaught, a Canadian firm, which was the only supplier of inactivated polio vaccine in its country. Each of the parties was one of the few potential entrants into the relevant market in which the other party was already trading. The Federal Trade Commission decided to exert jurisdiction on the proposed merger given that it would have had a relevant

[29] Institut Merieux S.A., 891 0098, 55 Fed. Reg. 1614 (Jan. 17, 1990).

impact in the US market. The review of the transaction was problematic, especially with respect to enforcement jurisdiction, since neither party had relevant assets in the US. Public international law bans countries from exercising enforcement jurisdiction beyond their national boundaries without the consent of the country in the territory of which the measure is to be enforced. For this reason, the Federal Trade Commission was obliged to seek cooperation of the Canadian competition authority to address and enforce effective remedies concerning assets located in Canada.[30]

B. *The position of the EC*

The criterion adopted by EC Merger Control Regulation 139/2004[31] to establish which merger operations fall under EC jurisdiction is the concept of "Community dimension". Article 1 of EC Merger Control Regulation 139/2004 lays down that the Commission has the power to appraise only concentrations with "Community dimension".[32] This concept is determined by EC Regulation 139/2004 with the help of financial criteria, which comprise a two-tier set of turnover thresholds.[33] Thus if a merger meets the financial thresholds it has "Community dimension" and, thereby, is subjected to EC jurisdiction.

The function of the financial thresholds is to enable the Commission to exercise its regulatory power with regard to merger operations, which are expected to substantially affect the competitive structure of EC markets. The thresholds set by EC Regulation 139/2004 refer to the revenue generated from the amount of goods and services sold to EC purchasers, no matter what distributive channels the parties use. The idea is that mergers among firms that are already well established in the market are more likely to produce anticompetitive effects within the EC. A firm may be considered well

---

[30] Deborah Owen and John Parisi, 'International Mergers and Joint Ventures: A Federal Trade Commission Perspective' [1990] Fordham Corporate Law Institute 1, 5–14.

[31] Regulation 139/2004 will only be applicable if there is a concentration. This issue is dealt with in article 3 (1): "A concentration shall be deemed to arise where a change of control on a lasting basis results form: a) the merger of two or more previously independent undertakings or parts of undertakings or b) the acquisition, by one or more persons already controlling at least one undertaking, by one or more undertakings, whether by purchase of securities or assets, by contract or by any other menas of direct or indirect control of the whole or parts of one or more undertakings" and continues Article 3 (2): "Control shall be constituted by rights, contracts or any other means which, either separately of an combination and having regard to the considerations of fact or law involved, confer the possibility of exercising decisive influence on an undertaking in particular by: a) ownership or the right to use all or part of the assets of an undertaking; b) rights or contracts which confer decisive influence on the composition, voting or decisions of the organs of an undertaking".

[32] Council Regulation no. 139/2004 of 7 April 2004 [2004] OJ L133/1.

[33] The financial thresholds was originally laid down by the old EC Regulation 4064/89 as amended by EC Regulation 1310/97 [1997] OJ L180/1. Jacques Bourgeois, 'EEC Control over International Merger' [1990] YEL 108.

established in the EC when the volume of its sales in the EC markets meets the financial thresholds. Thereby it is possible to say that the turnover thresholds incorporate the doctrine of effects.

The broad definition of "Community dimension" contained in EC Regulation 139/2004 enables the Commission to exercise virtually unlimited territorial powers.[34] Provided that the merging parties meet the turnover thresholds, the Commission has an exclusive jurisdiction over the merger, even if the transaction has only minimal anti-competitive effects in the EC. This problem was epitomised in JCSAT/SACAT where the Commission had jurisdiction over a planned joint venture among Japanese telecommunications firms as the parties met the turnover threshold. The Japanese firms had to notify the transaction to the Commission though it had no effects on EC markets because of technical and legal obstacles; accordingly, the Commission cleared the merger. Similarly, in Nestlé Pillsbury/Haagen-Dazs US the Commission, on the basis of the turnover thresholds, retained its jurisdiction over a merger between US firms despite the fact that the transaction affected only US domestic ice cream markets.

Likewise in Boeing/McDonald Douglas the Commission based its jurisdiction on the finding that the merging parties met the turnover thresholds, even though both of them had been incorporated in the US and neither had relevant assets in the EC. The Commission observed that the merger was likely to have a substantial impact on the EC markets. This prediction was based on the consideration of the large market shares held by the merging parties in the EC aviation transport market.[35] Boeing confirms that the exercise of the regulatory powers conferred by the EC merger control legislation is based on the doctrine of effects. Accordingly, the Commission is empowered to regulate a transaction among non-EC firms provided that the merger has direct, substantial and reasonably foreseeable effects within the EC.[36]

Once established that the EC merger control law incorporates the doctrine of effects, it remains to be seen whether this doctrine can be reconciled with the doctrine of implementation. Some legal scholars have proposed a broad interpretation of the doctrine of implementation, which includes not only those activities that are linked to the conclusion of a merger agreement; but

[34] Andre Fiebig, 'The Extraterritorial Application of the European Merger Control', (1998–99) 5 Columbia Journal Of European Law 79, 80.

[35] JCSAT/SAJAC (Case No. IV/M.346) Commission Decision. Nestle/Pillsbury/Haagen-Dazs US (Case No. IV/M.1689) Commission Decision. Boeing/McDonnell Douglas, Commission Decision [1997] OJ L336/16 (1997), para. 7.

[36] J.D. Banks, 'Lessons from Boeing/MacDonnell Douglas' [1998] ECLR 306. Antonio Bavasso, 'Boeing/Mc Donnell Douglas: Did the Commission Fly Too High? [1998] ECLR 243, 247 blamed the Commission has been blamed for stretching the territorial reach of the EC merger control regulation too far. Timothy Portwood, Mergers Under EEC Competition Law, (Athlone Press, London & Atlantic Highlands NJ, 1994) 37.

also those activities that are related to the performance of the said contract. In other words, implementation would include even the changes to the market structure resulting from a merger. As a result a merger between two non-EC firms importing into the EC would fall within EC jurisdiction. The merger would affect the competitive structure of EC markets by reducing the number of importers. A narrower interpretation of the doctrine of implementation, however, would restrain its ambit to the element of the actual coming together of the parties. Accordingly, EC Regulation 139/2004 would apply only to mergers between firms already physically present in the EC, while it would not apply to the reduction of importers trading in the goods produced by the merging parties as this is a mere repercussion of the transaction.

Another attempt to reconcile the two doctrines distinguishes between the formation and the implementation of a merger agreement. The conclusion of a merger agreement, so the argument runs, is different from its effects and only the effects are relevant to ascertain jurisdiction. The preoccupation of the Commission in merger control is to prevent the consummation of mergers that may have restrictive effects on the competition in the EC markets. It is necessary to consider the place where such effects are felt, rather than the place where the parties are located. So, consistently with the doctrine of implementation, EC Regulation 139/2004 should apply to mergers with anti-competitive effects regardless of the place where the merger agreement was signed.

The Court of First Instance clarified its views on the application of the doctrine of implementation in the field of merger control in the Gencor case. The Commission had blocked a merger, previously approved by the South African Competition Board, since the transaction would have brought about a collective dominant position in the platinum and rhodium markets between the merged entity and third parties. The Court on appeal against the decision of the Commission dealt first with the issue of the prescriptive jurisdiction. The question was whether the Commission had asserted jurisdiction consistently with the concept of Community dimension laid down by the EC merger control regulation. The Court found that only the turnover thresholds of the merging parties are relevant to ascertain whether the merger falls under the EC jurisdiction.[37] The Court then tried to reconcile the turnover thresholds with the doctrine of implementation. The requirement of implementation is met when the volume of sales of the merging parties exceeds the turnover thresholds, regardless of the location of the sources of

[37] CFI, Case T-102/96, Gencor Limited v. Commission [1999] 4 CMLR 971. Gencor Limited—Lonhro PLC, (Case IV/M.619) Commission Decision [1999] 4 CMLR 1076. CFI, Case T-102/96, above n. 106, para. 85. See also: Eleanor Fox,'The Merger Regulation and its Territorial Reach: Gencor Ltd. v. Commission', [1999] ECLR 334, at 336.

supply and production plants. Since the volume of the sales of the merging parties in the EC was in excess of the turnover threshold the Commission exerted its jurisdiction on the transaction in conformity with the doctrine of implementation. In simpler terms, according to the Court, the doctrine of implementation is equivalent to the criterion of the volume of sales incorporated in the turnover threshold.

In the following part of the judgment the Court addressed the issue whether under public international law the Commission legitimately asserted enforcement jurisdiction. EC judiciary has traditionally opted for the doctrine of implementation in order to assess whether the Commission has legitimately exercised jurisdiction with regard to cases falling under Articles 81 and 82 EC Treaty. Quite surprisingly, the Court of First Instance departed from the previous case law of the Court of Justice and relied upon the criterion of qualified effects to evaluate whether the Commission applied the EC merger control regulation in conformity with international law. The Court ruled that a country could legitimately exert jurisdiction over conduct which causes immediate, substantial and foreseeable effects on its national territory. Since all of these requirements were satisfied in Gencor, the Court concluded that the Commission did not breach international law when it asserted jurisdiction on the merger.[38] It may be worth noting that the wording of the test applied by the Court closely resembles the doctrine of effects applied by the US courts.

As for the exercise of enforcement jurisdiction, the appellant objected that the Commission infringed the international principles of proportionality and of non-interference. Such objections were dismissed by the Court holding that the principle of international comity, under which the principles of proportionality and of non-interference can be subsumed, can only be invoked in cases where there is a genuine conflict between the legal systems to which the respective regulating authorities belong. But, in the view of the Court such a conflict did not exist in Gencor. The South African competition authority consented, but did not require, the parties to enter into the merger agreement while the Commission prohibited the parties from implementing the merger agreement. In Gencor the Court of First Instance aligned

[38] Gencor Limited—Lonhro PLC, above n. 107, para. 90. For comments on this point see Porter Elliott, 'The Gencor Judgement: Collective Dominance, Remedies and Extraterritorial under the Merger Regulation' [1999] ECLR 638, 641; Fox above n. 110, 336. But, contra, see Cook and Kerse, who denied that in Gencor the Court of First Instance has openly endorsed the principle of effects. John Cook and Christopher Stephen Kerse, EC Merger Control, (Sweet and Maxwell, London 2000) 13. The position of the Court is a little surprising as the EC jurisdiction on this transaction could have been justified on the basis of the principle of nationality given that one of the merging party was a company incorporated under English Law. Francisco Enrique Gonzalez-Diaz, 'Recent development in EC Merger Control Law. The Gencor Judgement' (1999) 22 (3) World Competition 3, 14.

itself with the narrow approach already taken by the US Supreme Court in Hartford Fire regarding the relevance of international comity considerations in competition law matters.[39] The need for a genuine conflict makes it quite improbable that comity can be effectively applied with the purpose of resolving overlapping jurisdictions in merger cases.

In its judgment in Gencor the Court of First Instance has shed much needed light on the EC position regarding jurisdiction in merger cases. However, the legal community remains unconvinced by some rulings of the judgment. For example, the reliance on the doctrine of implementation to ascertain whether the assertion of EC prescriptive jurisdiction was consistent with international law is regarded as unsuitable for establishing whether the Commission has the power to regulate transnational mergers. The application of criterion of qualified effects in order to ascertain whether jurisdiction exerted by the Commission upon the basis of the jurisdictional criteria laid down by the EC merger control regulation is consistent with international law introduced an element of unnecessary discretion into merger control. Indeed, the Commission may comply with the EC merger control regulation and breach international law in the same case.[40] In light of Gencor two different levels of jurisdiction can be identified: the procedural jurisdiction, which refers to the pre-merger notification obligation, and the substantive jurisdiction, which concerns the appraisal of mergers. It appears that, in the view of the Court, the Commission should abide by the doctrine of effects only when exerting substantive jurisdiction in order to ensure that such exercise of jurisdiction is consistent with international law. On the other hand, as for procedural jurisdiction, the merging parties are obliged to notify the merger operations which meet the jurisdictional thresholds even if such operations are unlikely to have relevant effects in the EC.

The two levels of jurisdiction fit well into the less controversial cases regarding the scope of application of EC merger control law. Thus, if a merger falls short of the financial thresholds it is unlikely to have immediate, direct and reasonably foreseeable effects in the EC. Accordingly, the merging parties are not obliged to notify the authorities about the merger and the Commission has no regulatory powers over such a transaction. The opposite situation, in which the merger operation meets both the financial thresholds and the criterion of qualified effects, does not raise any particular concerns. It is agreed that the merging parties have to notify the merger and that that transaction falls within the substantive review of the Commission.

---

[39] CFI, Case T-102/96, above n. 106, paras. 91–101.

[40] Jan Piet Slot, 'Note on Gencor v. Commission' (2001) 38 CMLRev 1573, 1580, who argued that, instead, the doctrine of implementation would be more appropriate to regulate hardcore cartels in which national competition authorities have strong interests to apply their competition rules.

Yet, in between these clear-cut cases there exists a grey area concerning mergers, which, although they reach the turnover thresholds, are unlikely to produce qualified effects. The legal regime applicable to these merger operations may not be consistent with public international law. These transactions do not fall under the scope of application of the regulatory powers of the Commission and yet Article 4 of EC Regulation 139/2004 obliges the parties to notify the merger to the Commission. If it is true that the doctrine of effects sets out the limits within which the Commission can legitimately exercise its regulatory powers over mergers, the interpretation provided by the Court in Gencor as to the legal basis upon which the parties have the duty to notify the merger to the Commission may infringe international law. The imposition of the obligation to notify the merger is an act of asserting jurisdiction. It is also important to bear in mind that the fulfilment of such an obligation may be rather burdensome for the merging parties. They are obliged to fill in the CO form as well as, under the standstill clause, to refrain from putting into effect the transaction. Finally, if they fail to comply with these obligations they are liable to heavy fines.[41]

The Court of First Instance has attempted to justify the imposition of the notification obligation by pointing out that preliminary notification is necessary in enabling the Commission to examine the transaction in order to ascertain whether it falls within its regulatory jurisdiction.[42] However, this position seems to contradict the principle of proportionality, which is recognised by EC law and international law alike. This principle requires that the measures enacted by countries should not impose more severe obligations than are absolutely necessary to achieve the declared aims. The pre-merger notification obligations arguably do not satisfy these conditions as suggested by the fact they are not envisaged by other jurisdictions.

It is possible to adopt mechanisms which attenuate the negative implications of the pre-merger notification obligation. For example, the US law exempts certain mergers involving foreign firms from the obligation of notification imposed by the Hart Scott Rodino Act. The Notice of the Commission of 26 July 2000 on simplified procedure provides a special procedure that is applicable to some types of mergers that have no or negligible, actual or foreseen, activities in the EC.[43] The Notice empowers the Commission to bring the procedure to an end with a decision pursuant to article 6(1)(a) of EC Regulation 139/2004. EC Regulation 802/2004 allows parties to use a short

[41] Samsung/AST, (Case No. IV/M.920) Commission Decision.

[42] CFI, Case T.-102/96, above n. 106, para. 76. Ugo Draetta, 'International Law Aspects of Cooperation in Merger Review: Long and Short Term Solutions' [2002] Il Diritto del Commercio Internazionale 3, 6.

[43] Commission Notice No. 4062, [2000] OJ C217/32. Annex II Short Form for the Notification of Concentration pursuant to EC Regulation 139/2004 [2004] OJ L133/22.

form to notify a merger if certain conditions are met.125 however, one has to bear in mind that the availability of such mechanisms may not be of great help to firms. It is true that merging parties are not required to file a complete form CO; but, nevertheless, they might have to file a similar amount of information required by a standard notification. And the application of the simplified procedure is also an act of asserting jurisdiction.

As a whole the Gencor judgement has given further support and credibility to the practice so far followed by the Commission as to assertion of EC jurisdiction over transnational mergers. A further element that strengthens the credibility and legitimacy of the approach set out in Gencor is the fact that the EC is now closer to the position of the US authorities.[44]

VII. *The demise of the unilateral strategy*

The principle of objective territoriality and the doctrine of effects are the grounds of jurisdiction on which countries normally rely in order to assert jurisdiction in competition law matters. The US, as explained in previous sections, has keenly endorsed the extraterritorial application of their national competition laws upon the basis of the doctrine of effects. On the other hand, the EC is also willing to extraterritorially apply its competition law, although the position of the EC is more complex in respect to the grounds upon which it does so. It is indeed necessary to distinguish between the exercise of jurisdiction in cases concerning Articles 81 and 82 EC Treaty and in merger cases. As to the first category of cases, Advocate General Mayras in Dyestuffs, Advocate General Darmon in Wood Pulp and the Commission in the Eleventh Report on Competition Policy as well as in Wood Pulp have all expressly stated that the doctrine of effects set the territorial limits of the application of EC competition law. Yet, up to now, the European Court of Justice has not subscribed to this position; on the contrary, it has opted for the doctrine of implementation, which is considered as an expression of the principle of territoriality. The territorial application of EC law to merger cases is, on the other hand, regulated by the doctrine of effects. This doctrine

[44] Sarah Stevens, 'The Increased Aggression of the EC Commission in Extraterritorial Enforcement of the Merger Regulation and its Impact on Transatlantic Cooperation in Antitrust' [2001] Syracuse Journal of International Law & Commerce 263, 282. Amy Ann Karpel, 'The European Commission Decision on the Boeing-Mc Donnell Douglas Merger and the Need for Greater United States-European Union Cooperation in the Merger Field', (1997–98) 49 The American University Law Review 1029, 1032; Stevens, above n 127, 290. Federico Ghezzi, 'La disciplina delle concentrazioni e la promozione dei campioni nazionali tra diritto comunitario e normative nazionali antitrust' [2003] Rivista delle Società 1098. Robert Paul, 'The Increasing Maze of International Pre-Acquisition Notification' [2000] ICCLR 123, 123. Aziel Ezrachi, 'Limitation on the Extraterritorial Reach of the European Merger Regulation' [2001] ECLR 137. Eleanor Fox and Lawrence Sullivan, Cases and Material on Antitrust (West Publishing, St. Paul Minnesota 1989) 28.

is incorporated into the jurisdictional turnover thresholds laid down by EC Regulation 139/2004 and has been applied in Gencor by the Court of First Instance as normative parameters to assess whether the Commission had legitimately asserted under public international law enforcement jurisdiction in merger cases.

Legal scholars are still divided on whether the doctrine of effects is consistent with public international law, since it may breach the principle of sovereignty. Those belonging to the camp, which supports the doctrine, are aware of the problems that its application may cause. The risk is that countries may overstretch the territorial scope of application of their national laws and exert jurisdiction in situations that are linked to the territory of the regulating country only tenuously. Such an exercise of jurisdiction may be perceived by third countries as a threat to their sovereignty. Accordingly academics have developed a number of theories, inspired by the rule of reasonableness and the principle of international comity, with the purpose of tempering extraterritorial jurisdiction and allaying these risks.

These theories are, perhaps, incapable of restraining the application of the doctrine of effects within reasonable limits. First, the rule of reasonableness has been blamed for being too flexible and for leaving the courts with too wide a discretion. Secondly, the courts do not appear to be the best-equipped institutions to weigh the competing interests that are inherent in the balancing-interests test. When national courts are asked to balance national and foreign interests they are more likely to favour national ones over foreign ones. Moreover, the effectiveness of the comity considerations can be undermined by the political strength of the countries concerned. This problem was epitomised in Gencor when the Court of First Instance refused to take into consideration the national interests of South Africa, even if it is true that that country did not adopt a firm diplomatic stand to support the case of its national interests. It is uncertain whether the judgment of the Court may be read as a manifestation of legal imperialism. In contrast, in Boeing the Commission was decisively more willing to weigh the foreign interests affected by the merger, probably because South Africa was a less formidable opponent than US.

The history of EC/US cooperation in merger control provides other elements that should advise against overconfident reliance on the principle of comity. The EC/US cooperation framework, based upon comity considerations, is on the verge of collapse whenever the respective competition authorities are asked to review sensitive mergers. This happens when mergers touched on matters linked to sovereignty, such as national security and defence interests. On these occasions significant political tensions between the US and the EC were exposed. Both accused the other of having let industrial policy and other political considerations creep into the substantive assessment of the legality of mergers.

These last observations introduce the issue that the enforcement of merger control may be tainted by parochial considerations. Since merger control is linked to industrial policy, national competition authorities may take into account social and industrial policy considerations rather than strictly adhere to competition considerations. Competition authorities may also regulate mergers with the purpose of creating or fostering the formation of national champions. All these elements may fuel conflicts between countries affected by the mergers. Finally, it is important to bear in mind the quite restrictive interpretation of comity that was endorsed by the US Supreme Court and by the Court of First Instance in Hartford Fire and Gencor respectively. As a result of such narrow approaches, the room of relevance of comity considerations in the field of merger control has been considerably restrained.

The absence of appropriate instruments capable of restraining the unilateral extraterritorial application of national laws to transnational mergers can be regarded as a serious limitation of the unilateral strategy itself. If the doctrine of effects confers on countries the legal basis upon which to unilaterally intervene and remedy the anti-competitive effects which mergers may cause in their markets, a number of countries can potentially assert jurisdiction over the same transnational merger. Thus, it is possible to envisage a nightmare scenario where the parties have just obtained the approval from the competition authorities of the countries that have the greatest interest in investigating the merger. Then a remote third country applies its national merger control law to the transaction upon the basis of tenuous connecting factors. It threatens to block the merger and to impose a substantial fine on the parties. Such a threat may force the merging parties to sacrifice a significant amount of resources in order to settle all the competition problems raised by that authority.

The issue of the costs that firms incur because of the extraterritorial application of merger control laws has been recently addressed by a survey regarding the assertion of jurisdiction over merger control cases by the European Commission. The most interesting finding of the research is that an overtly extraterritorial exercise of jurisdiction may result in the externalisation of costs which may especially penalise foreign firms. On the other hand, the EC firms have indeed benefited from the one-stop shop systems ensured by the EC merger control regime since 1989, both in terms of slashing compliance costs and increasing legal certainty. Equally EC Regulation 139/2004 is of benefit to the EC's general interests. Yet, the extraterritorial application of EC merger control law may lead to harmful consequences for foreign firms, such as the suspension of merger imposed by the standstill clause and increased compliance costs and legal uncertainty.

Moreover, reliance on the unilateral strategy may bring about the likelihood of inconsistent decisions regarding the appraisal of mergers. Such a risk may be fuelled by a wide array of factors, such as the different substantive and procedural rules of each national merger control law or the structural characteristics of the relevant national markets. Competition authorities are particularly sensitive to the interests that are prevalent in their own jurisdiction. Thus, the competition authority of an importing country may appraise mergers differently from the competition authority of an exporting country. More precisely, the competition authority of an importing country favours the interests of consumers whereas the competition authority of the exporting country is more sensitive to the advantages that the manufacturers can gain from the merger. The danger is that a consumer jurisdiction may block a trans-national merger, even when this transaction has been already been approved by the competition authority of the exporting jurisdiction. In this case the consumer jurisdiction would disregard all those potential benefits that the manufacturers expect to gain from the merger.

The unilateral strategy is equally problematic with regard to the assertion of enforcement jurisdiction. Countries are willing to apply and enforce their national laws against persons and assets located abroad if that is necessary to protect their national economic interests, as epitomised by the efforts of the US authorities to extraterritorially enforce treble damage awards and pre-trial discovery orders. Yet such measures are seen by the third countries concerned as a serious intrusion into their territorial sovereignty as well as a curb on the power to self-determine their national economic policy. The reaction of these countries has taken the shape of diplomatic protests and blocking statutes, which only heightens the political tensions caused by the extraterritorial exercise of enforcement jurisdiction. The countries concerned are unlikely to retreat form such confrontation since what is at stake is their sovereignty. All these problems are exposed in Institut Meriuex, which illustrates that a competition authority is unable to act alone to adopt remedies which can effectively deal with the anti-competitive problems raised by firms located abroad. The cooperation of the authority belonging to the jurisdiction where the assets of the firm are located is essential in order to enforce the necessary remedies.

VIII. *Conclusion*

On balance, the unilateral strategy is unsuitable to effectively cope with all the global competition problems in the field of merger control. It is incapable to set the parameters within which a country may legitimately exert its jurisdiction without breaching the fundamental principle of sovereignty. It conduces to the risk of conflicts and rifts of different nature among countries as well as national competition authorities. It may also negatively affect the position of the parties to merger operations by increasing compliance costs and legal uncertainty. The internationalisation of merger control would be a more effective response to such problems. It is therefore advisable to leave aside the unilateral strategy and try to explore the possible avenues of international cooperation among national competition authorities. However, before discussing the proposals to establish mechanism of international cooperation it is convenient to first compare the different national merger control laws. The analysis of these laws will enable the reader to gain a more comprehensive understanding of all the differences between national merger control laws.

CHAPTER TWO

A COMPARATIVE ANALYSIS OF EC AND US MERGER CONTROL LAW: THE INSTITUTIONAL FRAMEWORK AND PROCEDURAL RULES

I. *Introduction*

The US and the EC are also the most vigorous and influential competition law enforcement jurisdictions. They have since long adopted statutes to protect the competitive structure of their home markets from restrictive business practices. The US introduced the first competition law in 1890 with the US Sherman Act. The first EC competition law provisions came into effect only in 1951 with the Treaty of Paris, which established the European Community of Coal and Steel. The Treaty of Paris, unlike the Sherman Act, did not have a general scope of application. Its reach was restricted "ratione materiae" to the business practices that occurred in the coal and steel sectors. Mergers consummated by firms competing in global markets are likely to fall within the jurisdiction of the US and/or the EC. It is therefore advisable to examine the most prominent aspects of the merger control laws of these jurisdictions and the approaches followed by their competition authorities. Within the substantive assessment of mergers, are the competition authorities allowed to take into considerations factors which are different from purely competition considerations, such as the impact of mergers on the level of employment?

II. *The history of the US merger control law*

The first US law to specifically deal with merger control was the 1914 Clayton Act. Previously the US competition authorities relied on the general provisions of the Sherman Act, which was passed by the US Congress as a response to the massive process of economic concentration[1] occurring within the

[1] See also: In July 2000, the Commission introduced a simplified procedure for treatment of certing concentrations. This procedure applies to threee categories of concentrations: "1. Two or more undertakings acquire joint control of a joint venture the turnover of which and or the turnover of the contributed activities is less than 100 million dollar within the EEA and the total value for assets transferred to the joint venture is less than 100 million dollar in the territory; 2. Two or more untertakings merger, or one or more undertakings acquire sole or joint control of another undertaking provided non of the parties do business in the same product in the same geographical market or in a product market which is upstream or downstream of the product market of another party; 3. Two or more undertaking merge, or one or more undertakings acquire sole or joint control of another undertaking and although

American industry during the 19th century. Such concentration was pursued by means of trusts, which, through the imposition of legally binding obligations, enabled the participant firms to coordinate their commercial policy and decide the level of prices and output. Due to this mechanism, individual firms controlled large shares of particular markets with a substantial decrease in competition. According to Professor Bork, the original purpose of the Sherman Act was to protect consumers from the increases in prices and the reduction of output caused by these trusts.[2]

But the early years of the application of the Sherman Act were disappointing as firms realised that mergers were appraised quite leniently. Therefore, firms kept on pursuing almost unaffectedly their concentration policies through the medium of mergers.[3] In 1914 the US Congress passed the US Clayton Act, which specifically introduced a mechanism for the appraisal of mergers. But a careless drafting of the provision setting the scope of application of the new law resulted in a restrictive definition of the relevant transactions, as only those merger operations executed with an acquisition of stock fell under the reach of the Clayton Act. On the other hand, merger operations carried out via acquisitions of assets fell outside the reach of the new law. It was only with the enactment of the 1950 Celler-Kefauver Act that this lacuna was eventually remedied.

III. *The history of the EC merger control law*

The Treaty of Rome of 1957 does not include any specific provisions on merger control. It was originally thought that mergers would enable EC firms to gain significant economies of scale and enhance their competitiveness in global markets against non-EC firms. However, this initial advantage

two or more parties have a horizontal or a vertical relationship, their combined market share is not 15 per cent or more for horizontal and 25 per cent or more for vertical relationships (…)". Commission notice on remedies acceptable under Council Regulation 4064/89 and under Commission Regulation 447/98 (2001) O.J. C68/3 (2001) C68/03. The notice sets out the applicable general principles the main types of commitments such as investiture, which have been accepted in the past, the specific requirements which proposals of commitments need to fulfil in both phases of the procedure and the main requirements for their implementation. Modification may be proposed before the notification, together with it, or within three weeks after the date of receipt of the notification.

[2] The issue of the purpose of the Sherman Act is controversial. Other possible purposes include: preserving the possibility of operators to compete with each other, preventing unfair distribution of wealth to the detriment of consumers, promoting innovation, maintaining the vitality of democracy and shifting wealth from large producers to small producers and farmers. Ernest Gellhorn, William Kovacic and Stephen Calkins, Antitrust Law and Economics, (Thomson West Saint Paul Minnesota, 2004) 23.

[3] Herbert Hovenkamp, Federal Antitrust Policy, (West Publishing, St. Paul Minnesota 1994), 433; Earl Kintner, Federal Antitrust Law: A Treatise on the Antitrust Laws of the United States, Volume IV (Anderson Publishing, Cincinnati Ohio 1984), 103.

led later to the problem of the emergence of market dominance positions generated by mergers. The first reaction of the Commission was to apply the general provisions of the EC Treaty. In the leading Continental Can case the Court of Justice ruled in favour of the application of Article 82 EC Treaty to regulate mergers.[4] However, this provision can apply only to cases where one of the merging parties has a dominant position[5] already in the relevant market and the merger itself is an abuse of that dominant position. In BAT/ Reynolds the Court ruled that Article 81 EC Treaty applies to merger cases provided that the acquiring party, as a result of the merger, acquire or is in the position to acquire the legal or the de facto control on the commercial conduct of the other party. However, the Court placed several restrictions on the possibility of invoking Article 81 EC Treaty in merger cases, as a result of which this provision applies only to merger operations implemented by an agreement concluded by the merging parties.[6] Consequently, mergers consummated through hostile takeover bids do not fall within its scope of application. Therefore neither Article 81 nor Article 82 EC Treaty[7] could be

[4] Case 6/72, Europemballage Corporation and Continental Can Company Inc. v. Commission [1972] ECR 215, paras 25–27. See also Giuliano Amato, Antitrust and the Bounds of Power, (Hart Publishing, Oxford, 1997) 78.

[5] See: case 322/81 Michelin v. Commission (1983) E.C.R. 3461 at 3503 (30). Case 85/76 Hofmann-La Roche v. Commission (1979) E.C.R. 461 (1979) CMRL, 211, where the Court rejected as irrelevant a number of additional criteria mentioned by the Commission, but indicated those which it considered important. Case 19/79 Miller v. Commission (1978) ECR 131, where the market share of the applicant was estimated at 6% of the German market and the Court accepted that in that case, there was a danger that trade between Member States would be appreciably affected. See joined cases T-24–26/93, Companie Maritime Belge Transport and others (1996) ECR, II-1201 (65–66); case IV/34-621 Irish Sugar Plc (1997) O.J. L.258/1 (11–112)—Case T-69/89, RTE v. Commission (1991) ECR II-485 and joined cases T-69/89, etc. Case SIV v. Commission (1992) ECR II. 1403 CMLR, 302. As we see, three conditions are necessary for the reaction of a collective dominant position significantly impeding effective competition: "1. There must be sufficient market transparency for all members of the dominant oligopoly to be aware, sufficiently precisely and quickly of the way in which the other members market conduct is evolving; 2. There must be adequate deterrents to ensure that there is a long-term incentive in not departing form the common policy, and 3. It must be established that the foreseeable reaction of current and future competitors, as well as of consumers, would not jeopardise the results expected form the common policy (…)". See. Case T-342/99 Airtours c. Commission (2002) ECR, II-2585, where the CFT annulled the Commissions dec. prohibiting the merger.

[6] Cases 142 and 156/84, British American Tobacco Company Ltd. and R.J. Reynolds Industries Inc. v. Commission, [1987] 3 ECR 4487, paras 31–64.

[7] Article 82 ex article 86 is concentrated to: "Any abuse by one or more undertaking of a dominant position within the common market or in a substantial part of its shall be prohibited as incompatible with the common market in so far as it may affect trade between Member States. Such abuse may, in particular consist in: a) directly or indirectly imposing unfair purchase or selling prices or unfair trading conditions; b) limiting production, markets or technical developments to the prejudice of consumers; c) applying dissimilar conditions to equivalent transactions with other trading parties, thereby plain them at a competitive disadvantage; d) making the conclusion of contracts subject to acceptance by the other parties of supplementary obligations which, by their nature or according to commercial usage, have no connection with the subject of such contracts". See also: J. Faull, A. Nikpay (ds.), "The EC

regarded as effective regulatory tools with regard to merger operations. It was only in 1989 that an ad hoc instrument for the appraisal of mergers was adopted: EC Regulation 4064/89. Subsequently, EC merger control regime has been thoroughly recast by EC Regulation 139/2004.[8] The new regulation has extended the cases in which it is possible to refer mergers from the Commission to the Member States and vice versa. It also reformulated the substantive test and amended the procedural rules with the aim of enhancing the quality and rigour of the assessment of mergers.[9] A further important innovation brought about by the 2004 reform is the intention of the Commission to publish Merger Guidelines in order to express its views on the different issues which may arise in merger control.[10] The Guidelines are prepared on the basis of the existing practice and case law and illustrate to firms how the Commission assesses mergers operations with the purpose of improving the transparency and legal certainty of merger control.[11]

IV. *Introduction to the EC/US bilateral cooperation*

In the early 1990's the EC and the US became aware that the competition problems arising from transnational business practices could not be success-

law of competition", Oxford University Press, 2007. M. Furse, "Competition law of the UK and EC", Oxford University Press, 2006. T. Eilmansberger, "How to distinguish good rom bad competition under Article 82. In searh of clear and more coherent standards for anti-competitive abuses", CMLR, (2005), 42. D. Ridyard, "Exlusionary pricing and price discrimination abuses under article 82–An economic analysis", ECLR, (2006), 286.

[8] Council Regulation (EC) No. 4064/89 on the control on concentrations between undertakings [1990] OJ L257/13; Council Regulation (EC) No. 139/2004 on the control on concentrations between undertakings, [2004] OJ L24/1.

[9] Trevor Soames and Sylvie Maudhuit, 'Changes in EU Merger Control: Part 1' [2005] ECLR 57.

[10] As of September 2006 the Commission has published only the Horizontal Merger Guidelines, [2004] OJ C31/5. In August 2006 a note of the European Commission's Economic Advisory Group for Competition Policy concerning non-horizontal mergers was published. Due to the complex problems raised by these transactions and to the lack of consensus on how to deal with these problems, the Advisory Group is sceptical about drafting detailed guidelines on non-horizontal mergers. Economic Advisory Group for Competition Policy merger subgroup, (2006) 'Non-horizontal mergers guidelines: ten principles'. The Commission, aware of these difficulties, is understandably hesitant to prepare non-horizontal mergers guidelines. Paul Hofer and Mark Williams, 'Non-Horizontal Mergers' (2007) The European Antitrust Review 6.

[11] Trevor Soames and Sylvie Maudhuit, 'Changes in EU Merger Control: Part 2' [2005] ECLR 75, 77. William Kovacic, 'Transatlantic Turbulence: The Boeing –Mc Donnell Douglas Merger and International Competition Policy' (2000–01) 68 Antitrust Law Journal 805, 831. Stefan Schmitz, 'The European Commission's Decision in GE/Honeywell and the Question of the Goals of Antitrust Law' (2002) 23 University of Pennsylvania Journal of International Economic Law 539, 567. Cristoforo Osti and Roberto Pardolesi, 'Falsi Amici: Le Concentrazioni in Europa e negli Stati Uniti' [2002] I Giurisprudenza Commerciale 153, 169. David Samuels and Emily Bendell Rating, 'Rating Enforcement' (2005) 5 Global Competition Review 2, 5.

fully addressed only through the application of national competition laws. It was thus necessary to put in place a formal instrument of cooperation to enable the respective competition authorities to coordinate their enforcement activities. The 1991 Cooperation Agreement and the 1998 Positive Comity Agreement established a framework for cooperation between the EC and US competition authorities. The purpose of these schemes is to promote cooperation and mutual assistance in the field of application and enforcement of competition law upon the basis of the principles of negative and positive comity. The EC/US bilateral cooperation has been quite a successful venture since its inception; nonetheless it failed to prevent the EC and US from having divergent views on the legality of the same merger operations on two different occasions. The US Federal Trade Commission approved the Boeing/Mc Donnell Douglas merger, while it was conditionally cleared by the EC Commission although it seemed to be ready to block the transaction. The General Electric/Honeywell merger was notified to the US Department of Justice in October 2000 and to the European Commission in February 2001. In May 2001 the Department of Justice concluded the review of the merger and conditionally cleared it; but the European Commission found that the merger would have adversely affected competition in several markets. Consequently General Electric/Honeywell became the first ever merger to be blocked by the EC after have being cleared by the US competition authorities.

V. *The institutional framework*

A. *Introductory remarks*

Since the above inconsistencies may be ascribed to the differences between the EC and US merger control laws, it is necessary to examine the merger control laws of these jurisdictions in order to verify the soundness of this hypothesis. The starting point of the proposed comparative analysis will be the institutional framework for merger control within the EC and the US. This concept includes the rules that determine the responsibilities and powers of the competent authorities in the field of merger control. In this regard, the EC and US diverge on two important aspects: the first one concerns the number of authorities involved in the administration of merger control. The second one concern which authority has the ultimate powers in the appraisal of mergers. The EC embraces an administrative regime, under which the Commission has the investigatory and adjudicative powers. On the other hand, the US opts for a prosecutorial regime, according to which, the competition authorities have investigatory powers, while the adjudicative powers are conferred upon the judiciary.

B. *The allocation of regulatory powers*

In the EC the competence to apply and enforce merger control law is vested in the Commission, which has also the power to formulate competition policies and participate in the law-making process. US merger control, on the other hand, is administered by the Department of Justice and the Federal Trade Commission. The former is an agency of the executive branch of the federal government and the latter is an independent regulatory agency. The Department of Justice has the power to review mergers between some specific categories of firms, such as banks, bank holding companies, airlines, newspapers and research & production joint ventures, to which special procedural standards apply. Importantly, other parties, such as state attorneys and private parties, are entitled to challenge mergers. Private parties may particularly motivated to bring the issue of the validity of mergers before courts due to the possibility of being awarded treble damages. The amount of human resources which the US Administration commits to merger control is higher than that of the European Commission. The latter employs 116 lawyers and 54 economists. In contrast, the US Department of Justice has 369 lawyers and 56 economists, while the Federal Trade Commission has 180 lawyers and 49 economists. The DG Comp, until the recent reform was implemented, lacked a sufficient number of professionals, in particular economists, to review all of the notified mergers. Such understaffing was all the more serious because the most controversial cases in merger control often concern issues at the cutting edge of economic research. Finally, in 2004 the Antitrust Division of the US Department of Justice had a budget of € 106,915, 226 and the budget of the Bureau of Competition of the Federal Trade Commission was € 68,560,000. In the same year the budget of the DG Competition of the European Commission was € 45,000,000.

C. *The EC administrative regime*

The Commission, an administrative institution, conducts investigations into the anti-competitive effects of merger operations and decides whether to approve or prohibit transactions.[12] EC Courts can intervene in merger control process only after that the Commission has reached a decision on a merger when the merging parties appeal that decision. Because EC Regulation 139/2004 does not expressly provide for any specific judicial remedy, the general principles of EC law apply, notably Articles 229, 230 and 233 EC Treaty. The Commission's decisions can be challenged before the Court of First Instance. The right to impugn these decisions is conferred by the Treaty to the person to whom the decision is addressed and to any persons to whom

[12] Articles 8 and 13 of EC Regulation 139/2004.

the decision is of direct and individual concern. This means that a decision of the Commission regarding a merger can be challenged both by the merging parties and by their competitors.[13]

Commission's decisions can be impugned for lack of competence, infringement of an essential procedural requirement, infringement of the Treaty and any rule of law relating to its application and, lastly, misuse of powers. It is also possible to appeal the judgments of the Court of First Instance before the Court of Justice, but only upon a point of law, such as error of assessment and violation of substantive and procedural legal rules. Some scholars have highlighted the inefficaciousness and weakness of the judicial control on the Commission's decisions. The scope of the appeal jurisdiction is rather narrow due to the restricted range of grounds for annulment open to the appellant. Also the length of the appeal process before the Court of First Instance, which is usually between 18–36 months, may discourage the parties from challenging decisions of the Commission.[14] A judgment which quashes a negative decision by the Commission should in theory allow the merging parties to execute the merger. However if the parties have waited two or three years for such a judgement, the market conditions might have been so substantially altered in the meantime that the transaction, as originally planned, would have no economic sense. In such a situation, the judgement of the Court provides little or no relief to the parties. The recent introduction of the fast track procedure, which attaches greater importance to the oral discussion of the case rather than to written pleadings, has reduced the length of the appeal process.[15] Nevertheless it may remain too long for the business world which requires legal certainty without delay.[16]

---

[13] The Commission decision regarding the Sony/Bertelsmann merger was impugned by competitors. CFI, case T-464/04 Impala v Commission. For a more detailed analysis of Article 230 EC treaty, see Josephine Steiner and Lorna Woods, Textbook on EC Law (Oxford University Press, Oxford 8th edition) chapter 28.

[14] Rachel Brandeburger and Thomas Janssen, 'European merger Control: Do the Checks and Balances Need to Be Re-Set' [2001] Fordham Corporate Law Institute 135, 177. David Evans and Michael Salinger, 'Competition Thinking at the European Commission: Lessons from the Aborted GE/Honeywell Merger' [2002] George Mason Law Review 489, 496. Eric Hochstadt, 'The Brown Shoe of European Union Competition Law', (2002) 24 Cardozo Law Review 287, 301.

[15] For example the appeal against the decision of the Commission to block the Schneider/Legrande concentration was decided in about one year after that the Commission adopted the questioned decision. See Jean-Marc Thouvenin, 'Concurrence (Concentration): aprés l'arrêt Airtours trois noveaux avertissements à la Commission' [2003] RMCUE 12, 13.

[16] Edward Swaine, 'Competition, Not Competitors, nor Canards: Ways of Criticizing the Commission', (2003) 23 University of Pennsylvania Journal of International Economic Law 597, 631; Robert O'Donaghue and Christoph Feddersen, 'Notes on Airtours v. Commission' [2002] CMLRev 1171, 1183. Pricewaterhouse Coopers, 'A Tax on Mergers? Surveying the Time and Costs to Business of Multi-jurisdictional Merger Review' [2003] Business Law International 275, at 290.

D. *The US prosecutorial regime*

The US merger control regime is prosecutorial regime in the sense that if a merger may substantially lessen the competition the competition authorities need a court decision in order to prohibit that transaction. The Department of Justice must bring an action before district courts, the jurisdiction of which is based on section 4 of the US Sherman Act and section 15 of the US Clayton Act. On the other hand, the Federal Trade Commission has to seek a preliminary injunction request before a federal district court; then it issues an administrative complaint that will be adjudicated by an Administrative Law Judge of the Federal Trade Commission.

Generally, the merger control proceedings instituted in the US are longer than the proceedings in the EC. A survey conducted by Pricewaterhouse Coopers on time and costs for firms in case of multi-jurisdictional review shows that the longest review in the US lasted 8,8 months, while in the EC the longest investigation did not go beyond 5 months. The slower pace of the US merger control procedure may be explained with the tighter statutory deadlines the Commission must comply with.

An important difference between the prosecutorial and the administrative regimes lies in the different standards of proof required to demonstrate the alleged anti-competitive effects of mergers. Apparently, in the prosecutorial regime the standard of proof is set at a higher level than in the administrative regime. A possible reason is that in prosecutorial regimes the negative decision to disallow a merger has to be adopted by an independent judicial authority before which competition authorities have to prove the anti-competitive effects of mergers. Accordingly, they have to submit sufficiently robust evidence to convince judges of the anti-competitive effects of the merger and withstand the defensive arguments put forward by the parties in the exercise of their rights of defence.[17]

E. *Determination of the scope of application of merger control: qualitative and quantitative criteria*

The US and the EC have enacted a number of qualitative and quantitative criteria with the purpose of delimitating the scope of application of their

[17] Patterson and Shapiro, above, argued that because of the independent judicial oversight prescribed by the US merger control law, the right of defence recognised to parties to judicial proceedings and the burden placed upon the acting authorities to demonstrate the likelihood of anticompetive effects, US competition authorities are unlikely to challenge a merger before courts upon the basis of controversial economic theories and inaccurate facts. These authors, writing immediately after the Commission decision on the General Electric/Honeywell, seem to embrace the view that the EC administrative regime would allow the Commission to block a merger upon the basis of grounds which would not be accepted under the US prosecutory standards. However, the recent developments of the EC case law should have at least reduce the alleged difference regarding the standard of proof.

merger control laws. The control in a firm can be gained through the acquisition of shares and/or assets, via contractual relations or via other means business transactions that fall within the reach of merger control. EC Regulation 139/2004 indicates that "concentrations" are the category of transactions caught by the regulatory powers of the Commission. The notion of concentration is illustrated by Article 3 of EC Regulation 139/2004 and by the 1998 Commission Notice on the interpretation of the concept of concentration. The key element of the notion of concentration is "the lasting change in the control of the undertaking concerned and therefore in the structure of the market", which can be achieved in different ways. A concentration takes place when previously independent undertakings merge, which, according to the Notice, covers the amalgamation or the absorption among two or more independent firms. In this case the rights and liabilities of the merging firms pass on to the merged entity, while the parties to the merger cease to exist as legal persons. In addition, mergers may also be the combination of previously independent undertakings leading to the de facto creation of single economic units. According to Article 3(1)(b) a concentration is also achieved when direct or indirect control of the whole or parts of an undertaking is acquired. Article 3(3) of EC Regulation 139/2004 defines control as the nexus of rights, contracts, and other means that gives, in law or de facto, the possibility to exercise decisive influence on the commercial strategies or activities of the firm concerned. It may be acquired directly or indirectly, solely or jointly by two or more undertakings, when each firm has the power to block action influencing the strategic commercial behaviour of a firm.[18] Finally, the concept of concentration also includes some types of joint ventures, namely the "full-function" joint ventures. These must be a viable autonomous economic entity operating on a lasting basis and must be characterised by dedicated management, sufficient staff and financial resources as well as access to the relevant market. In conclusion, it can be said that EC Regulation 139/2004 adopts a pragmatic approach for the definition of a merger, which focuses on the substance and effects of the transactions. The qualifying element of this concept is the changes to the structure of control over firms, irrespective of the form through which such changes are achieved.[19]

---

[18] European Commission Notice on the concept of full-function joint ventures Council Regulation (EEC) No 4064/89 on the control of concentration between undertakings.

[19] Kintner, above n 7, 112. Under the US competition law some categories are exempted from the scope of application of the relevant competition law provisions. Such exemptions include:—Joint ventures acting in the export trade, laid down by the Webb Pomerene Act (15 U.S.C. sec. 62) and the Export Trading Company Act (15 U.S.C. sec. 4001–3 and sec.4011–21)—Joint ventures set up in the field of research and development as well as production joint ventures provided by the National Co-operative Research and Production Act 1993 (15 U.S.C. sec. 4301–05)—Certain joint ventures agreed among daily newspaper publishers under the Newspaper Preservation Act of 1970 (15 U.S.C. sec. 1803).

In US law the definition of the categories of business transactions subject to merger control is contained in section 7 of the Clayton Act, as amended by the 1950 Celler-Kefauver Amendment. Any acquisition of stock and assets that is likely to have a restrictive impact on competition according to a standard that will be discussed later is caught by US law.[20] The term of acquisition is extensively construed, as it covers virtually all types of mergers and certain categories of joint venture as well. This wide approach was illustrated in Procter & Gamble where the US Supreme Courts ruled "all mergers are within the reach of (US Clayton Act) section 7 and must be tested by the same standard, whether they are classified as horizontal, vertical, conglomerate or other."[21]

The purpose of quantitative criteria is to establish whether a merger operation, falling under the category of transactions determined by the qualitative criteria, has enough strong links with a country to be subjected to the review of the competition authorities of that country. The EC quantitative criterion is the "Community dimension", which is based on a two-tiered financial threshold referring to the turnover achieved by the merging parties. However, the EC merger control legislation contains some exemptions to the "Community dimension" in the shape of the pre-referral and post-referral mechanisms. The pre-referral mechanisms are voluntarily triggered by merging parties who may ask the Commission to refer the merger to the competition authority of the Member State, within whose territory the adverse effects of the transaction are likely to be felt. The rationale underlying this provision is to allow the best placed competition authority to appraise the merger operation. The merging parties can also ask the Commission to assess a merger which does not meet the "Community dimension", but which is subject to review in at least three Member States. The post-referral mechanism is activated by the Commission of its own initiative or by a Member State's invitation. The

[20] Federal Trade Commission v. Procter & Gamble Co., 386 US 568.

[21] According to Article 1 of the EC Regulation 139/2004 a concentration has a Community dimension, and therefore falls within the jurisdiction of the Community, where: a) the combined aggregate worldwide turnover all of the undertakings concerned is more than EUR 5,000 million; and b) the aggregate Community-wide turnover of each of at least two of the undertakings concerned is more than EUR 250 million, unless each of the undertakings concerned achieves more than two-thirds of its aggregate Community-wide turnover within one and the same Member States. Moreover if a transaction fails to meet such requirements it can nevertheless considered as having Community dimension provided that: a) the combined aggregate worldwide turnover all of the undertakings concerned is more than EUR 2,500 million; b) in each of at least three Member States, the combined aggregate turnover of all the undertakings concerned is more than EUR 100 million; c) in each of at least three Member States included for the purpose of point (b), the aggregate turnover of each of at least two of the undertakings concerned is more than EUR 25 million; and d) the aggregate Community-wide turnover of each of at least two of the undertakings is more than EUR 100 million unless each of the undertakings concerned achieves more than two-thirds of its aggregate Community-wide turnover within one and the same Member State.

Commission can refer a merger operation to a Member State within the territory of which the adverse effects of the merger are felt. Conversely, Member States may ask the Commission to assess a merger which does not fall within the concept of the "Community dimension", but which affects trade between Member States and are likely to have restrictive effects in the territory of the Member States making the request. The quantitative criteria of the US Clayton Act, as amended by the 1976 Hart-Scott-Rodino Act, consist of a set of financial thresholds referring either to the size of the transaction or the size of the merging parties. A merger is caught by US jurisdiction when the acquiring person, as a result of the acquisition, holds an aggregate total amount of the voting securities and assets of the acquired person which is in excess of 226,8 $ million. A merger is caught by US jurisdiction even when the above thresholds is not met, provided that two conditions regarding the size of the parties are satisfied: any of the parties must have net sales or total assets not lower than 11,3 $ million, while the other party must have net sales or total assets not lower than 113,4 $ million.

The financial thresholds set by EC Regulation 139/2004 are higher than those laid down by the Hart-Scott-Rodino Act. An example may help readers understand the difference. Firms A and B decide to merge; in the last year the net sales generated by A amounted to $120 million, while the net sales of B do not exceed $50 million. The proposed merger operation meets the thresholds of the Hart-Scott-Rodino Act and it falls under the US jurisdiction. However, the worldwide turnover achieved by the merging parties is lower than the statutory thresholds regarding the combined aggregate worldwide turnover of all the parties. Indeed, upon the basis of a 0.85 ratio exchange euro/dollar it will be about €145 million and therefore it fall outside the scope of the EC jurisdiction. As a result of the higher level at which the EC financial thresholds are set only "true multinational mergers" seem to be caught by the EC jurisdiction. Therefore, a smaller number of merger operations are subjected to the EC merger control than the number of transactions that falls within the purview of the US competition authorities.[22]

[22] Thomas Kauper, 'Merger Control in the United States and the European Union: Some Observations' (2000) 74 St. John's Law Review 305, 316. Werner Berg, 'The New EC Merger Regulation: A First Assessment of its Practical Impact' (2004) 24 Northwestern Journal of International Law and Business 683, 698; Mauro Megliani, 'La riforma della disciplina comunitaria del controllo delle concentrazioni tra imprese', [2004] Il Diritto del Commercio Internazionale 685, 699. Trevor Soames and Sylvie Maudhuit, 'Changes in EU Merger Control: Part 3' [2005] ECLR 144, 146. Jason Garrick, 'International Horizontal Mergers: A Comparison of the European Union and the United States Regulatory Policy and Procedure' (1994) 7 Transnational Lawyer 299.

VI. *Procedural rules*

A. *Notification of merger operations*

The first aspect to be considered is the range of the factors triggering merger control. The EC and the US have opted for the ex ante merger control regime, under which mergers are normally appraised after the conclusion of merger agreements but before the implementation of the transaction. The great advantage of such regime is that the merging parties obtain a definitive response on the legality of the planned merger before the consummation of the transaction. Thus, should the competition authority decide to prohibit the merger the parties would not be forced to undo an already implemented transaction. The ex-ante control regime imposes upon the merging parties two different obligations. First, it imposes "a facere" obligation, which requires the parties to notify the merger to the competition authorities before consummation. The second obligation is a non "facere" obligation, which means that the parties must not implement transaction as long as the regulating authority is investigating the merger.

The mandatory pre-merger notification is the starting point of the EC and US merger control procedure. Under US law the parties, after the conclusion of a legally binding merger agreement or even after the drafting of a letter of intents, have a duty to notify the merger to the competition authorities. Article 2 (1) of EC Regulation 139/2004 stipulates that all mergers that have a Community dimension shall be notified to the Commission. The notification obligation is triggered by the "conclusion of the agreement, or the announcement of a bid, or the acquisition of a controlling interest". EC Regulation 139/2004 has made significant innovations to the old EC Regulation 4064/89 by extending the range of the triggering events of the notification obligation. The previous regulation ruled that the merging parties were obliged to notify the Commission only when they made a legally binding merger agreement. The new regulation allows parties to notify the Commission even before the conclusion of a binding agreement provided that there is a good faith intention to conclude the merger agreement. The term of good faith intention is read in the sense that the merging parties must have sufficiently concrete plans for the execution of the merger. This requirement is met by an agreement in principle, a memorandum of understanding or a letter of intent signed by all the parties. Moreover, the new regulation abolishes the seven days deadline by which, under the old law, the parties were required to notify the merger.

The new notification regime is thought to secure a number of benefits. First, the merging parties enjoy a certain degree of discretion in deciding when to notify. They can notify at any time from the moment their intention to execute the merger materialises in sufficiently concrete plans until a point before the consummation of the transaction. Where the parties opt for early notification they may expedite the review of the notified merger and reduce the compliance costs. Secondly, the new regime will be helpful for the international cooperation between competition authorities since the EC merger notification regime is now closer to that of the US and it is also consistent with the Recommended Practices of the International Competition Network. Such similarity should facilitate coordination and cooperation between the national competition authorities involved in the review of trans-national mergers.

B. *Investigation period*

The second constitutive element of the ex ante merger control is the waiting period, which is normally divided into two phases, during which the competition authority reviews the notified merger. Under EC law the initial phase of the waiting period starts the day the Commission receives the CO Form. This phase has to be completed within 25 working days, which can be extended up to 35 working days if the parties offer commitments. During this phase the Commission conducts preliminary investigations and verifies whether the merger—"raises serious doubts as to its compatibility with the common market". If the Commission declares that such serious doubts exist it starts the second phase investigation throughout which it carries out an in-depth examination into the merits of the merger. The Commission must close the second phase investigation and reach a final decision on the compatibility of the merger with the common market within the time limit of 90 working days from the opening of the formal investigation. This limit time must be extended up to 105 working days if the parties propose commitments within 55 working days of the start of the procedure. All the deadlines are expressed in working days, which should make it easier to calculate them. Article 10(3) of EC Regulation 139/2004 also contains a "stop the clock" provision which, in case the parties have offered commitments to meet the competition concerns raised by the Commission, extends the time limit for the second phase investigation by up to 20 working days upon request of either the Commission or the parties.

The US law provides that the first 30–day phase starts when the competition authority acknowledges the receipt of the notification form. The first phase is dedicated to preliminary investigations on the notified merger at the end of which if the acting authority has some doubts on the legality of the merger it may issue a Second Request order and asks the parties for more documents and information. The parties need to commit a wide range of resources to reply to the Second Request. From the day when the parties have satisfied the request of the authority with the submission of all the required information a further 20–days waiting period starts. During this second period the Department of Justice or the Federal Trade Commission have to assess the data given by the parties and decide whether to block or clear the merger. It is important to bear in mind that while the EC Commission cannot challenge the merger after the expiration of the statutory time limits,[23] US law does not provide for such limitations with respect to the power of US competition authorities to challenge mergers. These authorities have therefore the power to question the legality of mergers even after the expiration of the waiting period and after the implementation of the merger.

C. *Notification form*

EC Regulation 139/2004 and the US Clayton Act diverge as to the statutory content of the notification form. The EC form—the CO form-requires a large amount of data, ranging from a description of the relevant markets to an analysis of the competitive situation of the competitors.[24] The rationale behind this approach is that the parties should furnish the Commission from the very beginning of the procedure all the necessary information required to appraise the merger.[25] EC Regulation 802/2004 has introduced a short notification form, which requires fewer amounts of data from the merging parties. The parties can use the short form provided that the merger meets one of the conditions enlisted by the Annex to the Regulation, which normally happens when the merger is unlikely to raise serious competition problems.[26] On the other hand, under the US merger control regime, the parties discharge the pre-merger notification obligation by the submission of much less information.[27]

VII. *Differences between EC and US institutional framework and procedural rules: Possible consequences on the outcome of mergers review*

A. *Powers of the EC Commission*

The previous sections have described and compared the main features of the institutional frameworks and procedural rules of the EC and US merger control regimes. It emerged that, although these jurisdictions are converging with regard to many aspects of merger control, differences still exist between

[23] Commission Regulation (EC) 802/2004 of 7th April 2004, [2004] OJ L61/1.

[24] Annex to Commission Regulation (EC) 802/2004 relating to the notification of a Concentration pursuant to EC Regulation 4064/89.

[25] Stefan Schmitz 'How Dare They? European Merger Control and the European Commission's Blocking of the General Electric/Honeywell Merger' (2002) 23 University of Pennsylvania Journal of International Economic Law 325, 350.

[26] Annex II Short Form for the Notification of Concentration pursuant to EC Regulation 139/2004 [2004] OJ L133/22.

[27] Section 16 C.F.R., Part 803, Appendix Notification and Report Form for Certain Mergers and Acquisition. For a more detailed explanation of this issue, see below para 8.10, let. b).

them on other aspects. Such divergences may somehow affect the outcome of the appraisal of the same merger conducted by the EC and US competition authorities.

Among the factors that are thought to have such consequences, the most important one seems to be the fact that the EC law assigns several functions to the Commission: policy-maker and investigator, prosecutor and judge. The Commission is accordingly empowered to block unilaterally the merger without resorting to courts. Judicial scrutiny on the Commission decisions on the legality of mergers takes place only when merging parties challenge such decisions before the Court of First Instance. Until recently the external judicial control has not stringently limited the discretion of the Commission as suggested by the fact that the EC courts overturned for the first time a decision of the Commission to block a merger only in the Airtours judgement, 12 years after the inception of the EC merger control regime.[28] All these circumstances prompt some authors to voice concerns that the Commission has an excessive discretionary power and a low degree of accountability. The risk is that, due to the administrative regime, the Commission may base the decision to block a concentration upon a lower standard of evidence than that which the US competition authorities have to produce before an independent judicial body to block the merger.

These critiques have been fiercely rejected by the Commission, which maintains that the fairness of the process and the procedural rights are guaranteed in the EC administrative regime, although through different means from those adopted by US law. Indeed, while these values are safeguarded in US law through the judicial process, the EC protect them via a matrix of checks and balances, which constrains the discretionary power of the Commission within the limits of legality. For example, the decision with which the Commission closes the first phase investigations is communicated to the merging parties. The purpose of this provision is to allow parties to learn the legal and factual grounds upon which the doubts of the Commission as to the legality of the mergers are grounded. Another relevant example is the Statement of Objections that is issued by the Commission in the second phase investigations. This document crystallizes the legal, economic and factual data selected by the Commission as the basis of its opposition to the merger. The EC merger control Regulation confers on the parties the right of access to such data: thus not only are the parties entitled to a copy the Statement of Objections, but they can also access the files of the Commission. Such procedural rights should enable the parties to formulate their defensive strategies against the objections raised by the Commission more easily both

---

[28] Thomas Zweifel, 'Best and Worst Practices in European, US and Swiss Merger Regulation' [2003] JCMS 541, 557. Dimitris Giotakos, 'GE/Honeywell: A Theoretic Bundle Assessing Mergers Across the Atlantic' [2001] University of Pennsylvania Journal of International Economic Law 469, 507.

in the submission of written pleadings—after the notification of copy of the Statement of Objections—and verbally at the Oral Hearing.

Nevertheless, to some these checks and balances do not seem sufficiently strong to dispel all the concerns about the fairness of the EC merger control procedure. The period of time which the Commission allows the parties in order to prepare the replies to the Statement of Objections—usually two weeks—may be insufficient, especially if the issues raised by the Commission are controversial and complex. Besides, in the Second Phase investigation, after several months of investigations, the case handlers team within the Commission may have already taken strong views on the legality of the merger which may not be easily allayed. The strong commitment of the Commission to pro-competitive policies may affect the assessment of the anti-competitive effects of mergers as the Commission may be more likely to find restrictive rather than positive effects on competition. As a result, the merging parties may find it quite arduous reversing the position of the Commission and convincing it that the merger will not effectively result in the feared anti-competitive effects.

Criticism has been also levelled at the role of the Oral Hearing. This is labelled as the "day of the parties", and is the moment when the parties present their case. However, the Oral Hearing has been criticised for being too "informative" in the sense that the parties' presentations "cannot be effectively questioned" and that generally, "only informational questions are allowed". The powers of the Oral Hearing Officer, a Commission employee, are also criticised as the Officer does not decide either on the admission of evidence or what weight should be attached to the evidence. As he does not make substantive recommendation on the basis of evidence produced at the hearing, the Oral Hearing may be of little practical support for the investigations of the Commission. It bears more resemblance "to a seminar than a trial". It has mainly an educative function and its purpose is to make known the case of the merging parties to the other Directorate of the Commission and to those Member States that have an interest in the merger.

B. *Role of Competitors*

The role played by the rivals of the merging parties within merger control procedure is another aspect that is differently considered by the EC and the US. The Commission tends to attach great importance to the third parties' submissions, lest it might not be able to conclude the appraisal of mergers within the statutory deadlines.[29] The views of rivals are seen as a source of

[29] Swaine, above n 35, 627. For a detailed comparative analysis of the role of competitors in the EC and US merger control proceedings see Alan Ryan and Bob Schlossberg, 'The Role of Third Parties in Merger Investigation' in Transatlantic Merger Control (2006). James Turner,

valuable information given that, as insiders in the relevant markets, they are in the best position to supply the Commission with precious insights into how markets work. The participation of third parties to the merger control procedure is codified in Article 18(4) of EC Regulation 139/2004, which provides that persons other than the merging parties showing a sufficient interest in the merger have the right to be heard. The Commission usually lets third parties know the contents of the Statement of Objections served on the merging parties, either by giving them a summary or by providing a complete confidential version of the document or even a copy of it. The Commission also allows third parties to submit their own observations. In accordance with its interpretation of Article 18(4) of EC Regulation 139/2004 and Article 14(2) of EC Regulation 802/2004, the Commission will hear any person who is bona fide and able to give a relevant contribution to the facts and issues that constitute the subject matter of the proceedings. Third parties may also have the chance to take part in the oral hearing and put forward their objections against the proposed merger. Generally, third parties are not allowed access to the Commission's file; although, the Commission may give such access to the parties who have already been already informed of the Commission's objections against the merger, where access to its file will enable third parties to prepare their own submissions more effectively.[30] The file of the Commission is not usually available to the general public; thus, the possibility of third parties accessing these documents should be regarded as important.

Third parties sometimes seek to take advantage of the EC merger control procedural rules and actively participate in proceeding before the Commission. In General Electric/Honeywell, one of General Electric's legal counsels expressed annoyance at the significant role played by the competitors. Indeed, in General Electric/Honeywell as well as in Boeing/McDonnell Douglas, third parties produced their own data, gave their own testimony and expressed their views on the submissions and commitments advanced by the merging parties. Sometimes the Commission utilised the arguments developed by the third parties as grounds for prohibiting a merger. For example, the manufacturers of jet engines and avionics products who were strong opponents of the General Electric/Honeywell merger gave to the Commission some valuable suggestions regarding the economic theories which should be employed with the purpose of assessing the alleged competitive effects of

'Mega Merger, Mega Problems. A Critique of the European Community's Commission on Competition's Review of the AOL/Time Warner Merger' (2002) 17 American University International Law Review 131, 177.

[30] Jose Rivas, The EU Merger Regulation and the Anatomy of the Merger Task Force, (Kluwer Law International, London, Boston 1999) 40. Helen Power, 'The Honeywell monster' The Lawyer, 23 July 2001. Neal Stoll and Shepard Goldfein, 'A Tale of Two Regulators' [2001] New York Law Journal 226.

the proposed merger. The economists hired by United Technologies recommended to the Commission to apply the theory of bundling. The economic consultants of Rolls Royce brought to the attention of the Commission the issue that the vertical integration between General Electric and GECAS would have anti-competitive effects in the market for aircraft engines.

Yet, competition authorities must be aware that the views taken by competitors towards proposed mergers might be biased. The reason why competitors decide to intervene in merger control proceedings might be completely unconnected with any real competition concerns. The merged entity may turn out to be a fierce competitor to the remaining firms, whose profits as a result may be reduced. Not surprisingly, these firms try to strategically exploit merger review procedures with the purpose of blocking the merger. Alternatively, they may try convincing the Commission to open the second phase investigation or to impose onerous conditions on the parties, even when the merger may be advantageous for consumers. This is epitomised by the defensive strategies followed by GTE Corporation, Walt Disney Company and Sun Microsystems Inc. when all of them attempted to block respectively the MCI/ WorldCom, AOL/Time Warner and Microsoft/ Telewest mergers planned by their competitors. As a further example, the efforts of Lockheed and Arian Space to slow down the Boeing/Hughes merger were eventually successful as the Commission decided to start the second phase investigation.[31]

The Commission should avoid relying excessively on the arguments brought forth by third parties, since this stance could be interpreted as a sign of sympathy towards the preoccupations of competitors to the detriment of consumers' welfare. This is exactly the position expressed by the lawyers who acted on behalf of Boeing in Boeing/McDonnell Douglas. In their view the Commission tried to stop the merger as it would have posed a serious threat to the competitiveness of Airbus in the market. However, Commission officials who pointed out have promptly rebutted such allegations that the objections raised against the merger were exclusively based on purely competition law considerations.

The role played by third parties in the US merger control procedure is less significant since the US legislation does not confer on the competitors any formal rights to participate in the proceedings. More importantly, even if the US competition authorities are willing to take into consideration the information supplied by competitors, they have a more sceptical attitude

---

[31] WorldCom/MCI, (Case IV/M.1069) Commission Decision. AOL/Time Warner (Case IV/ M.1845) Commission Decision. Microsoft/Liberty Media/Telewest (Case IV/J27) Commission Decision. Boeing/Hughes (Case IV/M.1879) Commission Decision. cfr. Jenna Greene, 'Antitrust Action Moves to Europe. EU Seen as Friendlier Forum for Slowing Down Mega-Deals' 24 (2001) Legal Times no. 14.

when assessing such data. The US competition authorities are more wary that the observations put forward by rivals are often motivated by the fear of a tougher post-merger market. Their investigations therefore focus more on facts rather than on submissions. They usually do not base their case to block a merger on documents supplied by third parties, unless such documents are supported by a sound theory of competition harms and by hard facts. Evidence presented by third parties might not successfully withstand the cross-examination at a preliminary injunction hearing. The merging parties' competitors also have a limited ability to bring an action against mergers that may have anti-competitive effects; but they may obtain injunctive relief and treble damages after the consummation of the merger. States' prosecutors may also obtain injunctive relief and damages, although damages suits brought about by States have raised concerns. The decision of States to sue may be influenced by interests group which represent the competitors' merging parties that may oppose mergers for reasons other than the protection of competition.[32]

C. *Different timetable of merger control procedures*

The EC and US have differently shaped the time frame for merger control, especially with respect to the concluding phases of their procedures. Different timings may make more difficult the coordination between the US and the EC competition authorities, which may increase the risk of inconsistent decisions. The more rigid EC timetable is of benefit for businesses, given that it compels the Commission to complete the legality review of the merger within a reasonable time limit with as little inconvenience as possible for the merging parties. Yet, such rigidity may force the Commission to close its investigations within the statutory deadline even if it has not gathered all the information necessary for the appraisal of mergers. The Commission, with the approaching of the deadline of the investigation period, would face a dilemma. It may have to choose between closing the investigation, without being able to take a thoroughly informed decision due to the expiration of the time limits and risking taking an ill informed decision. The risk is that

---

[32] Jay Brown and Niamh Connery, 'Comparing U.S. and EU Merger Review: Procedures, Principles and Whether Adopting the "Substantial Lessening of Competition" Test in the EU will Produce Greater Harmony after GE/Honeywell'. William Kolasky, 'GE/Honeywell: Continuing the Transatlantic Dialogue' [2002] University of Pennsylvania Journal of International Economic Law 513, 534; Evans and Salinger, above n 31, 527. William Kolasky, 'Sound Economics and Hard Evidence: The Touchstone of Sound Merger Review' 2006. Joel Davidow, 'International Implications of U.S. Antitrust in the Government in the George W. Bush Era' (2002) 25 World Competition 493, 499. Filip Ragolle, 'Schneider Electric v. Commission: The Court of First Instance; Response to the Green Paper on Merger Review' [2003] ECLR 176, 180. Davies, Moltenbrey and Yde, above n 87; International Competition Policy Advisory Commette, Hearings, Washington DC, 3rd November 1998.

the Commission might choose the latter alternative and accordingly adopt a negative decision or opt for a hastily negotiated settlement. This procedural rigidity may also affect the examination of the undertakings offered by the parties by impeding appropriate evaluations of them. Mergers could be prohibited for procedural rather for substantive grounds. However, the novelties introduced by EC Regulation 139/2004 should have tempered the above lamented rigidity: under the new regime the Commission should be able to assess more comfortably the alleged anti-competitive effects of mergers.

The US merger control procedure seems to be more flexible and merging parties have a tighter control over the timing of the regulatory review, especially in the event of Second Request. In this case, it may be difficult to predict with a reasonable degree of certainty when the US authorities will complete the review of the merger. The review period starts again after that the parties have met all the requirements prescribed by the Second Request. So the control of the timing of the investigation is apparently shifted into the hands of the parties, who can agree to extend the second waiting period or force the acting authority to reach a decision on the merger within the original statutory review period. Second Requests, however, have raised concerns as it is thought that the US Competition authorities make Second Requests as broad as possible. In this case it takes longer for the merging parties to reply to all the questions and the regulators may gain more time for investigations. Moreover, foreign firms, especially those from legal system where discovery is unknown and therefore they are unused to litigations which require to produce many documents, dislike Second Requests. This might discourage foreign firms from investing in the US.

VIII. *Criticism of the EC Courts regarding Commission's administration of merger control*

The manner in which the EC merger control regime has been administered by the Commission has attracted the criticism of the competition law community. As explained above, the administrative regime combined with, at least until recently, an apparently lenient judicial scrutiny leaves to the Commission a wide margin of discretion as to the assessment of mergers. So on some occasions the Commission relied on inaccurate factual analysis and controversial economic theories. For example, in General Electric/Honeywell it applied the theory of conglomerate effects previously discarded by the US competition authorities. In Boeing/McDonnell Douglas the Commission referred to a declaration reported in a newspaper article without disclosing the source. Such concerns, however, have not remained unanswered and have been addressed by three recent judgements of the Court of First Instance concerning decisions taken by the Commission under the EC Regulation 4064/89.[33] In these judgments the Court blamed the Commission for the inaccuracies of its factual investigations, for the poor coherence of the economic analysis and for the reliance on insufficiently tested economic theories.

In Tetra Laval the Court of First Instance examines the application of the theory of conglomerate merger. Since, generally, such mergers have neutral effects on competition the Commission should have provided a convincing set of evidence of the anti-competitive effects of this category of mergers.[34] The Commission also erroneously did not take into consideration the possible infringement of Article 82 EC Treaty as a factor that would have discouraged the merged entity from putting into practice restrictive behaviour following the implementation of the merger. The Court did not share the same concerns as the Commission on the leverage effects. An earlier Article 82 EC Treaty decision had placed severe restrictions on the commercial freedom of Tetra Laval, which would have made it unlikely to adopt and implement leveraging strategies. In Schneider the Court criticised the methodology applied by the Commission to assess the competitive effects of the transaction under review. The merged entity, in the view of the Commission, would have obtained a dominant position in the relevant national markets because of the range of the products offered and because the overall impact the merger would have on all the relevant geographic markets. The Commission seemed to rely upon the idea of transnational market dominance to analyse the market power of the merging parties in each national market concerned. The Court was unimpressed by such an approach and it ruled that the evaluation of the market power of the merging parties in a specific national market should comprise only factors present in that market. However, the Court did not rule out the possibility of taking into account transnational effects if sufficient evidence of them were provided.

The Court also reproaches the Commission for its incoherent, inaccurate assessment of facts. In Airtours it ruled that the Commission mistakenly

---

[33] CFI Case T-342/99 Airtours plc v. Commission [2002] 5 CMLR 7; CFI Case T-310/01 Schneider Electric SA v. Commission [2003] 4 CMLR 768 and CFI Case T-5/02 Tetra Laval BV v. Commission [2002] 5 CMLR 1182. Jean Marc Thouvenin, 'L'arrêt Airtours du 6 Juin 2002: l'irruption du juge dans le contrôle des concentrations entre entreprises' [2002] RMCUE 482, 484, who lists some of the harshest terms used by the Court to review the impugned Commission decisions: particulièrement elliptique, quelque peu ambiguë, pas explicite, sans cohérence.

[34] CFI Case T-5/02, above n 127, para 155. Case IV/31043, Elopak Italia srl v. Tetra Laval(no.2),[1992] 4 CMLR 551. CFI Case T-5/02, above n 127, paras 217–225. Cfr. Laurence Idot, 'Deux interdictions annulées par le Tribunal: Tempête sur le contrôle des concentrations' Europe, December 2002 12, 13. CFI Case T-310/01, above n 127, paras 176–192. CFI Case T-342/99, above n 127, paras 74–181. CFI Case T-310/01, above n 127, paras 134–403.

held that the market conditions were such as to conduce a tacit collusion. In Schneider it found inconsistencies in the analysis of the Commission on the competitive structure of the relevant national markets. It also observed that the Commission overestimated the economic power of the merged entity within the relevant markets. In Tetra Laval the Court held that the line of reasoning followed by the Commission was erroneous and lacked sufficient evidence.[35] The Commission relied on horizontal and vertical links in order to demonstrate that the merging parties held a dominant position, but it did not adequately prove the existence of such links. Finally in Schneider the Commission infringed the rights of defence of the parties because of the charges in the Statement of Objections were different from the grounds invoked in the final text of the decision to justify the prohibition of the merger.[36]

The judgment of the Court of First Instance in Tetra Laval has been upheld by the Court of Justice. The Court of Justice confirmed the position of the Court of First Instance as to the extent of the judicial review on the decisions of the Commission. It also confirmed that the Court of First Instance has the power to review the interpretation of economic facts and data made by the Commission, with the only limit being that it may not substitute the economic assessment of the Commission with its own. Moreover, the Court of Justice approved the rulings of the Court of First Instance with regard to the standard of proof. The Commission has to provide convincing evidence, especially in merger control cases, which involve the prospective assessment of the alleged anti-competitive effects. The Commission should therefore focus on the factors that shape the competitive structure of the markets affected by merger operations. It should also provide a detailed examination of the causal links between the anti-competitive effects and the proposed mergers as well as of the likelihood that such effects may occur. The pieces of evidence upon which the Commission based its decisions should be particularly convincing where it relies on complex theories of competitive harm or where it applies economic theories to markets whose conditions do not appear to suit them. The statements of the Court of Justice on the width of the judicial scrutiny over the decisions of the Commission and over the standard of proof with which the Commission has to comply have been recently utilised by the Court of First Instance in the judgement concerning the appeal against the Commission decision to block the General Electric/Honeywell merger.

It can be inferred from these judgements that the EC Courts are ready to exercise a more stringent and effective judicial scrutiny of the appraisals of

[35] John Temple Lang, 'Two Important Merger Regulation Judgments: The Implications of Schneider-Legrand and Tetra Lava-Sidel' [2003] ELRev 259, 265.

[36] CFI Case T-310/01, above n 127, paras 437–465. ECJ Case C-12/03 P Commission v Tetra Laval. cfr. Bay Matteo and Ruiz Calzado Javier, 'Tetra Laval II: the Coming of Age of the Judicial Review of Merger Decisions' (2005) 28 World Competition 433.

mergers made by the Commission. This scrutiny may nevertheless provide limited relief for businesses for which the commercial viability of the transaction may have vanished during the merger review process and the appeal proceedings. However, the recent EDP case proved that the Court of First Instance is capable of deciding in seven month an appeal lodged against a merger control decision of the Commission. Be that as it may, judicial review may have a vital role in building-up of a body of case law in the field of EC merger control. This case law should provide the Commission and firms with a sort of benchmark in accordance to which the appraisal of mergers should be carried out, which in turn strengthens the legal certainty.

At the procedural level the Court of First Instance has clarified the powers and the burdens of the Commission and the merging parties within the merger control process. The Court acknowledges that a certain margin of discretion is implicit in the assessment of the economic facts carried out in merger control[37]. However, it points out that before prohibiting a merger it is incumbent upon the Commission to demonstrate that the notified merger will lead to the creation of, or the strengthening of, a dominant position and that the merger will have anticompetitive effects on the markets. Thus, in Airtours the Commission did not produce convincing evidence to support its view that the merger would bring about the creation of a collective dominance position. In Tetra Laval the allegation that the conglomerate merger may have anti-competitive effects was not corroborated with enough strong evidence. In Schneider the Court was not ready to accept the presumption that alleged trans-national effects might increase the negative impact of a concentration on each national market. Indeed, it urged the Commission to furnish serious evidence of the existence of such factors. As a whole, these judgments heighten the standards of proof with which the Commission is expected to comply in merger control cases. The ultimate result is that the standard of evidence in the EC merger control has been brought closer to the more sophisticated US standards.

IX. *The new EC Regulation 139/2004 and its impact on the EC merger control regime*

One of the reasons why the EC decided to reshape its merger control regime with the new EC Regulation 139/2004 was the need to address the problems raised by the Court of First Instance in the above judgements. The new Regulation, instead of carrying out a thorough recast of the old merger

[37] CFI Case T-342/99, above n 127, para 64; CFI Case T-342/99, above n 127, para 119. Case CFI T-342/99, above n 127, Case CFI T-310/01, above n 127, paras 178–179. Cfr. Berg, above n 65, 702; Mario Todino,'La riforma del controllo delle concentrazioni nel diritto comunitario', [2004] Contratto e Impresa/Europa 1068, 1084. para 63. Case CFI T-5/02, above n 127, para 155.

control regime with the separation between the investigative and the adjudicative functions of the Commission, favours a lower profile but more pragmatic stance. Indeed, it only strengthens the internal checks and balances and makes the timetable of merger control procedure more flexible. The less rigid timetable enables the Commission to carry out more careful and less rushed examination of facts, economic theories and commitments offered by the parties. The "stop the clock" provision gives the Commission much needed extra time for the analysis of particularly complex transactions. Each of these changes should improve the quality of the Commission appraisal of mergers.

EC Regulation 139/2004 also strengthens the investigative powers of the Commission, which now can obtain information by simple request or by decision. The Commission also has the power to enter the premises, land and means of transportation of the firms concerned; to examine books and other business documents; to seize and make copies of them, to seal premises and documents; to ask firm's staff for explanation regarding facts and documents. In addition, the Commission can impose fines on those who provide incorrect or misleading answer to Article 11(1) requests and on those who do not provide a complete answer to Article 13(2) explanation requests. These innovations align the Commission's investigative powers in merger control procedures with those provided by Articles 81 and 82 EC Treaty. In the light of the recent judgements of the Court of First Instance heightening the standard of evidence in merger cases, the changes introduced by the new regulation should improve the enforcement capabilities of the Commission. It may accordingly rely on its reinforced investigative powers to collect the necessary data to prove the anticompetitive effects of the mergers and consequently avoid an excessive reliance on the submissions of third parties. Moreover, EC Regulation 802/2004 renders the Commission's files more accessible to the parties and improves the degree of transparency of the enforcement activity of the Commission. This should enable the parties to know the elements upon which the objections of the Commission are based and, accordingly, prepare their defence.

X. *The soft law initiatives of the Commission to amend the EC merger control regime*

The Commission has strengthened the system of checks and balances of the merger control procedure with administrative initiatives such as the Best Practices. The aim of the Best Practices is to improve transparency of the handling of cases in the merger control procedure. Several measures have been introduced, such as meetings between the Commission officers and those whose interests are concerned by the merger. The Best Practices provide for "state-of-play" meetings between the merging parties and the Commission. These meetings are held at the key stages of the procedure and provide the parties with an insight into the views of the Commission on the competition problems raised by the merger. The merging parties will also be able to present their full case and answer directly any concerns raised by the Commission.

The Best Practices provide for triangular meetings among the Commission, the merging parties and third parties on a voluntary basis before the oral hearing. In triangular meetings all the parties concerned can exchange their views, even in a confrontational way, on the merger. The Commission can gather tested data and information upon the possible objections to the merger and may thus ascertain the completeness and correctness of the third parties' submissions. Finally, the Best Practices confirm and further specify the merging parties' right of access to the Commission files. More precisely, they have access to the key documents contained in the Commission file, such as the submissions of the third parties, within the limits of the protection of confidential information and business secrets of the third parties.

Another soft law instrument adopted by the Commission with the view of improving the standard of its investigation is the appointment of a Chief Economist. Deeper involvement of economists in the case handling was much needed after that some decisions of the Commission were criticised by the Court of First Instance and from academics for the poor level of economic analysis. Accordingly, the presence of a Chief Economist should guarantee the use of quantitative methodologies for the assessment of competitive effects of mergers. The Commission has also set a peer review panel. This panel should review the conclusions of the team of case handlers with a "fresh pair of eyes" in order to spot any weaknesses in the line of reasoning and evidence of the Commission. Yet the Commission has not further strengthened the role of the Hearing Officer after the measures adopted in 2001.[38] The appointment of the Chief Economist, along with the establishment of a peer review panel, is step in the right direction. They should avert the danger of shoddy application of merger control rules without the basis of sound economic models.

XI. *Conclusion*

The above paragraphs has analysed the institutional framework and the procedural rules of the US and EC merger control systems and has explicated the

[38] European Commission, European Commission strengthens the role of the Hearing Officers in competition proceedings, IP/01/736, Brussels 23 May 2001.

main differences between them. It has also suggested the differences, namely the role of competitors and the type of merger control regime, which may influence the substantive outcome of merger review. The debate on the difference between the EC and the US merger control procedural rules has been focused on the so-called 'capital vice' of the EC regime. This flaw is the concentration of several functions in the hands of the Commission, which acts at the same time as policy maker, investigator, prosecutor and decision-maker. Whereas this regime brings about rapidity in the merger review, such speed is achieved at the expense of predictability of the outcomes of the investigations and legal certainty. The Commission, probably because its discretionary power in the appraisal of mergers has not always been effectively restrained by judicial external checks, on some occasion applied controversial economic models and relied on unconvincing pieces of evidence.

However, the recent case law developed by the EC courts in relation to appeals lodged against negative decisions of the Commission seems to herald a turning point regarding the stance of the EC courts towards the regulatory activities of the Commission. The Court of First Instance has formulated quite harsh critiques about how the Commission enforces merger control. Such criticism has been later approved by the Court of Justice in the appeal trial regarding the Tetra Laval case. With these judgments the European Courts have manifested their intention to subject the regulatory activity of the Commission to a more pervasive judicial scrutiny and have raised the standard of evidence expected by the Commission. In order to assuage these criticisms the EC reformed its merger control regime in 2004 with EC Regulation 139/2004 and some administrative measures. The reform may contribute to enhance the right of defence of the interested parties before the Commission. The more flexible timetable may also allow the Commission to conduct a more detailed examination of the facts of mergers, the possible economic theories that can be applied to assess the alleged anticompetitive effects of the merger and the commitments offered by the parties. The appointment of a Chief Economist should also be acclaimed since it should ensure more economic analysis in the appraisal of mergers made by the Commission. Moreover, the standard of evidence of the EC merger control procedure has been clarified and brought closer to that which the US competition authorities have to comply with. As a whole, the reform should have at least reduced the source of potential conflicts between the EC and the US competition authorities, even if it has not addressed the issue of the separation of the functions of the Commission.

CHAPTER THREE

A COMPARATIVE ANALYSIS OF EC AND US MERGER CONTROL LAW: THE SUBSTANTIVE RULES

I. *Introduction*

This paragraph is concentrated to the comparative analysis of the US and EC merger control laws by focusing on the substantive rules. The second section gives a brief account of the substantive tests adopted by the US and the EC. The third section looks at the methodologies for the definition of relevant markets. The fourth section looks at the approaches of the US and EC competition authorities for the assessment of the alleged anti-competition effects of mergers. The fifth section compares the scope of application of the substantive tests adopted by US and EC.[1] The sixth and seventh sections examine the Boeing/Mc Donnell Douglas and General Electric/Honeywell cases and review the different positions taken by the EC and the US on these mergers. The eighth section outlines the different approaches adopted by these two jurisdictions for the regulation of mergers between large firms, namely in case of conglomerate mergers. The ninth section tries to identify the reasons of such a difference, which may be indicated in the different goals of competition law, in confidence in market forces, in the availability of post-merger remedies and in the treatment of efficiencies. The tenth section summarises the reasons which can be invoked to explain the divergent views between US and EC on merger cases. It also addresses the question whether the EC Regulation 139/2004 has eliminated any causes of the above divergences. The eleventh section draws conclusions.

II. *Substantive assessment of mergers: Introductory remarks*

A. *The US substantive test*

The purpose of merger control is to defend the competitive structure of markets from the risk of an accumulation of excessive market power in the hands of one or a few firms. The EC and US merger control laws employ different substantive tests to establish whether a proposed merger operation would have restrictive effects on competition and therefore should be prohibited.

[1] Antony Arnull, Alan Dashwood, Michael Dougan, Malcolm Ross, Eleanor Spaventa, Derrick Wyatt, European Union law, Thomson, Sweet and Maxwell, 2006. Barry Rodger and Angus MacCulloch, Competition Law and Policy, (Cavendish London 2001) 203.

The US law prohibits a merger when the consequences of the acquisition of stocks and assets, through which the merger is implemented "may be substantially to lessen competition, or tends to create a monopoly". This formula focuses on the prohibition of mergers the consummation of which may lead to a significant decrease in the competitive structure of markets. A merger is more likely to produce these effects when the market power of the merged entity in the post-merger markets is such as to enable it to raise prices and reduce output level.[2]

B. *The EC substantive test*

EC merger control law initially adopted the market dominance standard, which consists of two phases. First, the Commission had to establish whether the merger would create or strengthen a dominant position in the market; secondly, it evaluated the impact of the merger on the competitive structure of the markets concerned.[3] As explained above, the recent judgments of the Court of First Instance sparked the debate regarding the overhaul of EC Regulation 4064/89. The discussion concerning the amendment of the substantive provisions of the regulation mainly revolved around the question whether the market dominance test should be abandoned in favour of the substantial lessening of competition test.[4]

The switch to the substantial lessening of competition test would bring the EC much closer to the US and other important jurisdictions such as Canada and Australia. Firms trading globally would enjoy a level playing field in merger control in many jurisdictions with a following reduction in transaction costs. Another merit normally recognised in the substantial lessening of competition test is its flexibility and economics-based nature. As a result, its adoption would allow a more attentive position on the enhancement of consumers' welfare and on the efficiencies resulting from the mergers.

The majority of the replies received by businesses and counsellors pointed out that the advantages of the adoption of the substantial lessening of competition test would not compensate the disadvantages of the abolition of the market dominance test. In the initial period of application of the new test

[2] Stefan Voigt, 'Switching to Substantial Impediments of Competition (SIC) Can Have Substantial Cost-SIC' [2004] ECLR 584, 586.

[3] Article 2(1) of the EC Regulation 4064/89. The market dominance standard placed more attention on the structural examination of markets and required the Commission to firstly find a dominant position. Mike Walker, The New Merger Regulation and Horizontal Merger Guidelines: Will They Make a Difference?' Charles River Associates, 2006. Ioannis Kokkoris, 'The Reform of the European Control Merger Regulation in the Aftermath of the Airtours Case -the Eagerly Expected Debate: SLC v Dominance Test' [2005] ECLR 37.

[4] Proposal for Council Regulation on the control of concentration between undertakings, COM (2002) 711 final, 2006, paras. Submissions Received on the Green Paper on the Review of Council Regulation (EEC) No. 4064/89, 2006. Alexander Riesenkampff, 'The New EC Merger Control Test under Article 2 of the Merger Control Regulation' (2004) 24 Northwestern Journal of International Law & Business 715. 159–169.

firms would face more legal uncertainty and more unpredictability in merger control as it would not be clear whether the case law developed under the market dominance test would be still valid. All this might increase the discretionary power of the Commission. The EC acknowledged the soundness of such concerns and eventually opted for a compromise solution. It created the so-called 'significant impediment of competition test', according to which "a concentration which significantly impedes effective competition, in the common market or in a substantial part of it, in particular as a result of the creation or strengthening of a dominant position, shall be declared incompatible with the common market".

The new substantive test is a hybrid of the market dominance and the substantial lessening of competition tests. It emphasises the assessment of the effects of the merger though this element was already present in the old merger control regime as the second phase of the market dominance test. The compromising stance of the new EC 139/2004 Regulation is clear. It does not adopt, at least nominally, the substantial lessening of competition test, lest such a dramatic change might expose the EC merger control regime to the risk of legal uncertainty and unpredictability. The concept of market dominance survived the 2004 reform and is still valid under the new regulation, which allows the case law developed under the old regulation to remain valid. However, the role of market dominance is now downgraded since it is no longer the main component of the substantive test. Indeed, it is only a mere presumption, in the presence of which the Commission may assume that the merger would have anticompetitive effects.

The idea of market dominance also appears in the US. The US Horizontal Merger Guidelines state that a merger substantially lessens the competition when it alters the market structure to such an extent that it facilitates or creates the exercise of market power. The concept of market power is then defined as "the ability profitably to maintain prices above competition levels for a significant period of time". This is not far from the concept of market dominance embraced by the EC.

III. *Definition of relevant markets*

The first step in the assessment of mergers is the definition of the relevant markets on which the transaction will produce its economic effects. The US approach for the definition of relevant markets is illustrated by the Horizontal Merger Guidelines. A great importance is given by the Guidelines to demand-side substitution considerations, which are weighed against the "small but significant non transitory increase in price" test (SSNIP).[5] The EC

[5] The SSNIP is a multi-tasked test. First, it is assumed that an ideal monopolist in pursuance of the maximisation of profits decides a 5% price increase in the selling prices of its

Commission also applies the demand-side substitution approach by taking into consideration a wide range of factors, such as physical and functional characteristics and prices of products. It is only with the Commission Notice on market definitions of 1997[6] that the Commission has endorsed the SSNIP test. That said, the Commission Notice's methodology for the defining the EC relevant markets is similar to that of the US Horizontal Merger Guidelines. In this regard, it is possible to highlight their reliance on price-based and demand-side criteria and the fact that they define the relevant product market as the smallest set of goods or services for which a small, permanent increase in price would be profitable for the hypothetical monopolist.[7] The US competition authorities identify the relevant geographical market as the area in which the merging parties compete to sell their products to consumers. Under EC law the relevant geographic market is defined as the area in which there exist homogeneous competition conditions.[8] For the definition of relevant geographic markets the European Commission and the US competition authorities attach great importance to factors such as costs of transportation and the barriers to the importation of substitute products.

IV. *Evaluation of anti-competitive effects of mergers*

A. *The US approach*

After having identified the markets that are affected by the proposed mergers, the regulating authority examines the possible impact of the transaction on

---

products. Then the likely reaction of consumers is examined. If they continue purchasing the products of the monopolist, only the products sold by the monopolist are included in the relevant market. But, if consumers shift to another products in such a large proportion that the ideal monopolist is unable to profitably sustain the price increase because of the following lost of sales, the products to which consumers have switched are included in the relevant market. This exercise is repeated with other category of products until it is possible to identify the smallest group of products upon which the monopolist can impose a profitable price increaCook and Kerse, above n. 111, chapter 2, 135; Commission decision, Case IV/M.053, Aeréospatiale Sni and Alenia-Aeritalia e SeleniaSpa and De Havilland [1992] 4 CMLR M2, paras 8 ss.se.

[6] See also the EC Commission Regulation 447/98, which holds that "a relevant product market comprises all those products and/or services which are regarded as interchangeable or substitutable by the consumers by reason of the product characteristics, their prices and their intended use". European Commission Notice on the definition of relevant market for the purpose of Community competition law [1997] OJ C372/03, para 15 and following.

[7] Simon Baker and Lawrence Wu, 'Applying the Market Definition Guidelines of the European Communities' [1998] ECLR 273, 273; Henry Huser and Frederic Depoortere, 'Substantive Enforcement in Horizontal Mergers under the EC Merger Regulation' Antitrust Magazine Fall 2002, 44.

[8] This concept was first set out by the Court of Justice in an EC Article 82 judgement, Case 27/76 United Brands Co. v. Commission [1978] 1 CMLR 429, para 44. It is also codified in the Commission Notice on the definition of relevant market and in the form CO Annex to EC Commission Regulation 802/2004.

those markets. The US competition authorities have first to assess the degree of economic concentration in the relevant markets. US merger control law assumes that highly concentrated markets are likely to favour the formation of cartels, which is the main competition concern in this jurisdiction. The Horizontal Merger Guidelines provide an analytical instrument with which to measure market concentration: the Herfindahl-Hirschmann Index (HHI). This is obtained by adding the squared amount of market shares belonging to every firm in the market. The following results have to be evaluated against a scale laid down by the Horizontal Merger Guidelines, which envisage three different situations: a) The merger does not raise any competition concerns if the HHI does not exceed the 1,000 threshold. b) If the HHI is evaluated between 1,000 and 1,800 no presumption applies. Thereby, it is necessary to assess the legality of the merger on a case-by-case basis and to take into consideration further factors such as the ease of entry in the market, merger-specific efficiencies and failure of one of the parties. c) Lastly, if the HHI is in excess of 1,800 the merger is presumed to be illegal. However, it is possible to rebut such presumption by invoking the factors described above.

Originally, the US competition authorities attached great weight to market share data. In Philadelphia National Bank the US Supreme Court found that the high market share of the parties, along with the significant increase in market concentration, were sufficient grounds to block the merger. Later, the US Supreme Court abandoned this rigid approach in General Dynamics in which it disregarded the market share data as a strong indicator of anti-competitive effects.[9] The sole reliance on market share may not establish a relevant degree of market concentration and it is necessary to engage in a more thorough examination of the market structure to assess the alleged anti-competitive effect of mergers. As to such effects, the Horizontal Merger Guidelines indicate two possible forms of anticompetitive effects: unilateral and coordinated effects. A unilateral effect occurs when the merged entity can unilaterally increase prices or drive its rivals off the market. A coordinated effect occurs when there exists a risk of collusion between the merged entity and its remaining competitors. If a merger is likely to produce such negative effects, the regulating authority shall block the transaction unless the effects in question can be set off by other factors such as the risk of failure of the parties, the ease of entry of new competitors and the economic efficiencies concerned.

[9] United Stated v. Philadelphia National Bank, 374 US, 363. United Stated v. General Dynamics, 415 US 486.

B. *The EC approach*

As has been explained above, the concept of market dominance is an important element of the EC substantive test. Yet neither did EC Regulation 4064/89 nor does EC Regulation 139/2004 contain any definition of this concept. It is therefore necessary to have to recourse to the case law developed under the application of Article 82 EC Treaty. The leading case is United Brands, in which the European Court of Justice held that a dominant position "is a position of economic strength enjoyed by an undertaking which enables it to prevent effective competition being maintained on the relevant market by giving it the power to behave to an appreciable extent independently of its competitors, customers and ultimately of its consumers".

The Commission for the appraisal of a merger should also take into consideration the factors listed in Article 2 (1) of EC Regulation 139/2004. The market shares of the merging parties are considered as important indicia of the market power of the parties even though EC merger control law does not set any market share thresholds, above which the merger is considered to be anti-competitive. The only hint is in Recital 32 of EC Regulation 139/2004 which sets out that a merger operation is presumed not to raise any competition concerns if the market shares of the merging parties are less than the 25% threshold. But the recital does not lay down any presumption of illegality in case a merger exceeds this threshold.

The examination of the case law of the Commission gives an insight into the relevance that the market share data has in merger control. In the Alcatel/Telettra case, although the merging parties totalled a market share of more than 80%, the Commission did not block the transaction due to the buying power of the customer, a monopolistic purchaser. The incoming implementation of EC Directive 90/351 on public procurement was also crucial for the authorisation of the merger as the directive would have further facilitated the entry of new competitors in the market.[10] In Tetra Pak/Alfa-Laval

---

[10] See also: 1. The proposal of Directive amending Council Directive 78/855/EEC concerning mergers of public limited liability compagnies and Council Directive 82/891/EEC concerning the division of public limited companies as regards the requirement for an independent experts report on the occasion of a merger or a division (COM/2007/91 final); 2. The Directive 2007/63/EC of the European Parliament and of the Council of 13 November 2007 and 82/891/EEC as regards the requirement of an independent experts report on the occasion of merger or division of public limited liability companies. 3. The cross-border mergers Directive n. 2005/56/EC was approved by the Council and the European Parliament in November 2007 (Directive 2007/63/EC). In April 2008 the Commission tabled two proposal to amend the first and eleventh company law directives and the accounting directives; 3. The Directive 2006/68/EC of the Europena Parliament and of the Council of 6 September 2006 amending Council Directive 77/91/EC as regards the formation of public limited liability companies and the maintenance and alteration of their capital; 4. The Directive 2003/58/EC of 15.07.2003 amending Council Directive 68/151/EEC as regards disclosure requirements in respect of certain types of companies, ecc.

the Commission spelled out that, in some rare circumstances, such as when there are strong competitors in the market, even a 90% market share may not necessarily result in a dominant position being found.

On the other hand, the Commission has found a dominant position in situations where the merging parties did not have much high market share. In REWE/Meinl where a 37% market share was sufficient to establish a dominant position, a decisive role was played by the gaps existing between the market shares of the merging parties and those of their rivals.[11] The competitive advantages that would have been enjoyed by the merged entities, such as the more favourable location of shops, its system of central-managed-chain-store and above all its strong position in the procurement market, were equally important in finding it had a dominant position.

As a general rule, the Commission presumes the existence of a dominant position if the merged entity holds a market share more than 40%, provided that it is substantially larger than the market shares held by the next largest competitors. However important market shares may be for the analysis of the competitive structure of markets, these data may not always be infallible indicator of the market power of the merging parties. For this reason, the Commission, following the lead of the US competition authorities, is ready to take into consideration other elements.

With the 2004 reform the Commission adopted the HHI test with the purpose of examining the expected impact of the merger on the relevant markets. Upon the basis of the HHI test, the Commission distinguishes two situations: a) If the post-merger HHI is below 1,000, the transaction should not raise any serious competitive issues; b) If the post-merger HHI is between 1,000–2,000 with a delta below 250 or if the HHI is above 2,000 with a delta below 150, the transaction is unlikely to have anti-competitive effects.

Even when a transaction exceeds such HHI levels it may not cause anti-competitive effects if some of the special factors enlisted by the Commission are present. After having identified the degree of market concentration, the Commission proceeds by assessing the alleged anti-competitive effects of the merger and establishes whether the merger would or would not significantly impede effective competition. Interestingly, the second indent of article 2(1) of EC Regulation 4064/89[12] already required the Commission to assess whether the merger was likely to lead to significant impediment of competition. This provision was read in the sense that the Commission had to prove

[11] Case IV/M.042 Alcatel NV v. Telettra SpA, 4 CMLR 778, para 38. Case IV/M.068 Tetra Pak International SA and Alfa Laval AB, Commission Decision, para 23, 2006. Case IV/M.221 REWE Internationale Beteiligungsgesellschaft mbH, REWE-Verkaufsgesselschaft mbH and Julius Meiul AG, Commission Decision, [2000] 5 CMLR 256.

[12] Guidelines for the Assessment of Horizontal Mergers under the Council Regulation on the control of concentrations between undertakings (2004/C 31/3) [2005] OJ C31/5, section III 'Market Shares and Market Concentration Levels'.

a causal link between the dominant position imputable to the merger and the restrictive effects on competition. The European Court of Justice endorsed this position in Kali und Saltz, where it held that it was necessary to prove "a causal link between the concentration and the deterioration of the competitive structure of the market" in order to prohibit the merger.[13] It was then confirmed by the Court of First Instance in Airtours, which stated that the Commission has to "ascertain whether the concentration would have the direct and immediate effect of creating and strengthening a position of that kind (a collective dominant position), which is such as significantly and lastingly to impede competition in the relevant market. If there is no substantial alteration to competition as it stands, the merger must be approved".[14]

In light of the above, it can be said that with the new EC Regulation 139/2004 the Commission has a more flexible and sophisticated tool for the examination of the anti-competitive effects of mergers. This is more in line with the approaches followed in other jurisdictions and with the latest developments of economic thinking. Because Airtours, as will be explained below, had restrained the capability of the Commission to regulate the unilateral effects of mergers in oligopolies, the clarification of the boundaries of the substantive test was essential. The new test by incorporating the element of significant impediments of competition allows the Commission to analyse the competitive impact of the mergers without the legal straitjacket of the necessity of having to establish first a dominant position.

V. *A comparative analysis of the scope of application of the market dominance test and of the substantial lessening of competition test*

A comparative examination of the EC and US substantive tests for the appraisal of mergers must analyse the reach of these substantive tests. In simpler terms, the question is whether such substantive tests apply to the same category of merger operations. More precisely, does the scope of application of these two tests coincide? Is there any gap between the reach of the US and the EC tests? Do the market dominance test and the substantial lessening of competition test catch the same type of transactions? What are the innovations brought about by the new significant impediment of effective

[13] ECJ Case C.-68/94 & 30/95, France v. Commission [1998] 4 CMLR 829 para 116.

[14] Airtours plc v. Commission, above n 128, chapter 3, para 58. The Commission embraced this view since de Havilland (above n. 19) in which it hold that the creation of a dominant position was not per se prohibited by merger control law. Even if the parties have a dominant position in post-merger markets the transaction is not prohibited "if there exists a strong evidence that the position is only temporary and would be quickly eroded because of high probability of strong market entry."

competition test? Answering these questions can be important since the different scope of application of the substantive tests may explain the inconsistent positions taken by the US and the EC competition authorities in Boeing/Mac Donnell Douglas and General Electric/Honeywell. Since these cases were decided by the Commission under the old EC Regulation 4064/89, the proposed analysis will first focus on the scope of application of the old market dominance test. Then, it will examine the scope of application of the new significant impediment of effective competition test. Because the market dominance test required the Commission to establish a market dominant position it may be inferred that the EC law sets a higher level of concentration of market power for regulatory intervention. On the other hand, the US' substantial lessening of competition test seems to be more flexible and it appears to have a wider scope of application. Some hypothetical scenarios may help better understand these issues.

A. *Monopolist scenario*

Two leading firms in a market, both of which have a 35% market share, decide to merge. The post-merger market, in which the merged entity has a 70% market share, is a clear-cut situation both under EC and US law. From the viewpoint of EC merger control law, the merged entity has a dominant position in the market and then falls under the scope of application of its substantive test. The situation is similar if the US competition authorities assess the merger. The transaction with a HHI of 4,900 points is presumed to cause anticompetitive effects and, accordingly, is caught by the substantial lessening of competition test.

B. *Oligopolist scenario*

Economic literature distinguishes two forms of anti-competitive effects of merger in oligopolies: unilateral and coordinated effects. In the unilateral effects situation the incentives for pricing the products change only for the merged entity. As a result, this firm raises its prices in order to maximize its profits in the short period. Although the pricing incentives of the competitors remain unchanged, they set higher prices as a response to the price increase of the merged entity. These effects are more likely to occur in markets with a high degree of market concentration.

Coordinated effects occur with the existence of collusive practices amongst the firms trading in the market, such as agreeing, explicitly or tacitly, to charge prices at a supra optimal level. At the moment to decide how to behave firms face two conflicting incentives (the so-called prisoner's dilemma): the incentives to cheat and charge lower prices than those it has colluded with and the incentives not to deviate from the agreed prices. The latter are effective only if supported by credible threats of retaliation in case one firm cheats. Provided that such threats are felt, the firms, being aware of their interdependence of reaction, will find more convenient to collude and put into practice a cartel-like commercial strategy in order to maximize their profit.[15] The inquiry into the alleged coordinated effects should assess the possible impact of the merger on these incentives.

In the coordinated effects situation companies A and D have a 30% market share. There are also two major players, companies B and C, each of whom has a 20% market share. B and C decide to merge and the merged entity has a 40% market share. This merger can create a collective dominant position. Such situations arise when a dominant position is held by several independent firms, which decide their commercial strategies on considering the prospective conducts of their competitors, but without reaching any agreements. As explained by the US Horizontal Merger Guidelines, these mergers fall within the reach of the substantial lessening of competition test. With a 3,400 HHI result of the post-merger market in mind, the merger is likely to produce significantly restrictive effects on the competitive structure of markets.

EC merger control law does not make any express reference to the concept of a collective dominant position. It is therefore necessary to resort to the case law of the Commission and the EC Courts. In Nestlé/Perrier the Commission clarified that the merger control regulation may be read as covering single firm and collective dominance.[16] Therefore, the dominant position that can lead to restrictive effects on competition may be either single firm power or multi-firm power. The European Court of Justice confirmed the application of the merger control regulation to collective dominant position in France v. Commission.[17] The Court of First Instance in Airtours sets out the conditions upon which the finding of a collective dominant position must be based: a. Market transparency: in the market there must exist a sufficient degree of transparency so as to enable every firm to which a collective dominant position is imputable to be aware whether the other firms are abiding by the common policy. b. Viability: it is essential to establish the presence of adequate deterrents, whose function is to work as incentives for the colluding firms not to deviate from the common policy, such as retaliatory mechanisms. c. Profitability: the results expected from the adoption of

---

[15] Heiko Haupt, 'Collective Dominance under Article 82 EC and the EC Merger Regulation in the Light of Airtours Judgement' [2002] ECLR 434, 435.

[16] Nestlé SA and Source Perrier SA (Case no. IV/190) Commission Decision [1993] 4 CMLR M17, para 113.

[17] ECJ Cases C.-68/94 and C.-30/95 France v. Commission, Societe Commerciale des Potasses et de l'Azote and Entreprise Minière et Chimique v. Commission [1998]4 CMLR 829, paras 169–178. CFI Case T-342/99, above n. 127, chapter 3, para 62.

the common policy must not be prejudiced by the foreseeable reaction of current and potential competition and of consumers.

In the Airtours case the Court of First Instance probably closed the debate on the concept of the collective dominance by endorsing a more restrained interpretation of the concept than that adopted by the Commission.

In the unilateral effects situation three major firms are trading in the market: A, with a 30% market share, B, with a 15% market share, and C with a 13% market share. B and C decide to merge. The firm resulting from the merger will have a 28% market share. The US and the EC merger control law split on the assessment of the anti-competitive effects of this transaction. The US Horizontal Merger Guidelines expressly state that unilateral effects in non-collusive markets may lessen competition too. This situation occurs when the merger may render more profitable for the merged entity to unilaterally raise prices or reduce output. The Federal Trade Commission in Baby Food considered a unilateral effects situation. In this case the second and the third largest firms in the baby food market merged. Although the merged entity neither challenged the market position of the leading firm, nor had a collective or single dominant position, the US competition authorities blocked the merger as it would have reduced competition.[18]

On the other hand, it is more uncertain whether the hypothetical merger above is caught by the EC market dominance test. The merged entity does not have enough market power to be regarded as a single dominant firm and the structure of the market may not fit in a collective dominant position. However, merger with unilateral effects may lead to price increases and output restrictions to the detriment of the consumers' welfare. The requirement to establish the creation or strengthening of a dominant position laid down by Article 2 of the EC Regulation 4064/89, however, placed a serious constraint on the capability of the Commission to regulate mergers with unilateral effects.[19] In order to overcome this sort of legal straitjacket, the Commission tried to stretch the ambit of the concept of collective dominance to include also mergers with unilateral effects. The negative decision in Airtours /First Choice epitomizes such a line of reasoning.[20] The decision of the Commission was based on the assumption that in a highly concentrated post-merger market the remaining firms might have unilaterally adopted a parallel conduct for the determination of output capacity. The recourse to the unilateral effects analysis was probably the only available way to block the

[18] Federal Trade Commission v H.J. Heinz Co 246 F.3d 708, 720 (D.C. Circ.2001).

[19] Nathalie Jalabert-Doury, 'Concentrations et position dominante collective après l'arrêt Airtours: le point sur les concepts, les facteurs structurels et les critères', (2002) La Semaine Juridique, Cahiers du Droit de l'Entreprise, n. 5, 24th November 2001,1; Massimo Motta, 'EC Merger Policy and the Airtours Case' [2000] ECLR 199, 202.

[20] Airtours /First Choice, Case IV/M.1524, Commission Decision, 2006.

merger given that market conditions would not have permitted the finding of a collective dominant position. But, the prohibition of a unilateral effects merger was criticised by legal commentators. They argued that such situations falls short of the scope of the application of the market dominance test and it also restrained the freedom of firms to unilaterally and rationally adapt their behaviour to the commercial strategies of their rivals.

The decision of the Commission was then overturned by the Court of First Instance. The Court held that a merger likely to cause unilateral anti-competitive effects, without creating or strengthening a single or dominant position in the market, was not caught within the reach of EC Regulation 4064/89. On the other hand, such a merger does fall within the scope of application of the substantial lessening of competition test. As a result, there exists a gap between the scope of application of the EC-market dominance test and that of the US test regarding the unilateral effects in non-collusive oligopoly.[21]

C. *The EC Regulation 139/2004 and the unilateral anti-competitive effects in oligopolies*

The new merger control regulation should have filled in the gap by giving the Commission the power to prohibit merger operations that produce unilateral anticompetitive effects in oligopolies when they result in a significant reduction of competition, even if the merged entity does not have a dominant position. This is confirmed by the Recitals to EC Regulation 139/2004, which clarifies that the concept of significant impediment to competition also includes the anti-competitive effects resulting from un-coordinated behaviour of non-dominant firms. The application of the merger control regulation to unilateral effects mergers is further illustrated by the Guidelines on Horizontal Mergers. This document, mirroring the unilateral effects/coordinated effects dichotomy of the US Merger Guidelines, distinguishes between two anti-competitive effects of mergers: coordinated and uncoordinated effects. The former occurs when, as a result of the merger, the remaining firms are more likely to collude. The latter occurs when the merger eliminates important competitive restraints on the merged entity, which can exploit its increased market power without the need to co-ordinate with the remaining firms. For the unilateral effects to happen it is important that the merged entity has an appreciably larger market share than the next rival. The mergers that give rise to these types of effects shall be prohibited by the

[21] O'Donaghue and Feddersen, above n. 35, chapter 3, 1180; John Vickers, 'Competition Economics and Policy' [2003] ECLR 95, 99; But, contra, see Ulf Boege and Edith Mueller, 'From the Dominance Test to the SLC Test: Are There Any Reasons for a Change?' [2002] ECLR 495, 496. These authors argue that unilateral effects mergers are still caught by the market dominance test. In fact, if there was a lack of internal competition between the market leader firm and one of the parties to the transaction the merger could be prohibited in that it could lead to the creation or strengthening of a dominant position.

Commission. So, EC Regulation 139/2004, by enlarging the reach of the EC merger control regime to unilateral effects situations in oligopolies should have bridged the gap that previously existed between the scope of application of EC Regulation 4064/89 and US merger control law. The new EC merger control regulation should apply to the same range of merger operations as those falling within the scope of US law. However, such a gap only existed at a theoretical level, because the inconsistencies between the EC and US competition authorities on the assessment of mergers were caused by other problems. Indeed, in Boeing/McDonnell Douglas and General Electric/Honeywell it was the assessment of market foreclosure effects imputable to single-firm dominance which pitted the European Commission against the US competition authorities.[22]

VI. *The Boeing/McDonnell Douglas merger*

A. *The decision of the Federal Trade Commission*

In Boeing/McDonnell Douglas the Federal Trade Commission, apparently unconcerned by the reduction in the number of competing firms from three to two, cleared the merger. That transaction was unlikely to have an adverse impact in the market for large commercial aircrafts because of the weakness of McDonnell Douglas. It held that "Mc Donnell Douglas, looking to the future, no longer constitutes a meaningful competitive force in the commercial aircraft market" and its "prospects for future commercial aircraft sales are virtually non-existent."[23] Therefore, the Federal Trade Commission was convinced that the economic efficiencies expected from the merger would offset any competition concerns.[24]

B. *The decision of the European Commission*

Although the European Commission was equally unimpressed by the competitive strength of Mc Donnell Douglas, it examined the possible competitive impact of the transaction in the relevant markets paying particular attention to the effects of the combination of the assets of McDonnell Douglas and Boeing.[25] If Boeing decided to continue the production of McDonnell

---

[22] Kuhn Kai-Uwe, 'Reforming European Merger Review Targeting Problems Areas in Policy Outcomes', 2006.

[23] Statement of Chairman Robert Pitofsky and Commissioner Janet D. Steiger, Roscoe B. Starek III and Christine A. Varing in the Matter of Boeing Company / Mc Donnell Douglas Corporation, File no. 971-0051, 2006.

[24] Eric Stock, 'Explaining the Differing US and EU Position on the Boeing/Mc Donnell Douglas Merger- Avoiding Another Near Miss' [1999] University Of Pennsylvania Journal of International Economic Law 825, 874.

[25] Boeing/McDonnel Douglas, above n. 102, chapter 2, paras 61, 62, 71, 73, 98, 106 and 111.

Douglas aircrafts, the perspective of McDonnell Douglas might be, as a result, improved. On the other hand, if Boeing decided to discontinue the production it would have access to the customer base and technical capabilities of McDonnell Douglas; which would add extra productive capabilities and flexibility to Boeing's manufacturing lines. Moreover, Boeing would benefit from the acquisition of the thriving McDonnell Douglas defence sector. First, Boeing would exploit the technologies developed in the military sector by the acquired company in the civil field. Secondly, the Commission outlined that "Boeing will become the largest integrated aerospace company in the world". The acquisition of the McDonnell Douglas military sector would give Boeing access to the public funded research and development programmes, which would improve its financial strength. The synergies between the military and civil sectors would give more financial stability and would enable the merged entity to strengthen its capability to invest in the development of new products and to cope with the economic cycles in commercial aircraft market. The risk was that the merged entity might engage in an aggressive pricing policy, cross-subsidising the sales of the least successful aircrafts with the revenues gained from the sales of the most successful aircrafts.

Secondly, a further source of competition concern was the 20-year long exclusive supply agreements entered into by Boeing with three major US airlines. The Commission was worried about the increased range of products that the merged entity could offer to potential customers. It was such to "significantly increase Boeing's ability to induce airlines to enter into exclusive deals". However, these preoccupations were not shared by the US Federal Trade Commission, according to which these agreements would instead increase efficiency, as suggested by the fact that the exclusivity clause was proposed by the airliners.

Eventually the Commission cleared the transaction upon the condition that Boeing undertook a number of commitments to address the above concerns. The commitments included: licensing Government-funded patents to third parties, not concluding any more exclusive agreements for a period of ten years, increasing transparency for R&D activities, maintaining for a period of ten years the acquired company as a separated body and refraining from exerting undue or improper influence on suppliers.

VII. *The General Electric/Honeywell merger*

A. *The decision of the Department of Justice*

The US Department of Justice found that the merger parties had high market shares of the parties in the market for military helicopter engines and in the market for the provision of heavy maintenance, repair and overhaul services for aircraft engines and auxiliary power units. Therefore the merger would substantially lessen competition in the above markets in the shape of increased prices and decreased output. These problems were finally resolved by the commitments of the parties to divest part of their assets and the merger was conditionally cleared.[26] The Department of Justice was convinced that the merger would lead to significant efficiencies to the benefit of consumers, in terms of lower prices and a wider range of products choice.[27] The ability of the merged entity to offer a range of bundled product packages covering all the requirements of aircraft manufacturers and, therefore, to offer a "one-stop shopping" commercial policy to customers was viewed as a creation of efficiency.

B. *The decision of the European Commission*

The Commission took a different position and blocked the merger as it would have had anti-competitive effects in several markets: a) The market for large commercial jet aircraft engines due to the vertical integration between General Electric engines and Honeywell engine starters and bundling practices; b) The markets for avionics and non-avionics products, due to two types of conglomerate effects, the extension of the financial strength of General Electric to Honeywell products and bundling practices; c) The market for large regional jet aircraft due to horizontal overlaps; d) The market for corporate jet aircraft due to horizontal overlaps and vertical integration between General Electric activities and Honeywell lines of production; e) The market for small marine gas turbines due to horizontal overlaps.

Amongst the factors relied on by the Commission to corroborate its findings, the theory of conglomerate effects is the most controversial. A first type of conglomerate effects was ascribed to the financial power of one subsidiary of General Electric, GE Capital. As a result, General Electric had many competitive advantages, which its rivals were unable to match: the ability to offer heavy discounts for the launch of new products; the ability to commit to risky programmes in products development and the ability to guarantee significant financial support to airframe manufacturers such as platform-programme development assistance. Such financial strength may raise the competitors' manufacturing costs and weaken their position in the market. Another relevant factor was the vertical integration of General Electric's manufacturing lines with the aircraft purchasing, financial and leasing activities of GECAS, the world's largest purchaser of airplanes. The GECAS commercial policy is to purchase exclusively aircrafts equipped with General Electric engines

---

[26] US Department of Justice, Press Release, Justice Department requires divestitures in merger between General electric and Honeywell, 2006.

[27] Andreas Weitbrecht, 'EU Merger Control in 2001; the Year of the Controversy' [2002] ECLR 407,409; Charles A. James, 'Reconciling Different Enforcement Policies: Where Do You Go from Here?', 2005.

and it is also a launch or boost customer of the General Electric's products. Thereby, General Electric should be capable of influencing the airliners' decisions regarding the purchase of aircrafts and convincing them to buy only General Electric-powered airplanes. The extension of the financial strength of GE Capital and of the leasing activities of GECAS to Honeywell products (the so-called share-shifting) would have caused anti-competitive effects in the markets for avionics and non-avionics products. These markets, along with the markets for large commercial jet aircraft engines, would have been negatively affected by the second type of conglomerate effects, the bundling practices. In the view of the Commission, the dominance of the merged entity would ultimately result in foreclosure effects in the relevant markets at the end of quite a long causation chain. The merged entity, by virtue of its competitive advantages, would have gained market shares at the expenses of its rivals, which, constrained by rising costs and decreasing revenues, might leave the market.[28]

C. *The judgment of the Court of First Instance*

The negative decision of the Commission was subsequently confirmed by the Court of First Instance.[29] The Court agreed with the analysis of the Commission with respect to the anti-competitive effects of the merger in the markets for jet engines for large regional aircrafts, engines for corporate jet aircrafts and small marine gas turbines. However, it found that the Commission did not adequately proved the vertical anti-competitive effects of the merger in the market for large commercial jet aircraft engines. Equally, the Commission failed to prove that the merger, due to the conglomerate effects, would have negatively affected the market for avionics and non-avionics products.

Despite the errors in the line of reasoning of the Commission, the Court did not quash the appealed decision. When a decision is based on several grounds and each of which is a sufficient legal basis for the operative part of the decision, the decision can be annulled only if all the grounds are illegal. However, when the illegality affects only one ground, the decision can be annulled if that ground is decisive for the adoption of the operative part of the decision. The General Electric/Honeywell decision was based on several grounds but only a few of them were held to be illegal. Since the rest of the grounds invoked by the Commission to prohibit the merger were held not to be vitiated by errors and thus did provide a sufficient legal basis for the decision, the Commission decision was not annulled.

---

[28] General Electric/Honeywell, above n. 2, paras 343–348, 405–411, 419–427 and 438–442. See also Dimitri Giotakos, Laurent Petit, Gaelle Garnier and Peter De Luyck, 'General Electric/ Honeywell- An Insight into the Commission's Investigation and Decision', Competition Policy Newsletter, October 2001, 5.

[29] CFI Case T-210/01 General Electric v Commission, 2006.

D. *US criticism of the European Commission's decision*

Notwithstanding that, US commentators were sceptical as to many of the findings of the Commission. First, they rejected the thinking of the Commission that considered the cost of capital as an anticompetitive factor. The fact that General Electric had a high capitalisation did not necessarily mean it had cheaper access to capital markets. Large companies, while weighing the decision to fund a particular project or not, experience an opportunity cost too, which is made up by the unavailability of the financial resources for other plans. The access of General Electric to cheaper funding should be interpreted as an indicator of efficiency, instead of as an anticompetitive factor, since cheaper capitals may lower prices and promote innovation. Another unconvincing element in the reasoning of the Commission is the anti-competitive effects ascribed to the vertical integration between General Electric and GECAS. The US commentators played down the relevance of GECAS and its General Electric-only powered buying policy by outlining that GECAS accounts only for a 10% share in aircrafts purchasing and that such a small share could not justify any risk of foreclosure effects.

VIII. *Regulation of foreclosure effects*

A. *The theory of conglomerate effects*

Among the economic theories invoked by the European Commission as theoretical justification of the prohibition of the General Electric/Honeywell merger was the theory of conglomerate mergers. This is quite a controversial theory employed with the purpose of assessing the alleged anti-competitive effects of merger operations in those markets in which there are neither horizontal nor vertical overlaps between the merging parties. The Commission is convinced that conglomerate mergers may adversely affect the competitive structure of the relevant markets by leading to leverage or foreclosure effects. The theory is based on the assumption that the merged entity may use its market power in one of the pre-merger markets as a lever to increase its market power in another post-merger market through restrictive practices such as tying and bundling.[30] It has been also argued that a firm that is able

[30] Deborah Platt Majoras, 'GE-Honeywell: The US Decision', 2006. Charles James, 'OECD Roundtable on Portfolio Effects in Conglomerate Mergers. Range Effects in Conglomerate Mergers. Range Effects: The United States Perspectives' [2001] Fordham Corporate Law Institute 6, 17. Mette Alfter, 'Tetra Laval/Sidel and the Future of the EC Merger Control, Lawyers' Europe Winter 2003, 17. Gotz Drautz, 'Unbundling General Electric/Honeywell: The Assessment of Conglomerate Mergers under EC Competition Law', [2002] Fordham International Law Journal 885, at 886; Mario Monti, 'Antitrust in US and Europe: A History of Convergence' Washington DC, 14 November 2001.

to offer a wide range of products, which can meet all the needs of customers, may gain significant competitive advantages against its rivals. Following the consummation of the merger, this firm would have significant market power over a number of products for reasons that are unrelated to normal business performance or competition on the merits. The danger is that the rival of the merged entity, due to the market power of the latter, might be driven off the markets. This may reduce the range of choices to consumers and raise prices, which, logically, may harm consumers' welfare.

The theoretical framework elaborated by the Commission for the assessment of conglomerate mergers presupposes that the products of the merging parties belong to neighbouring or related markets. Under some circumstances, such a combination of products changes the structure of markets and gives the merged entity the ability and the incentive to change its pricing policy. This echoes the theory of Cournot, which predicts that a firm offering complementary products has the possibility to internalise price externalities due to the complementary links between its products. This means that in post-merger markets the price decrease of a product decided by the merged entity may result in increased demand for the other related product with a consequent increase in the profits of the combined entity. This pricing policy is implemented by the merged entity by tying the sale of one product with another. The merged entity is motivated to put into practice this commercial policy by the prospects of increasing its profits. The dominant position held by the merged entity in one of the pre-merger markets is considered as a necessary condition for the likelihood and the profitability of these practices.

B. *The theory of conglomerate effects in the case law of the Commission*

The first case in which conglomerate effects were considered was Aerospatiale-Alenia/De Havilland. The Commission banned the proposed merger since, amongst other things, the merged entity would have had a considerable financial strength and might have carried out a predatory pricing policy. Hints of the theory of conglomerate effects were also present in Boeing/McDonnell Douglas, where the Commission ruled that "the addition of products from McDonnell Douglas and the large increase in its overall resources would enhance Boeing's opportunities to engage in such pricing practices (cross-subsidising sales of the least successful aircrafts with the sales of the least successful ones) especially in view of its strong, and increasingly strengthening, cash flow positioned as outlined above".[31] Besides, "where a large fleet in service

[31] CAMBELL, Bilateral monopoly in mergers, (2007), n. 3, ALJ, pp. 5 ss. AL NAJJARI, DI BON, Cross-border mergers of limited liability compagnies. Some considerations on fiscal implication, (2007), pp. 215, FI. SHELANSKI, KATZ, Mergers and innovation in antitrust, (2007), n. 1, ALJ. ZAMAN, Cross-border mergers in Europe, (2006), pp. 124 ss, EJLR.

is combined with a broad product range, the existing fleet in service can be a key factor which may often determine decisions of airlines on fleet planning or acquisitions." In the decision-making process for aircraft purchases, airlines are sensitive to "cost savings arising from commonality benefits, such as engineering spares inventory and flight crew qualifications".

The theory was also invoked in the Guinness/Grand Metropolitan case, where the merged entity acquired a wide portfolio of leading brands in the beverage industry, which gave to it considerable price flexibility and many market opportunities. Amongst the marketing advantages that the merging parties would gain, the Commission cited "the possibility of Guinness/Grand Metropolitan of bundling sales or increasing the sales volume of one category by tying it to the sale of another category".

Undoubtedly General Electric/Honeywell constitutes the most famous case of application of the theory of conglomerate effects. The extension of the financial strength and vertical integration of General Electric to the Honeywell products and the bundled sales of jet engines with avionics and non-avionics products to be sold at discounted prices were identified as possible conglomerate effects stemming from the merger. The implementation of the merger would have adversely affected the markets for avionics and not-avionics products in which Honeywell was already a leading player with the risk that the competitors of the merged entity would be driven off the market.[32]

Finally, the Commission applied the theory of conglomerate effects in the appraisal of the Tetra Laval/Sidel merger. It should be noted that while in General Electric/ Honeywell the theory was applied to bundling complementary products, in this case the Commission applied the theory to bundling practices concerning substitute products.[33]

C. *The theory of conglomerate effects in the case law of the EC Courts*

The appeal lodged by the merging parties against the decision of the Commission on the Tetra Laval/Sidel merger gave the EC Courts the opportunity for the first time to express their views on the theory of conglomerate effects. The Court of First Instance has not expressly condemned the recourse to the theory; but it set the limits within which the Commission can rely on it with the purpose of the appraisal of mergers. It is first necessary that the markets concerned are neighbouring markets in one of which the merging parties have already a dominant position. Secondly, the consummation of the

[32] General Electric/Honeywell, above n. 4, chapter 3, paras 350–411, 412–416, 443–444.

[33] RBB Brief 001, above n. 89; Vincenzo De Nicolò, 'Europa e Concorrenza. Tre Casi di Fusione Critica', argues that the Commission should have addressed the competition problems raised by Tetra Laval/Sidel with horizontal merger analysis.

merger must bring about immediately changes to the competitive structure of the markets concerned, as a result of which the merged entity will be in a position to project its market power into the other relevant markets and gain in these markets a dominant position. Such a situation is likely to occur when the relevant markets are converging or when one of the merging parties is the leading supplier in the pre-merger market.[34]

From Tetra Laval/Sidel it can be inferred that the Court of First Instance does not reject the possibility of anti-competitive conglomerate effects arising in the medium or long-term. Such effects are not directly imputable to the structural changes caused by the merger, but are caused by future conducts of the merged entity, which will be facilitated by the modification to the competitive structure of market caused by the consummation of the merger. However, the Court clearly says that it is incumbent on the Commission to provide convincing evidence in order to prove that the alleged anti-competitive effects are likely to occur in the future. The Court confirmed its position concerning the theory of conglomerate effects in BaByliss, where the Commission was blamed for not addressing the question of whether the merger might cause anti-competitive conglomerate effects. It appears that this judgment reveals the intention of the EC Courts not to abandon the theory of conglomerate effects as a tool to analyse the alleged anti-competitive effects of merger operations.

The European Court of Justice substantially upheld the judgment of the Court of First Instance in Tetra Laval. The Court clarified that the appraisal of mergers involves a prospective analysis of how a merger can alter the competitive structure of a given market in order to establish whether the merger is likely to have anti-competitive effects. This requires the consideration of many causal links in order to determine which one is the most likely. Then the Court observed that this prospective assessment could be rather complex in case of conglomerate mergers. Firstly, these mergers generally do not produce anti-competitive effects. Secondly, the prospective examination of the alleged anti-competitive effects may embrace a long period of time. Finally, since the likelihood of the anti-competitive effects depends on the conduct of the merged entity, the causation chains between the merger and the effects are dimly discernible, uncertain and difficult to establish. In this respect, the quality of evidence provided by the Commission in order to block a merger is particularly important.

If the Commission believes that, in post-merger markets the merged entity is likely to carry out restrictive business practice, it has to support this

[34] CFI Case T-5/02, above 127, chapter 3, para 151. CFI, Case T-114/02 BaByliss v. Commission. Salans, Merger Control-Insufficient Commitments-Portfolio Effects, Competition Law Newsletter, May 2003. ECJ, Case C-12/03 P Commission v Tetra Laval BV. CFI Case T-210/01, above n 81, paras 333–339.

view with convincing evidence. Firstly, the standard of proof requires the Commission to take into consideration the possible incentives to engage in restrictive practices created by the merger. Secondly, the Commission has also to evaluate the possible illegality of such conducts under Article 82 EC Treaty. With respect to this point the Court of Justice and the Court of First Instance took different positions. The latter ruled that the Commission has to examine whether the incentives to adopt an anti-competitive conduct may be eliminated or reduced by the unlawfulness of that conduct, the likelihood of detection and the remedies that the Commission or national competition authorities can adopt. On the other hand, the Court of Justice ruled that the assessment required by the Court of First Instance would imply a detailed examination of the relevant legal provisions and enforcement policies. At the stage of the appraisal of a proposed merger such an assessment would be a speculative exercise and would not allow the Commission to base its decision on all the relevant facts in order to establish whether they support an economic scenario in which anti-competitive conducts are likely. Accordingly, in the view of the Court of Justice it is sufficient that the Commission takes into consideration, at least in a summary way, the factors that may prevent the merged entity from carrying out future restrictive business practices.

The Court of First Instance adhered to the principles developed by the Court of Justice as to the evaluation of conglomerate effects in the General Electric-Honeywell judgment. It ruled that the evidence given by the Commission did not support the finding that the merger was likely to restrict competition in the markets for avionics and non-avionics products because of conglomerate factors. In this respect, the conclusions drawn by the Commission concerning the anti-competitive effects of the merger on the market for SFE-standard products were not supported by convincing evidence. The Commission did not establish the intention of the merging parties to extend the restrictive business practice of General Electric in pre-merger markets to Honeywell products. And, as the Commission did not compare the revenues expected from such policies with the ensuing costs, the Court concluded that the Commission was unable to establish whether the policy at issue was in the commercial interest of the parties. The same critique was made of the findings of the Commission on the market for BFE and SFE-option products. Moreover, the Commission did not properly demonstrate the incentives that, in the post-merger market, would prompt airlines to choose the Honeywell products. The Court also criticised the line of reasoning of the Commission for a lack of precision, as it did not classify the Honeywell products into one of three relevant product categories while assessing the effects of the merger in each of the markets concerned. For this reason, it was impossible to establish the effects of the merger in such markets.

Then the Court evaluated the validity of the analysis of the Commission concerning the foreclosure effects imputable to bundling. Once again the

Commission had to prove the intention and capability of the merged entity to carry out these practices. The Court observed that some peculiarities of the aviation industry could render bundling difficult. In this regard, bundling should be possible only when engines and avionic and non-avionic products are selected by the same customers. A further obstacle to bundling is that normally these products are at different stages of the manufacturing process.

In any event, the analysis of the Commission on bundling was found to be marred by several errors that made the conclusions reached in its decision untrustworthy. With regard to pure bundling the Commission did not examine whether this policy would be effective; it did not evaluate the effects of the merger in the relevant markets and it did not furnish any example as to the future operation of these practices. Nor did the Commission take into consideration the possible deterrent effect of the illegality of the envisaged conduct. With regard to technical bundling, the Commission did not demonstrate that in the near future the merged entity would carry out these practices and that it would have restrictive effects on competition. Furthermore, it did not examine the possible technical integration between engines and the avionic and non-avionic products. According to the Court, the Commission did not support its analysis of mixed bundling with convincing examples to demonstrate the advantages that the merged entity could obtain from this practice. Moreover, the economic model relied on by the Commission was rather controversial and did not support the likelihood that the merged entity would engage in bundling. The Commission did not provide any evidence that the merged entity would take the strategic decision to sacrifice its profits in the short-term period in order to obtain larger profit in the long-term period. Thus, although in post-merger markets the merged entity could have had a wider range of products, the Commission failed to establish that the merged entity would have bundled the sales of engines with the sales of avionic and non-avionic products.

The Court was also unconvinced by the evidence supplied by the Commission to support the findings that the vertical integration between the General Electric engines and the Honeywell engine starters would have lead to foreclosure effects to the detriment of competing engines manufacturers. Since the alleged anti-competitive effects were imputable to future behaviour of the merged entity in the post-merger market, the Commission was expected to demonstrate that the merged entity was likely to carry out such conduct. Therefore, the Commission should have taken into consideration the incentives and the deterrents for the merged entity so behaving. In this respect, the Commission should have evaluated whether the possibility that the conduct of the merged entity would be banned and sanctioned under Article 82 EC Treaty may have prevented the parties from engaging in such behaviour. Given that the Commission failed to consider these points, the Court concluded that the Commission did not establish that the vertical overlap between engines and engine starters engine would result in anti-competitive effects in the market for large commercial jet aircraft engines.

D. *The theory of conglomerate effects in the US*

After illustrating the position of the EC judicature on the theory of conglomerate effects, it is worth noting that the US competition authorities were also concerned by conglomerate effects during the 1960's and 1970's. This period was characterised by an aggressive enforcement policy towards conglomerate mergers and the US competition authorities on some occasions resorted to the theory of conglomerate effects, better known in the US as the doctrine of entrenchment. The 1967 Procter & Gamble case was about a product extension merger with anti-competitive conglomerate effects. The acquired firm, which was already the dominant player in the relevant market, was to be absorbed into Procter & Gamble, a much larger organisation. The merger entity with its considerable size was likely to reduce competition in the market by raising entry barriers and discouraging smaller firms from competing. Because of its financial strength, Procter & Gamble could afford to make substantial investments in advertisement campaigns, whereas its closer rivals did not have the same financial capacity. The merged entity would be a very large firm, which, thanks to its economies of scale and scope, could enjoy a number of competitive advantages to the detriment of its competitors. Therefore, The US Supreme Courts found that the merger had negative effects on competition.[35]

E. *Comparing the EC and the US positions for the assessment of conglomerate effects*

Apparently, there exist some resemblances between the rulings of the EC Commission in General Electric/Honeywell and that of the US Supreme Court in Procter & Gamble, since they appear to subscribe to the same idea that "big is bad". The facts of these cases are similar: a large financially strong company seeks to expand its business into new markets by acquiring firms that are already trading in those markets. Both the EC and the US authorities viewed the proposed transactions with antipathy. They were also sceptical of the pro-competitive activities of these firms, such as offering discounts or favourable financial terms to customers. Seemingly, both of them ruled out that the possibility that the merged entity may use the expected economies of

---

[35] Federal Trade Commission v. Procter & Gamble Co, see above.

scope to offer a better service to customers. This aggressive enforcement policy has not withstood the criticism of the Chicago School, which attaches great relevance to efficiency-related considerations. They advocate the idea that the goal of competition law is economic efficiency; accordingly, competition law should protect competition rather than competitors. So, competition law authorities should block only mergers that are conducive to anti-competitive effects and which reduce economic efficiency. They should not be concerned with the mere size achieved by the merged entity; rather they should take into consideration the potential merger efficiencies. Conglomerate mergers, as has been demonstrated by economic studies, generally result in pro-competitive effects, such as a more efficient financial corporate policy and economies of scale and scope.[36] Therefore, competition authorities have no reason to prohibit this category of mergers. Moreover, only large firms can thrive in certain markets, such as the aerospace industry, since only large firms can have access to the finance needed to fund the necessary investments for the developments of new products. Thereby, the sacrifice of smaller inefficient firms in these markets can be justified by efficiency considerations.

However, the EC Commission considers the approach of the School of Chicago as too Darwinian. Indeed, the EC chases the enhancement of efficiency and consumer welfare through the maintenance of a high degree of competition in the market, with the presence of many competitors which should ensure lower prices and innovation. A laissez-faire approach that allows market players to carry out their strategies free from any competition law constraints would lead to the creation or strengthening of dominant firms. The formation of large firms, which are able to drive smaller firms off the market in the long-term, would negatively affect the competitive structure of the market, since the disappearance of the smaller competitors is likely to result in higher prices and less innovation. Apparently, the fears of the Commission are that the merged entity in the post-merger markets may adopt business practices that may put in jeopardy the commercial viability and the existence of smaller competitors.

---

[36] Thomas Leary, 'A Comment or Merger Enforcement in the United States and in the European Union', 2006. Paolo-Maria Smirne, 'Antitrust e Joint-Ventures: Il Punto sull'Esperienza Italiana e sul Modello Comunitario' [2003] Giurisprudenza Italiana 1298, 1299. Thomas Leary, 'A Comment or Merger Enforcement in the United States and in the European Union', 2006. Paolo-Maria Smirne, 'Antitrust e Joint-Ventures: Il Punto sull'Esperienza Italiana e sul Modello Comunitario' [2003] Giurisprudenza Italiana 1298, 1299. Mario Monti, 'The Future for Competition Policy in European Union. Merger Control: Issues Highlighted in the Context of GE/Honeywell Merger' speech presented at Merchant Taylor's Hall, London 9 July 2001, Simon Baker and Derek Ridyard, 'Portfolio Power: A Rum Deal' [1999] ECLR 181, 182.

F. *Critical review of the foundations and practicability of the theory of conglomerate effects*

The theory of conglomerate effects lends support to the latest development of the economic thinking of the post-Chicago scholars. The Chicago School assumes that there is only one monopoly profit to be gained and that the monopolist can obtain this profit simply through supra-competitive pricing in the tying monopolistic market. This assertion is valid, provided that the tied market is competitive. But, if the competition in the tying and the tied market is imperfect, tying may adversely affect the competitive structure of the tied market. Under some circumstances bundling practices may be used in order to extend market power from the tying market to the tied market.

This situation is addressed by the Post-Chicagoan scholars, who regard the likelihood that the transaction is likely to raise rivals' costs as the crucial factor for the assessment of mergers between firms trading in complementary or vertically related products. Michael Whinston has shown that the conditions upon which bundling practices may have adverse effects on competition, namely foreclosing effects. This may happen when a monopolist in the market for the tying product has committed to offer only tied sales. In such a situation he can extract a monopoly profit if he manages to sell a considerable amount of the tied product. This strategy can be profitable if it sufficiently reduces competitors' expected revenue either by impeding them from entering the market or driving them off the market. Essential conditions for this strategy to be successful are that the market for the tied product is not perfectly competitive and the competitors' willingness to make sufficient sales to remain in the market. Choi has also indicated that with mixed bundling strategies, which makes a reduction of the price of tied products conditional upon the decision of customers to buy these products, a merged entity can maximise the Cournot effects. This strategy, however, may foreclose competitors which manufacture only one of the tied products from the market.

The theoretical foundations upon which the theories of the Post-Chicago School are based are not undisputed, since they often rely on empirically untested mathematical models. Theories of foreclosure and leveraging effects are quite complex; economists still have to agree on theoretical models for the analysis of such competition problems and crucial empirical data to test the validity of these models may lack. Besides, the Post-Chicago analysis of the competitive effects of bundling fails to distinguish between harms to competitors that result also in harm to competition from the harms to competitors that are the consequence of the ordinary dynamics of competition.

Furthermore, the theory of conglomerate effects does not seem capable of correctly identifying the competition problems of mergers. It is uncertain whether portfolio effects may contribute to foreclosure practices. The assertion that the availability of a wider range of products would conduce foreclosure effects is not supported by any sound economic theory. Moreover, bundling itself is not necessarily an indicator of anti-competitive aims. It can also be associated with a number of economically rational and pro-competitive reasons. Therefore, in the absence of any evidence of predatory intention, linking bundling practices to foreclosure effects is a highly speculative exercise.

Leveraging, on the other hand, may not produce any direct anti-competitive effects. In the short-term leveraging practices lead to increase in consumer welfare, given that bundling schemes results in lower prices for customers. Indeed, anti-competitive effects may take place at the end of quite long causal links, some phases of which are far from being certain. The probability of such effects is subordinated to hypothetical events, the assessment of which implies a certain degree of speculative prediction. It is unsure whether the merged entity will use the financial resources made available by the cost savings attained by the merger in order to subsidise a predatory exclusionary policy. It is also uncertain whether such conduct will marginalise or drive competitors off the market. In this respect, it must be observed that both in Boeing/Mc Donnell Douglas and General Electric/Honeywell the main rivals to the merging parties were large, financially healthy companies which were unlikely to succumb to predatory prices policies. Moreover, the typical customers of the parties to the above were sophisticated purchasers, who would not be willing to allow the merged entity to gain control over prices and developments of products.

The model developed by the Commission for the appraisal of conglomerate effects requires the evaluation of a number of factors, the correct assessment of which may not be within the capacity of a competition authority. According to this model, a merger may be blocked when in the long-term it is likely to produce negative effects, such as the foreclosure of competitors and price increases, which overwhelm the short-term benefits. The US competition authorities prefer a less predictive approach. Instead of engaging in predictions on the possible effects of mergers in a long-term scenario, they focus on the near-term benefits.

In conclusion, the EC and the US competition authorities have a different approach for the regulation of conglomerate merger and, more generally, of mergers between big firms. The EC Commission is convinced that such mergers may have a negative impact on competition and has taken a strict approach to these merger operations; while, the US competition authorities are much less concerned by such mergers and attach more importance to the immediate effects that these mergers may have. That said the question that has to be addressed now is whether such different policies are due to the different substantive merger control rules or whether they can be imputable to other reasons.

IX. *The EC and US different approaches to regulation of mergers between large firms: Possible explanations*

The different wording of the substantive tests cannot be regarded as the only explanation for the different views taken by the US and EU competition authorities in Boeing/Mc Donnell Douglas and General Electric/Honeywell. An examination of the case law regarding the application of US merger control law reveals that, at least for a certain period, the US competition authorities employed the substantial lessening of competition test to prohibit conglomerate mergers. The EC Commission's tendency to block conglomerate mergers should not therefore be explained solely by the need to establish a market dominant position. Rather, it may be also imputed to cultural and philosophical ideas underpinning merger control laws.

A. *Goals of competition law*

A convenient starting point to test the above hypothesis can be the examination of the goals of competition law. The understanding of the goals that each country assigns to its own competition law is important, as these goals may affect the interpretation of the competition rules. The range of possible goals of competition law is fairly wide and may include, for example, the enhancement of economic efficiency, the prevention of the excessive concentration of market power, the fairer distribution of wealth, the protection of consumers and of small and medium enterprises, the maintenance of a high level of employment and the integration of the single market. Importantly, competition law goals are not unchangeable they may differ in different times, depending on political priorities and prevailing economic theories.

An evaluation of the goals that historically have been assigned to US competition law may be helpful at this point. Since its enactment one of goals of the US Sherman Act was the protection of small and medium firms against larger competitors. Thus, in the 1960s the US Supreme Court in Brown Shoe stated that the motivation behind the enactment of the US Clayton Act was the "desire to promote competition through the protection of viable, small, locally owned business".[37] The primary preoccupation of those applying US competition law in this period was to maintain the competitive process, to promote diversity, to ensure market opportunities for smaller firms, and to

[37] Brown Shoe Co. v. United States, 8 L ed. 2d, 510; See also US Federal Trade Commission v. Procter &Gamble Co., 386 U George Priest and Romani Franco, 'Psicoanalisi di una Divergenza' [2002] Mercato, Concorrenza e Regole 151. Craig Paul and De Burca Grainne, EU Law, (Oxford University Press, Oxford, ultimate edition. Eleanor Fox, 'US and European Merger Policy- Fault Lines and Bridges. Mergers that Create Incentives for Exclusionary Practices' (2002) 10 George Mason Law Review 471, 474; Stock, above n. 1, 89, 831. S. 568 (1967); United States v. Von's Grocery Co., 384 U.S. 270 (1966).

restrain the formation and exploitation of excessive market power. The then dominant idea was that a high degree of market concentration was firstly harmful for consumers as it would reduce their freedom of choice; but secondly that it was harmful for smaller firms which, as result, could be exposed to the exclusionary practices of larger competitors. These observations explain why during this period the US competition law took quite an aggressive approach towards the emergence of a few large competitors in the markets. However, when Chicago School began gaining ground the pendulum of the priorities of US competition law swung towards the maximisation of consumers' welfare. The Chicago School argues that the only goal of competition law should be the efficient allocation of resources, which is considered as synonymous with the protection of consumers' welfare. From the standpoint of competition law, it is therefore necessary to establish whether a given business practice is conducive to output reduction or price increase or not, and hence whether it is efficient or inefficient. Only the inefficient practices, in the view of the Chicagoans, can be regulated by competition authorities.

The EC Treaty assigns a number of goals to EC competition law, embracing the protection of consumers as well as the protection of small and medium enterprises against the market power of the dominant firms. EC competition law was inspired by Ordoliberalism, according to which every economic player present in the market should be able to compete with each other free from any possible constraints imposed by the dominant firms. The perception of dominant firms being a threat to competition dates back to the origin of the EC, when the national markets were dominated by publicly owned firms, whose monopoly positions constituted a serious obstacle to the entry of potential competitors. The importance that Ordoliberalism attaches to the protection of small and medium enterprises is based on the assumption that the active presence of a number of smaller firms will ensure a more competitive market structure with beneficial fallouts for consumers' welfare. Consistently with these ideas, the Commission does not favour the formation of large leading firms whose market power might distort the competitive dynamics of markets. A further reason that explains such a strict stance is that EC competition law has also to promote the integration and the creation of the EC single market. Dominant firms when exercising their market power may raise private barriers in the commerce amongst Member States and divide national markets, which infringes the fundamental freedoms of the EC Treaty.

It seems that the US and the EC share the same pure competition goal of the enhancing of economic efficiency. However, while the former is mainly focused on the goal of consumers welfare, EC competition law also pursues the other goals set out by the EC Treaty and for this reason it has to be coordinated with the other EC policies. This taxonomy may influence the fashion according to which merger control is administered in these jurisdictions. In this regard, an aspect that is affected is the definition of competition harms. The US has adopted a result-oriented approach to identify relevant competitive harms. In accordance to the views of Chicago School, the diminution of efficiencies, such as output reduction and price increases are regarded as the competition harms that the US competition authorities have to regulate. Thereby, competition authorities should prohibit those practices, which encourage collusive and coordinated behaviour amongst firms likely to cause the above negative effects.[38]

The above statements must not be read in the sense that for the EC the protection of competitors is more important than the protection of competition itself. EC competition law is clearly focused on the interests of consumers. As has been stressed by the current European Competition for Competition Policy, Neelie Kroes, the aim of the EC competition law is to protect competition, not competitors and the protection of competition is the best way to protect consumers. Competition law is also instrumental in the integration of European markets as it ensures a fair playing level where efficiency and innovation are encouraged because competition is solely on merits.

The EC approach for the enhancement of the welfare of consumers, arguably, pays more attention to the fairness of the competition process, rather than to its outcomes. It primarily seeks to protect the competitive structure of markets against the risk of excessive accumulation of market power in the hands of a few firms since effective competition cannot exist without competitors. Indeed, the EC believes that consumers' welfare may be harmed if the merged entity is a large firm capable of eliminating its rivals. Thus the EC has developed a wider concept of competitive harms that embraces any distortion of competition, including exclusionary conducts. This concept covers those strategic conducts carried out by dominant firms for reasons unrelated to the merits of competition, the effect or aim of which is to drive competitors off the market or fetter rivals' market access. 156 Merger operations resulting in dominant firms that are likely to implement exclusionary conducts should be banned by the Commission.

---

[38] Elspeth Berrym Sylvia Hargreaves, Europan Union law, Oxford University press, 2007. Eleonor Fox, 'What is Harm to Competition? Exclusionary Practices and Anticompetitive Effects' 70 Antitrust Law Journal 377(2002). Kroes Neelie, 'Developments in anti-trust policy in the EU and the US', speech addressed at The C. Peter McColough Series on International Economics, The Council on Foreign Relations New York, 15th September 2006. European Commission, DG Competition discussion paper on the application of Article 82 of the Treaty to exclusionary abuses (2005), para 54: "it is competition, and not competitors as such, that is to be protected".

B. *Different perception of market forces*

The US and the EC also have different views on the reliance on market forces in order to counterbalance the abusive exercise of market power. Inspired by the Chicago School, the US competition authorities are more confident in the capability of competitors and customers to react successfully against anticompetitive conducts. In the appraisal of conglomerate effects, facing the dilemma whether to attach greater importance to short-term benefits or to the alleged long-term loss of consumer welfare, they tend to favour the former. The US competition authorities adopt a "wait and see approach" toward speculative harms and are more sensitive to the short-term foreseeable effects of merger.[39] The evaluation of alleged anti-competitive effects of mergers within a long-term scenario is a problematic exercise being based on guesswork and speculative assessments for which the competition authorities may not be well equipped.

The EC position is, at the same time, more cautious and more aggressive than that of the US. More cautious, because the Commission is less confident than its US counterparts in the ability of market players to withstand abusive exercise of market power by dominant firms. Understandably, the Commission is quite wary of approving mergers, where the likely outcome is the creation or the strengthening of the market power of the merged entity. For instance, in Boeing/Mc Donnell Douglas the Commission held that in the medium-long term the integration of the acquired firm with the manufacturing assets of Boeing would have given to it a significant competitive advantage on its competitors. Similarly in General Electric/Honeywell, the Commission blocked the merger, even though it would have led to immediate price decreases, since in the long-term the merged entity with its strengthened market power could have forced its rivals to exit the market.

C. *Availability of post-merger remedies*

The US legal system makes available to the competition authorities and to those affected by a merger operation the possibility of contesting the transaction even after the conclusion of the regulatory review. The US law do not set any statute of limitation with respect to the power of competition authorities to impugn a merger. Moreover, the prospective of recovering treble damages

[39] Neal Stoll and Shepard Goldfein, 'A Tale of Two Regulators' (2001) 3 New York Law Journal, 236. Ysuf Akabar, 'Grabbing Victory from the Jaws of Defeat: Can the GE/Honeywell Merger Facilitate International Antitrust Policy Cooperation?', (2002) 25 World Competition 131. Thorsten Käseberg, 'Are Merger Control and Article 82 EC in the Same Market?- The Assessment of Mergers Which Facilitate Exclusionary Conduct under EC Merger Control' [2006] European Competition Law Review 409, 419.

may provide an incentive to private parties to bring before courts the question of the legality of merger operations.

On the other hand, EC law does not allow the Commission to investigate and prohibit mergers after the expiration of the statutory waiting period, nor give potential private litigants the stimulus of treble damages. So, the Commission, facing the risk that in post-merger markets the merged entity may carry out restrictive business practices, has two options: it may immediately address this problem by blocking the merger or approving it, though with the adoption of suitable remedies; or, it may opt for postponing its intervention when the merging parties do carry out a restrictive business practice and assess it under Article 82 of the Treaty. As for the first option, the EC Courts have set out in Tetra Laval v Commission and in General Electric v Commission how the Commission should assess mergers the alleged restrictive effects of which are not directly imputable to the consummation of the transaction itself, but to successive conducts of the merged entity induced by post-merger market conditions.

Probably, the major problem with the application of Article 82 of the Treaty is the effectiveness of remedies available to the Commission. The Commission may impose pecuniary penalties; yet, these penalties, however high they may be, may not restore the competitive market conditions that existed before a merger. Article 7 of the EC Regulation 1/2003 confers upon the Commission the powers to impose behavioural and structural remedies in Article 82 infringement cases. However, the enforcement of the commitments imposed under the EC Regulation 139/2004 can be more easily monitored by the Commission compared with remedies imposed under the EC Regulation 1/2003. The Commission may verify compliance with the former through an arbitration procedure, within which the burden of proof is placed upon the merged entity. Moreover, the Commission is entitled by Articles 6(3) (b) and 8(6) (b) to revoke the decision which approve the merger in case the merged entity does not discharge its commitments.[40]

The Commission, seemingly aware of these difficulties, is not really confident in post-merger regulatory intervention as a tool to address and eliminate the causes of the potential anti-competitive behaviours created by the consummation of mergers. Thereby, it prefers to regulate restrictive practices from when the mere likelihood of their occurrence may arise, due to the alteration of market structures which is brought about by mergers. Merger control is the tool chosen by the Commission to ascertain whether a merger operation may facilitate restrictive business practices in the post-merger markets. The scarce confidence in ex-post regulatory intervention

---

[40] Koen Lenaerts, Dirk Arts, Ignace Maselis, Proedural law of the European Union, Thomson, Sweet and Maxwell, 2006.

may also explain the strict approach of the Commission towards mergers that can create efficiency. The danger is that the merged entity might use its increased competitive strength to sustain anticompetitive conducts in the post-merger market.[41]

D. *Treatment of efficiencies*

The US law allows weighing efficiency-related considerations, provided that the requirements set out by the Horizontal Merger Guidelines are met. The Guidelines provide that in order to be relevant, the efficiencies must be cognisable or must specifically originate from the proposed transactions, that they cannot be achieved via less anti-competitive means than the merger, and that they must be substantial or of such magnitude to set off the negative effects of the merger.[42] In Procter & Gamble the US Supreme Court ruled: "Possible economies cannot be used as a defence to illegality". Legal commentators are divided on the meaning of this statement. Apparently the Court seems to suggest a cautious resort to efficiencies, although lower courts generally rely on efficiency considerations.

The EC has taken quite a hostile approach towards merger efficiencies as proved by the fact that so far the Commission has never cleared any merger operations on the basis of efficiency considerations. Under EC Regulation 139/04 efficiency considerations seem to have a limited room. The Commission may evaluate "the development of technical and economic progress" expected by the merger, provided that such benefits are "passed on to consumers" and do not "form an obstacle to competition".[43] The second requirement–the efficiencies must not constitute any obstacle to competition- was strictly interpreted by the Commission, which in Danish Crown stated that: "the creation of a dominant position in the relevant market identified above, therefore, means that the efficiencies argument put forward by the parties cannot be taken into account in the assessment of the present merger".[44] So, the Commission, once established that the merger is likely to lead to the creation or the strengthening of a dominant position, it is unwilling to take into consideration the efficiencies that can be generated by the merger.

---

41 According to some scholars, the preoccupations of the Commission about the ineffectiveness of Article 82 of the EC Treaty are groundless. This provision does not impose on competition law enforcers the burden of proving the exit or marginalization of competitors as a result of leveraging conducts. Consequently, Article 82 allows the regulatory intervention even before that these adverse effects occur. Sven Völcker, 'Leveraging as a theory of competitive harm in EU Merger Control' [2003] CMLRev 581, 594.

42 Horizontal Merger Guidelines, above n. 44. See also Peter Camesasca, 'The Explicit Efficiency Defence in Merger Control: Does it make the Difference?' [1999] ECLR 14, 21.

43 Stephen Weatherill, Cases and materials on EU law, Oxford University press, 2006.

44 Case IV/M.1313, Slagteriselkabat Danish Crown AmBa and Vestjyke Slagterier AmBa, [2000] 5 CMLR 296 para 198.

The sceptical stance of the Commission towards efficiencies on some occasions has turned into a theory of an efficiency offence. This theory is based on the assumption that the merged entity, because of the considerable competitive advantages gained through the merger, might drive its competitors off the market. This is precisely what the Commission said in General Electric/Honeywell where it ruled that the superior financial strength and vertical integration would have given to the merged entity competitive advantages which were not replicable by their competitors. A similar view was also taken in Boeing/Mc Donnell Douglas with respect to the synergies between the military and commercial sectors, which would enhance the financial conditions of the merged entity and the capability and flexibility of its manufacturing facilities. These findings are rejected by the US scholars, who, in light of the teachings of the Chicago School, are convinced that the ultimate effect of a decision to block a merger because of the savings cost gained by the parties is to protect competitors rather than competition.

With the Guidelines on Horizontal Mergers the Commission has sought to clarify the role of efficiencies. The Guidelines explain that the Commission carries out a comprehensive assessment of the impact of the merger on competition within which it balances anti-competitive effects against efficiencies stemming from mergers. If the efficiencies of the merger compensate its anti-competitive effects the transaction does not impede competition significantly and the Commission cannot block it. This may occur when efficiencies which will be generated by the merger increases the ability and the incentives of the merged entity to act pro-competitively to the benefit of consumers. In this case the expected efficiencies will offset the anti-competitive effects the merger may produce. The Guidelines have introduced a three-pronged test with the aim to setting out the requirements which efficiencies have to comply with in order to be relevant. These requirements are as follows:

a) Efficiencies have to be passed on to consumers in terms of lower prices or new or better products. For example, cost savings in production and distribution may give merged entity incentives to reduce prices;
b) There must be a direct causal link between the merger and the efficiencies, which cannot be achieved to a similar extent with less anticompetitive means;
c) Efficiencies must be verifiable and sufficiently substantial to offset potential harms to consumer welfare. It is upon the merging parties that invoke the efficiencies to prove to the Commission that the expected merger efficiencies are likely to occur and that they meet the above requirements.[45]

[45] Guidelines for the Assessment of Horizontal Mergers, above n. 44. paras 79–88. Some commentators fear that the burden of proof on the parties may be higher the burden of proof the Commission has to comply with in order to prove that a merger may significantly impede

The Guidelines state that in order to clear a merger on the basis of efficiencies considerations the efficiencies must be of such a magnitude to compensate the alleged competitive harms of the transaction. Therefore, the more serious thealleged anticompetitive effects are, the more difficult it will be to persuade the Commission that the envisaged efficiencies are strong enough. In case the merged entity has a monopoly position or a very high market power the merger is unlikely to be approved by the Commission on the grounds of efficiency consideration.

However, it is still unclear whether and to what extent efficiency considerations will play a relevant role in the appraisal of mergers. The "passing on to consumers" requirement may not be easy to fulfil. Charles Pitofsky in a paper addressing the treatment of merger efficiencies under the US Clayton Act has labelled this requirement as a "killer qualification".[46] Unsurprisingly, the 1997 Review of the Horizontal Merger Guidelines abrogated it. The passing of efficiencies on to consumers can be proved with certainty only when the merger takes place in a nearly competitive market. But, if the competitive structure of a market is unchanged by the merger operation, it is pointless to evaluate expected merger efficiencies. A strict interpretation of the "passing on to consumers" requirement makes little economic sense in practice. From the viewpoint of the merging parties some basic questions can arise: why should firms merge? Why should they engage in the regulatory merger review process, which requires the dedication of a large amount of resources, if potential efficiencies need to be passed on to consumers?

To understanding the "passing on consumers" requirements, it may be helpful to consider Article 81.3 of the EC Treaty, which as condition to exempt restrictive agreements prescribes that a fair share of the efficiencies generated by the above conducts must accrue to consumers. According to the Commission this requirement is met when the restrictive agreements have at least neutral effects on consumers, with the positive effects being equal to the negative ones. Such a condition is more likely to occur when the restrictive effects of the conducts are not significant. A similar position has been adopted by the Commission for the assessment of efficiencies in merger cases. The crucial factor for the evaluation of efficiency claims is that consumer must not be worse off following mergers. This condition is unlikely to be met when mergers leads to the concentration of high market power in the hands of the merged entity.

Efficiency considerations seem to be relevant only in the appraisal of those mergers that are expected to produce minor anti-competitive effects and

competition. Mette Alfter, Simon Bishop and Eric Mahr, New Horizontal Merger Guidelines: Plugging the Gap or Opening the Floodgates?' [2004] Business Law International 385, 398.

[46] Charles Pitofsky, 'Proposal for a Revised United States Merger Enforcement in a Global Economy' [1992] Georgetown Law Journal 195, 207.

ensure significant efficiency gains. A recent survey has shown the type of mergers that are more likely to generate the kind of efficiencies which can meet the requirements set out by the Commission's Guidelines. Reduction of marginal costs leading to price reductions generally stem from transactions between firms with minor market power. However, such a merger is unlikely to have adverse effects on competition which need to be compensated with efficiencies.[47]

The Commission has listed a number of gains that the merging parties may derive from the consummation of a merger operation such as the increased economic power of the merged entity, the vertical integration that allows privileged access to the supply of upstream products, and the access to important facilities and financial capital. Yet, these factors may be harmful for the remaining firms since they may undermine their ability to place competitive pressure on the merged entity and prevent it from raising prices and reducing output. These benefits are usually generated by merger operations between financially strong firms that are already the dominant or, at least, the leading players in the relevant markets. Thereby, the Commission may continue considering these factors as symptoms of market power and may base on these elements the negative decisions to block a merger, instead of considering them as potential gains as the US competition authorities normally do.

Finally, it may be interesting to examine which category of efficiencies the Commission is ready to recognise. Before the enactment of EC Regulation 139/2004 Commission officials illustrated their views on this issue by distinguishing between structural efficiencies and strategically driven efficiencies. A structural efficiency is a "long-term and structural reduction in the marginal cost of production and distribution, which comes as a direct and immediate result of the concentration, which cannot be achieved by less restrictive means and which reasonably will be passed on to consumers as a permanent basis in terms of lower prices and increased quality". Only the efficiencies that meet these requirements are relevant for the Commission. Such conditions are not satisfied by the cost savings that are achieved through the elimination of duplications, because they normally do not result in sustainable price reductions. Even if such gains can guarantee increased margins for the merged entity, they are more likely to be employed to subsidise predatory pricing policies than to be passed on to consumers.

To sum up, the Commission recognised only productive efficiencies, while it disregarded allocative efficiencies. This is a narrow perception of the relevant efficiencies created by mergers, especially if compared with the position

---

[47] Michel Rainelli, 'A propos du règlement européen n° 139/2004 relatif au contrôle des concentrations entre entreprises: une vision sceptique de la prise en compte des gains d'efficacité' [2006] Revue International de Droit Economique 45, 53.

endorsed by the US competition authorities. Productive and transactional efficiencies are gainful to consumers in that they lower the costs of goods and services. Equally, allocative efficiencies are of benefit to consumers since they bring the allocation of resources closer to the Pareto optimum. Both cost savings and structural efficiencies lead to sustainable beneficial prices reductions. Therefore, the distinction between allocative and productive efficiencies is not based on any sound economic theories.

X. *Final thoughts on convergence and divergence between EC and US merger control laws*

The comparative analyses of US and EC merger control laws have revealed convergences and divergences between these jurisdictions. The US and the EC still diverge as to the legal regime of the merger control process, the contents of the notification form, and as to the goals of merger control. Convergences include the pre-merger compulsory notifications, the events triggering the notification obligation, the methodologies defining the relevant markets, the regulation of collective dominant positions and, to a certain extent, the substantive tests. Under the old EC merger control regulation, there existed two situations in which the EC and US competition authorities had or may have taken different views on the appraisal of mergers. The first situation of possible inconsistency concerned the gap between the scope of application of the old EC market dominance test and the US substantial lessening of competition test, as the former did not cover unilateral effects mergers in non-collusive markets. Yet, such a situation never resulted in conflicting decisions and with the new substantive test adopted in EC Regulation 139/2004 this potential source of conflict has now been erased. The second situation of possible inconsistency regards the regulation of foreclosure effects, especially in cases of mergers amongst large firms. This situation has already resulted in differing views adopted by the US and EC competition authorities, which have been expressed in Boeing/Mc Donnell Douglas and General Electric/Honeywell.

A number of ideas have been developed with the purpose of finding a justification for these conflicting views. The different wording of the market dominance test and the substantial lessening of competition test might be indicated as a valid explanation for these inconsistencies. It is true that some aspects of the practices followed by the Commission were somehow imposed by the market dominance test. In this respect, it can be said that the necessity to establish a dominant position induces the Commission to define the relevant markets in narrow terms. Thus, after finding several small fragmented relevant markets, the Commission may find it difficult to carry out a thorough assessment of the competitive impact of mergers upon these markets.

Therefore, it may find it more convenient to apply the theory of conglomerate effects even if the mergers are likely to affect only horizontal relations. Moreover, the market dominance test was also thought to place serious limitations on the capability of the Commission to recognise merger efficiencies. Since the dominant position was the crucial factor in the appraisal of mergers, after establishing that a merger may create or strengthen a dominant position the Commission, understandably, was unlikely to be enthusiastic about taking into consideration merger efficiencies. The adoption of the significant impediment of competition test, with its more marked focus on the examination of the competitive effects of the merger, should have softened the traditionally strict position of the Commission on the relevance of efficiencies in merger review.

During the 1960s' and 1970s' the US competition authorities applied the theory of conglomerate effects with the same vigour as the Commission. This stance was abandoned with the rise of the Chicago School which held that the objective of competition law should be the enhancement of economic efficiency. From then on, conglomerate mergers, since they usually have a neutral impact on markets, have no longer been of concern for competition authorities. Therefore it cannot be said that this theory is indissolubly linked to the dominance test as competition authorities of jurisdictions which have a different substantive test from that of market dominance, such the US authorities, made recourse to the theory. In sum, the different substantive tests cannot be regarded as the only reason for inconsistencies between the EC and US. Alternative explanations should be sought aliunde, such as at the institutional and the policy level of cultural and philosophical ideas underlying merger control laws.[48]

Competition law goals should be ranked amongst the factors that can have an effect on the outcome of the regulatory review of mergers. The EC and the US have made different choices concerning which values competition law should pursue and which tools should be used in the pursuance of such values. As said before, the application and enforcement of the US merger control policy is currently strongly influenced by the Chicago School. The Chicagoans believe that the only goal of competition is economic efficiency and that the self-correcting nature of markets is an effective remedy against abusive exercises of market power. Thereby, they advocate a narrow

[48] Interestingly, two surveys conducted among American and European industrial organisation economists seem to confirm that there exist different views on a number of competition issues on the two sides of Atlantic. In particular, American economists appear to be more disposed to believe that markets and firms should operate free from any regulatory intervention than their European colleagues. Karl Aiginger, Mark McCabe, Dennis Mueller, Christoph Weiss 'Do European and American Industrial Organization Economists Differ?' [2001] Review of Industrial Organization.

ambit for regulatory intervention, which should be restrained to genuinely inefficient practices. In this regard, the Chicago School does not justify the decision of competition authorities to block a merger when the alleged competitive harms of the transaction are based on speculative predictions. On the contrary, competition authorities should intervene only when the restrictive effects on competition are effectively felt.

EC merger control law follows the teachings of the Ordoliberalism School, which adheres to the idea that competition, and thereby economic efficiency, is guaranteed by the presence in the market of several firms. EC competition law also has to be coordinated with the other objectives set out by the EC Treaty, in particular the integration of the single market. The Commission tends to attain these goals with a 'dirigiste' approach, with which it tries to impose and maintain a market structure that ensures competitive dynamics. The aim of the regulatory intervention of the Commission is to contain the risk of the creation or the strengthening of dominant firms in the market. Such large firms may put in jeopardy the market viability of smaller firms and then negatively affect the correct working of markets. Moreover, large firms are likely to carry out commercial policies that may effectively close off national markets and infringe the fundamental freedoms of the EC Treaty. The Commission's lack of confidence in the market forces is a further factor that can explain its active approach in mergers control. The Commission blocks mergers which are predicted to increase the market power of the merging parties in the long-term, irrespective of the possible benefits for consumers expected in the immediate future. This is why the Commission is unconvinced that regulatory intervention in post-merger markets may successfully regulate the restrictive business practices that have been put in place by the merged entity.

XI. *Conclusion*

The above discussion has indicated that the different views taken by the EC and the US competition authorities in General Electric/Honeywell and Boeing/McDonnell Douglas should be imputable to different factors. These factors concern the procedural and substantive rules as well as the institutional aspects of the respective merger control laws of these two jurisdictions. The recent reform of EC merger control law has attenuated the previous strictness of the timetable of merger control procedures and has introduced efficiency considerations. Arguably, these innovations should have eliminated some of the potential sources of conflicts. Furthermore, it is worth mentioning the latest judgments of the EC Courts which have clarified the extent of the judicial scrutiny over the decisions of the Commission and which have clarified the standard of evidence on which the Commission is expected to base its decisions. As a result of these recent developments, the administration of EC merger control should be brought closer to the US merger control regime, especially with respect to the evidence competition authorities are expected to produce to justify their decision on the appraisal of mergers. Another relevant development in EC merger control concerns the theory of conglomerate effects. Although the recent case law has not rejected the theory as a tool for the assessment of the effects of merger operations, the EC Courts have recommended that the Commission should apply the theory of conglomerate effects more carefully. In this respect, the Commission should furnish convincing evidence to support its findings concerning the anti-competitive conglomerate effects of mergers. All these innovations should have shed much needed light on some of the more controversial issues in EC merger control. Some of the issues touched upon by these innovations had previously attracted the criticism of the US competition community. So, the overhaul of the EC merger control regime may also lead to the reduction of the likelihood of conflicts between the EC and US authorities in merger control. Notwithstanding that, it cannot be ruled out that in future the EC and US competition authorities will be still divided on the appraisal of a given merger, especially if the transaction concerned will affect nationally sensitive interests.

CHAPTER FOUR

A COMPARATIVE ANALYSIS OF MERGER CONTROL LAWS ENACTED BY OTHER JURISDICTIONS

I. *Introduction*

The previous two chapters have exposed the differences and similarities between the EC and the US merger control laws. However, a transnational merger may need more than the regulatory approval of the EC and US competition authorities: it has also to be authorised by the competition authorities of the other countries in which it may produce effects. For example, the proposed acquisition of Pechiney, the French aluminium producer, by Alcan of Canada was subject to the regulatory review of many national competition authorities, notably by the US, EC, Brazilian, Australian and Canadian competition authorities.

It is therefore desirable to conduct a comparative analysis of the most important elements of the merger control laws enacted by different jurisdictions from the US and the EC. The analysis highlights the different solutions and options adopted by each country, which the merging parties and their advisors have to take into consideration. To grasp all these differences may be a complex task and it raises transaction and compliance costs.

The structure of the present chapter is as follows. The second section compares the different institutional frameworks for merger control, in particular how countries allocate regulatory powers, from the investigative to the decision-making functions. The third section considers the rules that govern the merger control proceedings before the various national competition authorities. The fourth section is about the substantive tests and standards which each national competition authority apply to assess the validity of mergers. The fifth section analyses the consequences for competition authorities and merging parties caused by different national competition laws. The sixth section draws conclusions.

II. *Institutional frameworks*

The institutional frameworks designed by jurisdictions for the administration of merger control can be divided into two different types: the administrative and the prosecutorial regimes. Several jurisdictions have opted for the administrative regime and some of them concentrate the investigative and decision-making functions within the same entity. The Federal Law on

Economic Competition of Mexico confers on the Federal Competition Commission, an independent administrative body, the powers to conduct investigations, adjudicate on the legality of merger operations and impose sanctions. This model is also embraced by South Korea, which assigns the exclusive responsibilities for merger control to an administrative body, the Fair Trade Commission. Yet, in other administrative regimes, the power to review mergers is given to ministerial authorities. For example, under the law of Kenya, the Ministry of Finance is entitled to decide on the legality of merger operations upon the basis of the non-binding recommendations formulated by the Monopolies and Prices Commission, an internal department within the Ministry.[1] A further variant of the administrative regime envisages the separation of the investigative and decision-making functions, which are assigned to two different bodies. This model is adopted by Chile, whose Fiscalia Nacional Economica has the authority to carry out investigations, whereas the decision-making powers are reserved to the Antitrust Commission.[2]

The prosecutorial regime is generally chosen by common law jurisdictions, with the exceptions being New Zealand and the United Kingdom. The UK Competition Act of 2002 has designed a two-tier system for the administration of merger control. The Office of Fair Trading carries out the preliminary investigations and if it finds that a merger is likely to substantially lessen competition and that it is not possible to adopt suitable remedies, it will refer the transaction to the Competition Commission. This body is empowered to carry out in-depth investigations and has adjudicatory powers too. The decisions taken by the Office of Fair Trading and the Competition Commission can be appealed before the Competition Appeal Tribunal. As for New Zealand, the Commerce of Act of 1986 confers upon the Commerce Commission enforcement and adjudicative powers in relation to mergers.

The Competition Act of Canada opts for a prosecutorial regime under which the Competition Bureau conducts investigations and assesses the alleged anti-competitive effects of mergers. If this authority fears that a merger may have adverse effects on competition it has to apply to the Competition Tribunal to block the transaction.[3] According to the Australian Trade Practices Act of 1974 and the Trade Practices Regulations of 1974, the

[1] Restrictive Trade Practices, Monopolies and Price Control Act, Chapter 504, Laws of Kenya, art. 29–31; Oliver Fowler, Kenya, in William Rowley and Donald Baker (eds.) International Mergers (Sweet and Maxwell, London 2000).

[2] See Decree law No. 211 of 1973 of the Ministry of Finance, as amended by Law 19610 of 1999, reproduced in in William Rowley and Donald Baker (eds.) International Mergers (Sweet and Maxwell, London 2000), 10–15.

[3] Competition Act, Sections 91 to 103 (R.S. 1985, c. C-34) reproduced in in William Rowley and Donald Baker (eds.) International Mergers (Sweet and Maxwell, London 2000), 45, Appendix 1.

Australian Competition and Consumer Commission has only investigative powers. If it takes the view that the transaction may have anti-competitive effects, it has to seek from the Federal Court of Australia an injunction to impede the consummation of the merger.

Curiously, the merger control law of South Africa combines elements of prosecutorial and administrative regimes. On the basis of quantitative criteria it determines which mergers are reviewed under the administrative regime and the operations that are reviewed under the prosecutorial regime. Small and intermediate mergers are subjected to the administrative regime and are investigated and adjudicated by the Competition Commission. On the other hand, large mergers are appraised under the prosecutorial regime, which means that the Competition Commission conducts investigations and that the Competition Tribunal decides on their legality.

III. *Procedural rules*

A. *Jurisdictional criteria*

The first aspect to be examined is the criteria adopted by the different national laws with the purpose of identifying which business operations fall within the scope of their merger control laws. As a general rule, countries rely on criteria referring to the size of business operations to delimit the reach of merger review. A possible option is the establishment of financial thresholds that are based on the amount of turnover generated by the merging parties; the volume of sales achieved by the parties; and the value of the assets the merging parties have in the relevant market. An alternative approach is the jurisdictional criteria that incorporate the size of the market shares of the merging parties.

The Swiss merger control law adopts a two-tier financial threshold according to which a merger is caught by the jurisdiction of the Swiss Competition Commission if it meets either the worldwide financial or the domestic turnover threshold. Under the Competition Act of Argentina, a merger is subjected to the review of the Argentinean competition authority when the net sales of the merging parties exceed the statutory thresholds. The competition law of Ukraine establishes a comprehensive system of financial thresholds, some of which are calculated on a worldwide basis, some of which are on a national basis.[4] However, the incorporation of financial thresholds into the

[4] Article 2 of Law of Ukraine 'On Restricting Monopoly and Preventing Unfair Competition in Business Activity' reproduced in William Rowley and Donald Baker (eds.) International Mergers (Sweet and Maxwell, London 2000), 62–15, Appendix 1. William Rowley and Donald Baker, 'Introduction' in William Rowley and Donald Baker (eds.) International Mergers (Sweet and Maxwell, London 2000).

jurisdictional criteria is not free from problems, especially if they are calculated globally. The risk is that a country may assert its jurisdiction on a merger that, though it meets the financial thresholds of a country, it may cause only negligible competition problems in the markets of that country.

A number of jurisdictions combine the criterion of the financial thresholds and the criteria of market share. The Turkish competition law applies to those transactions whose merging parties have a total market share exceeding 25% in the relevant product market or have total turnovers in excess of the statutory financial threshold.[5] A similar model is embraced by the Brazilian Lei de Defensa da Concurrencia, which lays down a two-pronged jurisdictional test that is based alternatively on market share or on turnover thresholds. A merger fall under the Brazilian jurisdiction when the merged entity has a 20% market share or when the turnover achieved in Brazil by any of the merging parties in the preceding year exceeds the statutory threshold.[6]

The jurisdictional criteria based on the market shares of the merging parties exclude from the scope of jurisdiction all those transactions that are unlikely to pose any serious threats to competition, as the merged entity may not have considerable market shares. But, such an advantage is gained at the expense of legal certainty as these criteria require the definition of the relevant markets affected by the merger and the assessment of the market shares of the merging parties. It is thought that such assessment is a subjective, fact-intensive exercise, which can be difficult, especially when no specific guidance on this issue is provided. As has been rightly observed, "reasonable minds may differ concerning the definition of relevant markets".[7]

Finally, the jurisdictional criteria may incorporate factors connected to the local economy. The Venezuela competition law prescribes that only the merger operations, the parties of which generate combined gross sales in the preceding year exceeding the statutory threshold, fall within its jurisdiction. The relevant statutory threshold is expressed in tax units, set annually by the Superintendence. Similarly, the relevant financial thresholds of Mexico are calculated upon the basis of the general minimum wage, determined each year by the Federal Government, whereas the relevant financial threshold of the Russian law refers to the monthly minimum wage.

---

[5] Act on the Protection of Competition No. 4054/1994.

[6] Law No. 8884 of 11 June 1994. Christianne S. Zarzur, Lilian Barreira, Thiago Bonini and V. da Rocha, Brazil, in Maher Dabbah and Paul Lasok (eds) Merger Control Worldwide (Cambridge University Press, Cambridge 2005) 171.

[7] Kevin Kennedy, Competition Law and the World Trade Organization: The Limits of Multilateralism' (Sweet & Maxwell London 2001) 245.

B. *Merger notification regime*

As for the regime concerning the notification of mergers, the majority of jurisdictions have chosen a mandatory regime, under which the merging parties are obliged to notify the merger within a statutory time limit and to refrain from implementing the merger pending the investigation. The mandatory notification jurisdictions have different deadlines by which the notification obligation must be discharged. They may also have different events triggering the notification obligation. In South Korea the merger has to be notified to the Federal Trade Commission with a 30-day time limit, starting from the date on which the underlying transactions are concluded. The Argentinean law sets out that the obligation to notify may arise even before the conclusion of a definitive agreement. The Japanese law provides for different notification requirements and thresholds depending upon the categories of transactions and whether the merger operations concern solely Japanese firms.[8]

Interestingly, Russian merger control law provides both for a pre-merger and a post-merger mandatory notification. The mandatory pre-merger notification regime applies when the value of the assets of the merging parties is higher than the statutory financial thresholds. The mandatory post-merger notification regime applies to the categories of business operations indicated by the law. The Swiss law opts for a flexible deadline regime: it does not prescribe any specific time limits within which the parties have to notify the merger; however, they cannot proceed with the implementation of the merger before obtaining the approval of the competition authorities.

Under the voluntary regime, the merging parties are free to decide whether and when to notify the transaction, even if it is strongly advisable to notify the merger to the competition authorities who have the legal right to assess the legality of mergers that may raise competition concerns.[9] Brazil, Venezuela, New Zealand and Australia have all adopted the voluntary notification regime. New Zealand and Australia have also enacted a pre-emptive authorisation scheme according to which the merging parties may apply to the competition authority in order to obtain an authorisation or a clearance of the merger. This mechanism is of great importance because with authorisation the competition authorities waive their legal rights of investigation into the merger. After the authorization the competition authorities are not allowed to question the legality of merger operations, which thus gain a sort of immunity status. In the South African merger control system the mandatory

[8] Act Concerning Prohibition of Private Monopolization and Maintenance of Fair Trade. Nitsuo Matsushita and Eriko Watanabe, Japan, in Maher Dabbah and Paul Lasok (eds) Merger Control Worldwide (Cambridge University Press, Cambridge 2005) 713.

[9] Andrew Renshaw and Alicia Van Cauwelaert, 'Global Deals; Managing the Global Competition Issues".

and the voluntary notification regimes co-exist: the former applies to large mergers, whereas the latter applies to intermediate and small mergers.

C. *Investigation period*

Another aspect of merger control procedure on which national laws can be divided is the length of the reviewing period. One extreme of the range of possible options is Mexico which adopts a tight time-framed procedure by establishing a series of peremptory deadlines by which the Federal Competition Commission has to close its investigations. The Canadian merger control legislation also provides for strict time limits for the investigation periods. The length of these periods vary depending on whether the parties have used the long or short notification form to report the transaction to the Competition Commissioner. At the other extreme, the Brazilian Lei de Defensa de Concurrencia does not establish any deadlines for the appraisal of mergers. Such a flexible approach is also endorsed by the competition law of Kenya, which does not include any legal provisions setting the time limits of the reviewing period. The only statutory requirement by which the Monopolies and Prices Commission has to abide is the requirement to take a decision on the merger within a reasonable period of time.

D. *Notification forms and filing fees*

The content of notification forms is another controversial issue on which national laws are divided. In this respect, the merger control laws of Brazil and Turkey are amongst the most demanding, as they require the submission of a large amount of detailed data.[10] This is a relevant issue, since the different requirements for notification filings may have important consequences on the compliance costs of the merging parties.

The filing fees charged by competition authorities upon the receipt of the notification form are also of particular importance, especially from the viewpoint of firms. From a survey recently conducted by PricewaterhouseCoopers it emerges that the amount of the fees may greatly vary depending on the acting jurisdictions. The US competition authorities exact the highest sum, while the European Commission does not charge any filing fees. In the same survey PricewaterhouseCoopers also measured the amount of time that is normally taken by national competition authorities for the review of merger operations. According to the survey, the merger control proceedings before the Brazilian and the US competition authorities are the longest ones. On the

[10] Ulf Boege, 'Multi-Jurisdictional Merger Review' [2002] Fordham Corporate Law Institute 129, 130. See also Celia Hampton, 'EC Merger Control: Summary of a CEPR discussion paper by Tomaso Duso, Damien J. Neven and Lars-Hendrik Roeller' CLI July/August 2003, 18.

other hand, the Mexican and German competition authorities are praised for reaching decisions on the legality of mergers in the least amount of time.

IV. *Substantive rules*

A. *Substantive tests for the assessment of mergers*

There exist three general models of substantive tests for the appraisal of mergers, apart from the newly-minted hybrid EC test. These are: the substantial lessening of competition test, the market dominance test and the public interest test. The majority of common law countries follow the US and have the substantial lessening of competition test. Apart from Malta and Cyprus, which prefer the market dominance test, the substantial lessening of competition test is adopted by Ireland, the United Kingdom, Canada, Australia, and New Zealand. Civil law countries such as Argentina, Brazil, Japan, Peru and Ukraine also adopt the substantial lessening of competition test. The market dominance test, however, is used by many Member States of the EC, with the exceptions of Ireland, Latvia and the United Kingdom. It is also adopted in Macedonia, South Korea and Russia.

The third general model is the public interest test. This open-ended standard allows the balancing of purely competition considerations against wider interests, such as the preservation of the level of employment and the promotion of exports. The Pakistani Monopolies And Restrictive Trade Practices Ordinance of 1970 rules that mergers are appraised according to the public interest test. The Monopoly Control Authority can ban a merger when it is necessary to protect the public interest, which includes the promotion of economic growth and consumer welfare. The Indonesian law prohibits acquisitions leading to monopolistic practices or unfair business practices that are harmful to the public interest.[11] Finally the Philippine Constitution rules that monopolies are regulated or prohibited when public interest so requires.

Some jurisdictions have designed a hybrid regime, which put together different elements of each general model. The South African Competition Act provides that mergers are appraised not only against the substantial lessening of competition test; but also upon the basis of public interest grounds. The Swiss competition law combines elements of the market dominance test with elements of the public interest test. The government has the legal right

[11] Law no. 1 of 1995 on Limited Liability Companies in conjunction with Government Regulation No. 27 of 1998 on the Merger and Acquisition of Limited Liability Companies (GR 27/1998) and Law No. 8 of 1995 on Capital Markets and Law no. 5 of 1999. Picazo Buyco, Tan Fider and Santos, Philippines, in Maher Dabbah and Paul Lasok (eds) Merger Control Worldwide (Cambridge University Press, Cambridge 2005) 888.

to authorise a merger even if it creates or strengthens a dominant position, provided that the authorisation is necessary to fulfil compelling grounds of public interests. Australia merger control law adopts the substantial lessening of competition test for the assessment of competitive effects of merger operations. Moreover, the Australian law also prescribes a public interest test for the authorisation procedures. Section 90(9) of the 1974 Trade Practices Act empowers the Australian Competition and Consumers Commission to ascertain whether the merger will bring in any pubic benefits. Unfortunately, the Act fails to define the meaning of the term of "public benefit" under Section 90(9). In any case the term should be interpreted extensively to include wider interests than the welfare of consumers.[12]

The merger control law of Kenya also makes recourse to the criterion of public interest to set off the potentially anticompetitive effects of merger operations. These public interests grounds consist in the increased efficiencies and competitiveness of Kenyan exports, which should be contrasted with the possible negative effects on the competition in its domestic markets and with the possible decrease in employment due to the introduction of new technologies. The competition law of Zambia provides perhaps the most interesting example of hybrid substantive test. The Zambian national competition authority can in theory apply the three general models of substantive tests. But, normally, it applies only the substantial lessening of competition test and the public interest test. The reason why it usually disregards the market dominance test is that otherwise it would have to ban those mergers whose negative effect in creating a dominant position is outweighed by socio-economic benefits.

B. *Competition harms*

Moreover, countries may have different views on the concept of competitive harms. The previous chapter has exposed the different views taken by the EC and the US in this respect. The US, due to an effects-oriented perception of competition injuries, is principally concerned with conducts resulting in prices increase and output reduction. The EC has historically showed a more pronounced sensitivity towards exclusionary conducts. Developing countries

[12] Russel Victor Miller, Australia, in William Rowley and Donald Baker (eds.) International Mergers (Sweet and Maxwell, London 2000) 3–9; Allan Fels, Sharon Henrick and Martyn Taylor, Australia, in Maher Dabbah and Paul Lasok (eds) Merger Control Worldwide (Cambridge University Press, Cambridge 2005) 76. Eleanor Fox, 'We Protect Competition, not Competitors' (2003) 26 World Competition 149, 164. Hilde Smets and Patrick Van Cayseele, 'Competing Merger Policies in a Common Agency Framework' (1995) 15 International Law Review of Law and Economics 425. Ernest-Ullrich Petersmann, 'Legal Economic and Political Objectives of National and International Competition Policies: Constitutional Functions of WTO "Linking Principles" for Trade and Competition' (1999) 34 New England Law Review 145, 153.

sometimes consider unfair competition as competition harm. Therefore, their competition laws ban those business practices that infringe the standard of fair competition. Because of the weak competitive structure of their markets, the freedom of firms to compete without any restraints might result in considerable proportions of individual markets concentrated in the hands of a small number of traders.

C. *Goals of competition law*

The last aspect that is worth considering is the different competition law goals. Since national competition laws are the outcome of a nexus of ideas and experiences that are peculiar only to one specific country, each jurisdiction may entrust different goals to their respective competition law. For example, the EC assigns priority to the promotion of economic and political integration and to the enhancement of the competitiveness of EC-based firms. The US competition law is perceived as an instrument for the maximisation of economic efficiency. In Japan competition law favours domestic producers to the detriment of consumers. In developing countries the objective of competition law is to impede firms from carrying out unfair competition practices. A survey demonstrates that in multi-jurisdictional reviews divergences in the applicable law, especially in the objectives of competition law, are conducive to negative consequences. Indeed, the merging parties have to submit different information to each of the competition authorities involved. The result will be a sub-optimal protection of global consumer protection.

V. *Major implications of differences in national merger control laws*

This chapter along with the previous two chapters has portrayed the wide spectrum of solutions adopted by national merger control laws. National laws may differently regulate the more important aspects of merger control: from the allocation of regulatory powers to the criteria for determining whether merger operations fall within their jurisdiction; from the identification of the events that trigger the obligation to notify the merger to the information that must be supplied with the notification form; from setting the deadlines by which the investigations must be closed to the formulation of the substantive tests for the appraisal of mergers. Countries sometimes opt for hybrid solutions by combining different elements from different models: mandatory notification regimes may coexist with voluntary notification regimes; the market dominance test or the substantial lessening of competition test may be applied in combination with the public interest test.

The general picture that emerges is discouraging and the current framework for the appraisal of transnational mergers can be compared to a sort of legislative Tower of Babel, where each national competition authority seems to speak a different language. The lack of uniformity increases the likelihood that transnational mergers may be subjected to multi-jurisdictional reviews with different procedural and substantive rules. The patchy regulation of these transactions requires considerable efforts from the merging parties in order to correctly understand the national rules applicable and identify the obligations they have to discharge in every jurisdiction concerned.

All this is likely to place two different burdens on the merging parties. The first one is more immediate and concerns the identification of the competent national competition authority and the applicable law. The merging parties have to determine which competition authorities to notify about the proposed merger and whether such a notification is compulsory or only voluntary. They have also to determine the data they have to supply with the notification form. Intuitively, such discrepancies raise the compliance and transactional costs of the parties. The majority of respondents to the PricewaterhouseCoopers survey have indicated that the different information requested by each national competition authority is the most important difference between merger control laws. These differences result in a large amount of professional time and financial resources that the merging parties have to commit to the regulatory review of the merger. The survey also calculates the volume of the external costs which are on average incurred in the merger review process of a € 3,9 million value transnational merger subject to regulatory review in 8 jurisdictions. The costs for the initial filing amount to € 3,3 million. PricewaterhouseCoopers has also separately calculated the costs generated in the phase of preliminary investigations and the costs incurred in the second stage of formal investigations. In the former the average costs are estimated to be about € 545,000. But if the review of merger enters the second phase of formal investigations the costs are expected to rise sharply. The costs generated by the formal investigations conducted by the EC Commission and by the US competition authorities are circa € 4 million for each of the proceedings.

The second burden is less immediate and probably less likely to materialise, though no less onerous. The different substantive tests that are applied by the regulating competition authorities may result in the danger of inconsistent decisions on the legality of mergers, which may reduce the legal certainty of the merger review. The risk of conflicting decisions may also depend on the different goals of the various national competition laws. The EC and the US merger control laws, although sharing the same broad objective to enhance economic efficiency, have taken different views on which strategy should be deployed to pursue this objective. Developing countries tend to have a wide perception of the tasks of competition law, which range from disciplining restrictive business practices carried out by private firms to pursuing the elimination of governmental market access restrictions, from the deregulation and privatisation of industry to the accommodation of social unrest brought about by the injection of competition into markets.

VI. *Conclusion*

The second chapter of this book has already criticised the unilateral strategy. The exposition of the differences existing between national merger control laws, contained in chapters three, four and five corroborates such criticism. The simultaneous application of national merger control laws, which may differ on a number of points, is not an efficient approach for the regulation of transnational mergers since it fails to effectively address global competition problems. Besides, it has counterproductive effects both on firms and on relationships between countries. As has been shown, the unilateral strategy raises the compliance costs and increases the risk of legal uncertainty for the merging parties; it also may cause diplomatic tensions between countries. It is now time to explore the feasibility of alternative approaches for the regulation of transnational merger: notably, those approaches which focus on the internationalisation of competition law.

CHAPTER FIVE

THE BILATERAL STRATEGY

I. *Introduction*

The previous chapters have criticised the unilateral strategy for its ineffectiveness to address global competition problems. This chapter starts the analysis of the different ideas that have been proposed regard to internationalisation of competition law. Such ideas may be subsumed into the bilateral strategy and the multilateral strategy. The bilateral strategy embraces those agreements entered into by two countries, whose aim is to promote the cooperation and coordination between the national competition authorities of the two signatory parties. The multilateral strategy, on the other hand, includes the agreements entered into by a higher number of countries.[1]

This chapter focuses on the bilateral strategy, while the multilateral strategy is examined in the following chapters. The structure of the chapter is as follows. The second section provides an overview of the historic background of the bilateral cooperation. The third section briefly describes the contribution of the OECD to bilateral cooperation.[2] The fourth section examines the US/EC bilateral cooperation agreements and evaluates the achievements of this cooperation arrangement. The fifth section introduces the topic of regional trade agreements that include competition rules.[3] The sixth section

---

[1] OECD 'Making International Markets More Efficient Through "Positive Comity" in Competition Law Enforcement' OECD Journal of Competition Law and Policy, Vol. 5 No. 3, 38, 43; Charles Stark, 'International Cooperation in the Pursuit of Cartels (1997–98) 6 George Mason Law Review 533, 536.

[2] The OECD report of 2005 succintly summarised this positition: "(...) modernisation of the enforcement process, by eliminating notification and prior approval of exemptions while sharing enforcement responsbibility with National agencies, is designed, among other things, to redirect resources so that DG Comp can concentrate on complex, community wide issued and investigations. Modernisation shares competence with National institutions in a different way than the community usually does. It does not follow the paradigm of a directive from Brussels to be implemented through National laws. There are no EU-level directives requiring national governments to adopt a particolar substantive competition law, and modernisation does not require substantive harmonisation. Rather, it buidls on the fact that National competition system, so that over the years most National governemnts have adopted substantive rules that are generally consistent with those of the EU without being require to do so (...)".

[3] Robert C. Reuland, 'Hartford Fire Insurance Co., Comity and Extraterritorial Reach of United States Antitrust Law (1994) 29 Texas International Law Journal 159, 193. Brian Peck,' Extraterritorial Application of Antitrust Law and the US-EU Dispute Over the Boeing and Mc Donnell Douglas Merger: From Comity to Conflict? An Argument for a Binding International Agreement or Antitrust Enforcement and Dispute Resolution' (1998) 35 San Diego Law

looks at the above regional trade agreements. The seventh section is about the Europe Agreements entered into by the EC with the neighbouring countries. The eighth section provides an assessment of the cooperation schemes contained by regional agreements. The ninth sections weigh the advantages of bilateral cooperation agreements against their disadvantages. The tenth section discusses the viability of bilateral strategy as regulatory approach for the assessment of anti-competitive effects of transnational merger and draws conclusions.

II. *The origins of bilateral cooperation*

Historically, the first generation of bilateral cooperation agreements incorporated a narrow idea of comity, so-called negative comity. The primary objective of these agreements was to avoid jurisdictional conflicts. Later, with the progress of international cooperation, countries developed a second generation of bilateral cooperation agreements, which are more complex and comprehensive and are based on a broader idea of comity, so-called positive comity.

A. *The first generation of bilateral cooperation agreements*

This category of cooperation agreements rests upon the principle of negative comity which includes a number of non legal rules of politeness and good manners. These rules recommend countries to conduct their international affairs in such a manner as to pay regard to the legitimate interests of other countries. This principle can be relevant to settle cases of concurrent jurisdictions, when two or more countries claim jurisdiction in the same situation. It suggests that the jurisdiction with the superior or more reasonable claim should prevail over the other concurrent jurisdictions.[4] But the effectiveness of the principle in resolving jurisdictional disputes is undermined by its vagueness and its lack of legally binding force.[5]

Review 1163, 1175. Robert Shank, 'The Justice Department's Recent Antitrust Enforcement Policy: Toward A "Positive Comity" Solution To International Competition Problems?' (1996) 29 Vanderbilt Journal of Transnational Law 155, 175.

[4] OECD 'Making International Markets More Efficient Through "Positive Comity" in Competition Law Enforcement' OECD Journal of Competition Law and Policy, Vol. 5 No. 3, 38, 43; Charles Stark, 'International Cooperation in the Pursuit of Cartels (1997–98) 6 George Mason Law Review 533, 536.

[5] Robert C. Reuland, 'Hartford Fire Insurance Co., Comity and Extraterritorial Reach of United States Antitrust Law (1994) 29 Texas International Law Journal 159, 193. Brian Peck, 'Extraterritorial Application of Antitrust Law and the US-EU Dispute Over the Boeing and Mc Donnell Douglas Merger: From Comity to Conflict? An Argument for a Binding International Agreement or Antitrust Enforcement and Dispute Resolution' (1998) 35 San Diego Law Review 1163, 1175. Robert Shank, 'The Justice Department's Recent Antitrust Enforcement

The first generation of bilateral cooperation agreements can be regarded as a forum in which the parties exchanged their views on competition problems.[6] They also ensured a basic framework for the coordination of the enforcement activities of separate competition authorities. Within this framework, each authority should take into consideration the interests of the other party in order not to harm them. Examples of these agreements include the 1976 US-Germany Antitrust Accord[7] and the 1982 US-Australia Agreement.[8]

B. *The second generation of bilateral cooperation agreements*

What distinguishes the second generation bilateral cooperation agreements from the first generation agreements is that they do not pursue the minimum objective of preventing jurisdictional conflicts. Instead, they create frameworks for closer coordination between the enforcement activities of national competition authorities.[9] Such agreements are founded on the principle of positive comity, which allows positive acts of cooperation and reciprocal assistance between competition authorities. This principle is based on the presumption that the country, in which the negative effects of a restrictive business practice are felt, should renounce its right to regulate this practice if the competition authority of a third country is in a better position to regulate it. This situation arises when a restrictive practice is performed in one country but its effects affect another country. In this case positive comity enables the country whose economic interests are harmed to seek the cooperation of the country where the practice has been carried out. Accordingly, the former may request the competition authority of the latter to open or expand enforcement activities in order to remedy the restrictive practice.[10]

The first international instrument to incorporate the principle of positive comity was the 1991 EC/US Cooperation Agreement.[11] Other examples of second generation agreements are the 1995 US-Canada Agreement; the 1999

Policy: Toward A "Positive Comity" Solution To International Competition Problems?' (1996) 29 Vanderbilt Journal of Transnational Law 155, 175.

[6] OECD, Making International Markets More Efficient Through "Positive Comity" in Competition Law Enforcement' above n. 1, 43.

[7] Agreement between the European Commission and the Government of the United States of America regarding the application of positive comity principles in the enforcement of their competition laws [1999] IV CMLR 502.

[8] Article I.2 of the 1998 Agreement. John Parisi, 'Enforcement Cooperation among Antitrust Authorities' [1999] ECLR 133, 135.

[9] Claudio Cocuzza and Alessandro Montini, 'International Antitrust Co-operation in a Global Economy', [1998] ECLR 156, 159. Robert Pitofsky, Antitrust Cooperation Global Trade and US Competition Policy, in Jones and Matsushita (eds.) Competition Policy in the Global Trading System (Kluwer Law International, The Hague 2002) 57.

[10] European Commission, XXXth Report on Competition Policy 2000, 121.

[11] Exxon/Mobil (Case No. IV/M. 1383), Commission Decision (2001)OJ L 103/1; Exxon Corporation and Mobil Corporation, File No. 91 0077, Docket No. C-3907.

US-Israel Agreement;[12] the 1999 US-Japan Agreement;[13] the 1999 US-Brazil Agreement;[14] the 2000 US-Mexico Agreement; the 1999 EC-Canada Agreement; the EU-Japan Agreement; and the EC-South Africa Trade Agreement.[15]

C. *De facto application of the principle of comity*

Positive comity can also be used when no formal cooperation agreements has been signed. This is the so-called de facto use of positive comity, an example of which is given by the Kodak/Fuji case debated before the WTO Dispute Settlement Body. Following the complaint of Kodak about practices hindering its access to the Japanese market, the US Trade Representative made a positive comity referral to the Japanese Fair Trade Commission, even though no positive comity agreements existed between the US and Japan. The US invited the Japanese competition authority to open investigations into those practices which, although carried out in Japan, harmed the US economic interests, by impeding US firms from entering the Japanese market.[16]

---

[12] European Commission, XXIXth Report on Competition Policy 1999, Sec (2000) 720 Final, 115.

[13] Commission report to the Council and the European Parliament on the application of the Agreement between the European Communities and the Government of the United States of America and the Government of Canada regarding the application of their competition laws—1 January 1999 to 31 December 1999 in European Commission, XXIXth Report on Competition Policy 1999 319, 321.

[14] AstraZeneca/Novartis, (Case No. IV/M. 1806) Commission Decision (2004) OJ L110/1; Federal Trade Commission, Novartis, AstraZeneca and Syngenta, File No. 001 0082, Docket No. C-3979.

[15] Commission report to the Council and the European Parliament on the application of the Agreement between the European Communities and the Government of the United States of America and the Government of Canada regarding the application of their competition laws—1 January 2000 to 31 December 2000 in European Commission XXXth Report on Competition Policy 2000, 293. Commission report to the Council and the European Parliament on the application of the Agreement between the European Communities and the Government of the United States of America and the Government of Canada regarding the application of their competition laws—1 January 2000 to 31 December 2000, above n 46, 291. Commission Notice, Guidelines on Vertical Restrictions, (2000) OJ C291/1. See for instance, Commission Notice Guidelines on the Application of Article 81 of the EC Treaty to technology transfer agreements (2000) OJ C101/2; Commission Notice, Guidelines on the Application of Article 81 of the EC Treaty to horizontal cooperation agreements (2001) OJ C3/2; Guidelines on Horizontal Mergers, above n 44, chapter 4. Commission report to the Council and the European Parliament on the application of the Agreement between the European Communities and the Government of the United States of America and the Government of Canada regarding the application of their competition laws—1 January 2001 to 31 December 2001 in XXX1st Report on Competition Policy 2001, 333.

[16] Maureen Brunt, 'Australian and New Zealand Competition Law and Policy' [1992] FordhamCorporate Law Institute 131. John Mollard, 'Asean Overview' The International Financial Law Review Guide to Merger and Acquisition (2004); Lawan Thanadsillapakul, 'The Harmonisation of ASEAN Competition Laws and Policy from an Economic Integration Perspective' http://www.thailawforum.com/articles/theharmonisation.html (visited 2 October 2006). Damien Géradin and Nicolas Petit, 'Competition Policy and the Euro-Mediterranean Partnership' [2003] European Foreign Affairs Review 153, 155.

III. *Contributions of the OECD to the development of international cooperation*

Countries in negotiating cooperation agreements have benefited from the work of the OECD, which was a real precursor to international cooperation. Its non-binding Recommendations have set out the basic principles for international cooperation amongst competition authorities. The first edition of the Recommendations on enforcement activities concerning trans-national restrictive business practices was issued in 1967 and has been revised on different occasions. A quick reading of these documents provides an insight into the constitutive elements of international cooperation according to the thinking of the OECD. International cooperation comprises the notification of investigations or proceedings when the matter affects important interests of the other party, the exchange of information between competition authorities (within the limits of legitimate interests and the protection of confidential information), and consultation schemes for the coordination of enforcement activities.

IV. *The EC/US bilateral cooperation*

A. *The 1991 Cooperation Agreement*

Amongst the many bilateral cooperation agreements concluded, particular attention will be given to the EC/US bilateral cooperation agreement. The EC/US bilateral cooperation is chosen as a case study to evaluate the achievements of the bilateral strategy because these two jurisdictions have a long history of cooperation and because the most important examples of inconsistencies between national merger control regimes involve the EC and the US competition authorities.[17]

The cornerstone of EC/US bilateral cooperation is the 1991 Cooperation Agreement. The objective of the agreement is to "promote cooperation and coordination and lessen the possibility or impact of differences between the parties in the application of their competition laws". Article II lays down that the parties have the reciprocal obligation to notify the enforcement activities carried out by their competition authorities that may affect important interests of the other party. The purpose of the notification obligation is to

[17] Europe Agreements have been signed with Poland,[1993] OJ L348/2; Hungary, [1993] OJ L347/2; Slovakia, [1994] OJ L359/2; the Czech Republic, [1994] OJ L360/1; Bulgaria, [1994] OJ L358/3; Romania, [1994] OJ L357/31; Estonia [1998] OJ L68/3; Latvia [1998] OJ L26/3; Lithuania, [1998] L51/3; Slovenia, [1999] OJ L51/3.

enable one party to take into consideration the interests of the other party.[18] However, in case of mergers or acquisitions the scope of application of the notification obligation is limited to the transactions in which at least one party is a company organised or incorporated under the law of the US or of the Member States of the EC. Article III provides for exchange of information and periodical meetings between the competition authorities. Article IV deals with cooperation and coordination in enforcement activities. The competition authorities of one party will assist the competition authorities of the other party in their enforcement activities, provided that it is not contrary to the important interests of the assisting country. They may also agree to coordinate their enforcement activities if it is in their mutual interests such as in the case in which the parties are interested in carrying out enforcement activities on related situations. The most important points of the 1991 Agreement are contained in Articles V and VI. Article VI codifies the principle of negative comity that prescribes that at any stage of their respective enforcement activities each party should take into consideration important interests of the other party. A non-exhaustive list of relevant factors for evaluating the interests of other parties is also included in Article VI. Article V sets out the principle of positive comity, whereby one competition authority may request the other to initiate appropriate enforcement activities against businesses within the latter's jurisdiction if the negative effects of that business's restrictive practices are felt within its territory.[19] Following the request, the competition authority of the notified party will consider whether or not to begin new enforcement activities or expand ongoing enforcement

[18] For instance, Article 64 of the Europe Agreement with Romania sets out the three types of restrictive business practice as follows: a) all Agreements between undertakings, decision by associations of undertakings and concerted practices between undertakings which have as their object or effect the prevention, restriction or distortion of competition; b) abuse by one or more undertakings of a dominant position in the territory of the Community or of Romania as a whole or in a substantial part thereof; c) any public aid which distorts or threatens to distort competition by favouring certain undertakings or the production of certain goods. See also: Christophe Hillion, 'The Partnership and Cooperation Agreements between the European Union and the New Independent States' [1998] European Foreign Affairs Review 399. Thomas Gomart, 'Le Partenariat entre l'Unione Européenne et la Russie a l'épreuve de l'élargissement' [2004] RMCLUE 349, 350. Massimo Silvestri, 'Le Partenariat Euro-Mediterranéan' [2002] RMCLUE 183, 184. A.M. Van den Bossche, 'The International Dimension of EC Competition. The Case of the Europe Agreements' [1997] ECLR 24.

[19] European Commission, White Paper on the preparation of the Associated Countries of Central and Eastern Europe for integration into the internal market of the Union, above n. 97, at 150; Karel Van Miert, 'Competition Policy in Relation to the CEEC. Achievements and Challenges' Competition Policy Newsletter, (June 1998) 1. Damien Géradin and Nicolas Petit, 'Règles de concurrence et Partenariat Euro-méditerranéen: Echec ou succès' [2003] RIDE 47, 92. See for instance Article 36 of the Euro-Mediterranean Partnership Agreement with Morocco and Article 64 of the Europe Agreement with Romania. See also: Article 53 of the Partnership and Cooperation Agreements with the Russian Federation or Article 49 of the Partnership and Cooperation Agreements with Ukraine. Laurence Idot, 'Mondialisation, Liberté et Régulation de la Concurrence' [2001] RIDE 175, 193.

activities on the notified anticompetitive activities. So, if a merger between two EC-based firms is thought to have anticompetitive effects in the US markets, the US competition authorities may invoke Article V and ask the EC Commission to investigate into the legality of that transaction.

B. *The 1998 Cooperation Agreement*

The concept of positive comity has been refined by the 1998 Agreement, the purpose of which is to avoid anticompetitive conducts which may negatively affect trade and investments flow. It also aims at reducing the adverse effects of such conducts on competition and consumer welfare. The greatest innovation of the 1998 Agreement is the presumption that, under some circumstances, the party, which has made the positive comity request, will normally suspend its enforcement activities over the period, not exceeding six months, during which the requested party conducts its investigation. Article III establishes that such a request may be advanced even if the conduct at issue does not infringe the competition law of the other party. The abolition of the double illegality requirement should facilitate positive comity requests. So the competition authority of one party may be requested to investigate into a conduct even though that conduct is not prohibited by its national competition law and despite the possibility that the former may not be interested in carrying out enforcement activities. The requested party may also have the legal power to remedy the anticompetitive conduct.[20]

---

[20] The risk that the cooperative process pursued by national competition authorities may be not legitimate is raised by Edward M. Graham in 'Internationalizing Competition Policy: An Assessment of the Two Main Alternatives' [2003] Antitrust Bullettin 947, 968. Anne-Marie Slaughter, 'The Real New Order', (1997) 76 Foreign Affairs 183. Under EC law the issue of the power of regulators to engage in international relations with their counterparts was addressed in relation to the 1991 EC/US Cooperation Agreement. The French Government contested before the European Court of Justice the decision of the Commission to conclude the above agreement with the US. The Court found that this decision infringed article 228.1 of the EC Treaty, which lays down that the Commission has only the power to negotiate agreements with third countries, whereas the power to conclude international agreements is conferred on the Council. Then the Court annulled the Commission's decision to conclude the agreement (ECJ Case C-327/92, France v Commission [1994] ECR 3641). Thomas Lampert, 'International Co-operation Among Competition Authorities' [1999] ECLR 214, 216. For an analysis of the EC/US bilateral cooperation through the lensis of transgovernmentalism, Christopher Whytock, 'A Rational Design Theory of Transgovernmentalism: The Case of E.U.- U.S. Merger Review Cooperation' (2005) 23 Boston University International Law Journal 1 Allard Ham, 'International Cooperation In the Antitrust Field and In Particular the Agreement Between the United States of America and the Commission of the European Communities', [1993]. James R. Atwood, 'Positive Comity-Is It a Positive Step? [1992] Fordham Corporate Law Institute 79, 88. Walid Abdelgawad, 'Jalons de l'internationalisation du droit de la concurrence: vers l'éclosion d'un ordre juridique mondial de la Lex Economica' [2001] RIDE 161, 169. Kathleen Luz, 'The Boeing-Mc Donnell Douglas Merger: Competition Law Parochialism and the Need For a Globalized Antitrust System' (1999–00) 32 George Washington Journal of International Law and Economics 155, 173. Roger P. Alford, 'The Extraterritorial Application of Antitrust Laws: A Postscript on Hartford Fire Insurance Co

Yet, the new agreement does not apply to merger control. The strict deadlines with regard to the obligation of competition authorities to decide on the legality of notified mergers set by the US and the EC merger control laws are incompatible with the deference and discretion that are inherent in the exercise of positive comity. Moreover, a country may not be ready to ask a foreign competition

C. *Practical assessment of the EC/US bilateral cooperation in merger control*

The EC/US Cooperation Agreement is praised for attaining many achievements. It created a framework within which officers of the EC Commission and their colleagues from the US competition authorities can better coordinate their enforcement activities. In 1999 the EC and the US signed an administrative agreement that enables the members of the competition authorities of one party to take part in proceedings before the competition authority of the other party. Visits of staff of the authorities of one party to the authorities of the other party are often arranged. Officials from the US competition authorities are sometimes present in the decision-making meetings of the Commission and vice versa.[21] In BOC/AirLiquide officials from the Federal

v California' (1993–94) 34 Virginia Journal of International Law 213, 226. Spencer Weber Waller, 'Public Choice Theory and the International Harmonisation Of Antitrust Law', The Antitrust Bulletin, Summer 2003 427, 435. Eleanor Fox, 'International Antitrust and the Doha Declaration' (2002–03) 43 Virginia Journal of International Law 911, 917. Sandra Ferson Young, 'An International Antitrust Dilemma: An Analyses of the Interaction of Antitrust Laws in the United States of America and the European Union' (2002) 36 John Marshall Review 271, 271. Kennedy, above n. 19, chapter 5, 122; Eleanor Fox, 'Competition Law and the Millennium Round' (1999) 2 Journal of International Economic Law 665, 666. The so-called Munich Group was composed by: W. Fikentscher, E.M. Fox, A.Heinemann, U.Immenga, H.P. Kunz-Hallenstein, E.U. Petersmann, W.R. Schluep, S.J. Soltysinski and L.A. Sullivan. Filippo Amato, 'International Antitrust: What Future?' (2001) 24 World Competition 451, 459. Wolfgang Fikentscher, 'An International Antitrust Code' (1996) 27 International Review of Industrial Property and Copyright Law 755, 757. Wolfgang Fikentscher, 'A Trans-national Antitrust Convention and the Recent European Antitrust Proposals: Exercises in Economic Anthropology' in Clifford Jones and Mitsuo Matsushita (eds.), Competition Policy in the Global Trading System (Kluwer Law International, The Hague 2002) 366. Daniel Gifford, 'The Draft International Antitrust Code Proposed at Munich: Good Intentions Gone Awry' (1997) 6 Minnesota Journal of Global Trade 1. Philip Marsden, A Competition Policy for the WTO, 56 (London: Cameron May 2003) 56. The members of the group of experts, chosen amongst both academics and Commission Staff , included: Immenga, Jenny, Petersmann, Elhermann, Pons, Abbot, Lamoureux, Marchipont and Jacquemin.

[21] Competition Policy in the New Trade Order: Strengthening International Co-operation and Rules, (Luxembourg: OOPIC, July 1995). See also, Andrew Mitchell, 'Broadening the View of Trade Liberalisation: International Competition Law and the WTO' (2001) 24 World Competition 243. Communication to the Council Submitted by Sir Leon Brittan and Karel Van Miert, "Towards an International Framework of Competition Rules", COM (96) 296 final, (June 8th, 1996). Josef Drexl, 'International Competition Policy after Cancun: Placing a Singapore Issue on the WTO Development Agenda' (2004) 27(3) World Competition 419, 420. Ignacio Garcia Bercero and Stefan Amarasinha, 'Moving the Trade and Competition Debate Forward' [2001] Journal of International Economic Law 481, 485.

Trade Commission attended the oral hearing before the Commission. In MCI Worldcom/Sprint staff from the EC Commission attended a "pitch meeting" between the Department of Justice and the merging parties. These meetings normally take place when the competition authority is about to decide whether to block or to approve the transaction. In many cases the US competition authorities and the European Commission coordinated the assessment of the alleged anti-competitive effects of mergers. For example, in Exxon/Mobil members of the Federal Trade Commission and the European Commission worked closely together in the appraisal of the transaction. The European officials examined the documents held by the Federal Trade Commission. Since the merging parties waived their confidentiality rights, the Federal Trade Commission and the European Commission were also able to exchange confidential information. In Allied Signal/Honeywell the European Commission and the US Department of Justice discussed the definition of the product and geographical markets as well as the suitability of the divestitures proposed by the merging parties. This subject was particularly relevant for the European Commission since the majority of the assets that the merging parties pledged to divest were located in the US. Cooperation regarding the remedies was also important in AstraZeneca/Novartis. The Federal Trade Commission and the European Commission discussed which remedies to adopt in the markets for cereal fungicides and maize herbicides. The commitments proposed by the parties concerned different regional markets;[22] bilateral cooperation was important since it enabled the Federal Trade Commission and the European Commission to ascertain whether the

[22] See for a comment on the case Mark Furse, 'Competition Law and the WTO Report: "Japan-Measures Affecting Consumer Photographic Film and Paper" [1999] ECLR 9. Mexico-Measures Affecting Telecommunications Services, WT/DS204/R April 2 2004, adopted by the WTO Dispute Settlement Body on June 1, 2004. Robert Wisner and Nick Gallus, 'The Emergence of the WTO Competition Law: The Mexico Telecommunications and Canada. Wheat and Grain Decisions' [2004] ITLR 91, 93; Carol George, 'WTO Panel Condemns Anti-Competitive Behaviour in International Telecom Case: Mexico-Measures Affecting Telecommunications Services- WT/DS204/R' [2004] ITLR 106; Philip Marsden, 'Trade and Competition: WTO decides first competition case with disappointing results' CLI May 2004, 3, who criticised the application of the Reference Paper made in this case since, in is view, the WTO Appellate Body has given preminence to market access rather than to preservation of competition. This approach, especially in absence of rigorous analysis, may facilitate abuses. The rivals of the firm, the conduct of which is complained, may strategically exploit the WTO rules in order to obtain access to things they would build by themselves. Philip Marsden, 'Dealing with International Exclusion. The Right Focus for the WTO Working Group on Trade and Competition Policy' (1997) 21 (2) World Competition 91, 102. John O. Mc Guinness, 'The Political Economy of International Antitrust Harmonization', (2003) 45 William and Mary Law Review 549, 562. John H. Shenefield, 'Coherence or Confusion: The Future of the Global Antitrust Conversation' (2004) Antitrust Bulletin 385, 431. Daniel Tarullo, 'Norms and Institutions in Global Competition Policy' [2000] American Journal of International Law 478, 490.

commitments were contradictory or not and whether the buyer had obtained the assent of the competent competition authorities.

Apparently, transatlantic cooperation decisively influenced the outcome of the merger review in Oracle/PeopleSoft. Initially, the US Department of Justice and the European Commission agreed that the merger would have produced anti-competitive effects in the market for business software applications used by large companies to automate financial management systems and human resource processes.[47] But the US District Court rejected the application lodged by the Department of Justice to block the merger.[48] The Court found that the Department of Justice failed to define the relevant market in which the restrictive effects would have taken place. Eventually, the European Commission embraced the view of the District Court and on the basis of the new evidence revealed in the US trial cleared the merger. What is remarkable in Oracle/PeopleSoft is the interaction between the US and the EC competition authorities. The bilateral cooperation agreement allowed the Commission to take into consideration the evidence gathered in the US proceedings, which was important in the case debated before the Commission. Following a more detailed examination of this evidence, the Commission decided to align its views with those of the US Court and cleared the merger.[49]

The EC/US Cooperation Agreements certainly bring mutual benefits to both parties, which are identified "in terms of enhancing our respective enforcement activity, avoiding unnecessary conflicts or inconsistencies between those enforcement activities, and in terms of better understanding each other's competition policy regimes". It also fosters a marked convergence in the application of the EC and the US competition law· As examples of such convergence, it is possible to cite the adoption, on the part of the EC, of the economics-based approach for the appraisal of vertical restrictions; the Guidelines published by the Commission to clarify its position on particular issues; the reformulation of the substantive test for the appraisal of mergers. An influential US competition law scholar has commented that the level of cooperation and coordination between the US and the EC is so high that it would be difficult to improve it. Officers from the US Department of Justice have underlined the substantial convergence between US and EC competition policies in many areas. Former EC Commissioner Mario Monti has acknowledged that the convergence between the US and EC competition laws is facilitated by transatlantic cooperation and that such a cooperation is particularly relevant in the field of merger control, in which the national competition authorities have to assess the competitive effects of the same transaction. Finally, bilateral cooperation reduces the risk of conflicting decisions too, though Boeing/Mc Donnell Douglas and General Electric/Honeywell indicate that this risk still exists.

Also US competition law is converging towards EC competition law on certain issues. For example, US competition authorities have become more concerned about mergers leading to the creation of monopolies. So, the Federal Trade Commission opposed to the merger between Office Depot and Staples since the merged entity would have had a dominant position in the market for office supply.

Yet, the US and EC competition authorities may still have divergent positions which impedes them from reaching common views on the appraisal of mergers. Such divergences are all the more important, as there exists no mechanism to resolve the conflicts between the competition law enforcers involved.[23] Despite the success of bilateral cooperation, the EC and the US still divide on the assessment of a number of competition law issues. As of speaking in 2002, William Kolasky identified as many as five potential sources of disagreement: the role of efficiency considerations in merger control, fidelity rebates, predatory pricing, the doctrine of essential facilities and monopoly leveraging. On a few occasions such different approaches resulted in disagreements between the EC and the US competition authorities. For example, in General Electric/Honeywell they disagreed on the issue of monopoly leveraging. US law condemns this practice when the dominant firm is likely to obtain a monopoly position in a neighbouring market. But Article 82 EC Treaty bans every practice by which a dominant firm extends its market power into a neighbouring market even if it does not obtain a dominant position. Accordingly, the European Commission disallowed General Electric/Honeywell because, among other things, it would have enabled the merged entity to engage in leveraging conducts. As explained above in chapter four, the Commission based its findings on a controversial theory, the theory of conglomerate effects that had been long abandoned by the US competition authorities. It seems that the different approach regarding the role of efficiencies considerations surfaced and influenced the assessment of Boeing/McDonnell Douglas as well. The initial unenthusiastic attitude of the Commission towards the merger may arguably be explained with the sceptical attitude of EC merger control towards efficiencies. However, the divisions between the EC and the US competition authorities are not always attributable to the application of different theoretical models. Indeed, on some occasions, such as in Ciba-Geigy/Sandoz, it was the dialogue between them that faltered, given that they were unable to find a common position on competition problems and necessary remedies. The European Commission and the Federal Trade Commission feared that the proposed transaction would have

---

[23] For an explanation of the reasons why the Cancun Conference failed see Bart Kerremans, 'What Went Wrong in Cancun? A Principal-Agent View on the EU Rationale towards the Doha Development Round' [2004] European Foreign Affairs 363. Philip Marsden, 'Trade and Competition. Competition after Cancun- A Personal View' CLI, October 2003 22, 23. Eleanor Fox, 'Toward Antitrust and Market Access' (1997) 91 American Journal of International Law 1, 14. Eleanor Fox, 'International Antitrust: Against Minimum Rules, for Cosmopolitan Principles' (1998) 43 Antitrust Bulletin 3, 8.

created similar competition problems in certain markets, namely the market for crop protection and animal health. However, whereas the European Commission was satisfied with the commitments proposed by the merging parties, the Federal Trade Commission took a more severe stance and approved the merger only after imposing more stringent conditions. On considering the different commitments accepted by the European Commission and by the Federal Trade Commission, some scholars have argued that in this case the Federal Trade Commission did not take into consideration the views of the Commission.

The EC and US competition authorities try to minimise these divergences and have observed "disagreements are the exception rather than the rule". Even if the US and EC competition laws are similar, the respective competition authorities may nevertheless evaluate the same facts in a different manner. This point was made by Professor Mario Monti, who stated that each competition authority is expected to carry out its own assessment of merger operations. The fact that the regulating competition authorities belong to countries that have concluded a bilateral co-operation agreement does not guarantee that they have identical views on the legality of the same merger. Inconsistent decisions may not necessarily be imputable to parochial considerations. Rather, they may be ascribed to the possibility that competition authorities assess facts differently and make different predictions of the expected competitive effects of mergers. That said, it is true that the overwhelming majority of cases handled by the US and EC competition authorities have been decided without conflicts. It is also worth noting that the transatlantic dialogue did not cease during the Boeing/MacDonnell Douglas confrontation when the climate of reciprocal accusations of parochialism reached its height. Even then the Federal Trade Commission and the European Commission continued collaborating and jointly discussing the competition problems of Guinness/Grand Metropolitan. Notwithstanding the different views, the European Commission and the US Department of Justice cooperated intensively even during the review of General Electric/Honeywell.[24]

As a whole, the EC/US bilateral cooperation has reached a remarkable level of coordination and convergence, though not strong enough to avoid the possibility of inconsistencies. More efforts are therefore desirable to further strengthen the bilateral cooperation. A right step in this direction may be the establishment of the EC/US Merger Working Group, which in 2002 published the Best Practices on Cooperation in Merger Review. This document contains a number of measures to render bilateral cooperation in

[24] UNCTAD Set, above n. 2, Part IV, section B, (i) 1. See also Debra Miller and Joel Davidow, 'Antitrust an the United Nations: A Tale of Two Codes' (1982) 18 Stanford Journal of International Law 347.

merger review more effective, such as the synchronisation of the investigations timetable. The Best Practices also recommend facilitating the exchange of information between the EC and the US competition authorities. They should exchange non-confidential information and discuss their views on issues such as market definition, the assessment of competitive effects and the treatment of efficiencies. The Best Practices also encourage the merging parties to waive their confidentiality rights on the information they have provided during the investigations. This would allow the exchange of these data between the EC and US competition authorities.

V. *Regional Trade Agreements*

Contributions towards the internationalisation of competition are also made by regional agreements, the objective of which is the implementation of regional trade integration schemes. The reason why regional agreements are discussed in this chapter is that they have some important aspects in common with bilateral agreements. Both are concluded by a limited number of countries, which are geographically contiguous and which may have strong economic or political links.

The topic of the merger control regimes incorporated into regional trade agreements cannot be exhaustively discussed without making any reference to the EC regime. This represents the most successful and brilliant regional framework for the regulation of transnational mergers. Twenty-five countries have conferred upon a supranational body- the European Commission- the task to appraise mergers the size of which go beyond the statutory dimensional criteria. The EC competition law has been taken as a model by a number of countries which, following the European suit, created or are planning to create regional frameworks for the regulation of restrictive business practices. This section of the book will briefly look at competition rules incorporated into regional trade agreements, whereas the next section will examination the competition rules in the association agreements concluded by the EC with its neighbour countries.

A. *The Australia New Zealand Closer Economic Relations Agreement*

The 1983 Australia New Zealand Closer Economic Relations Agreement established a free trade area between Australia and New Zealand, the so-called Trans-Tasman market, which should eliminate any barriers between the national markets of these countries. In this respect, the agreement instructs the parties to harmonise their national competition laws. The implementation of this agreement has triggered a process of convergence between the competition laws of New Zealand and Australia. So in 1991 New Zealand amended its own merger control legislation to bring it closer to the Australian law. In the 1994 Agreement Australia and New Zealand convened to extend the territorial scope of application of their national competition laws to any conduct liable to affect trade between the two countries. Accordingly, the Australian Trade Practices Act 1974 and the New Zealand Commerce Act apply to the misuse of substantial market power or dominant positions within the Trans-Tasman market. The 1998 Protocol includes a provision that puts into practice the principle of positive comity as to restrictive business practices carried out in the Trans-Tasman market. The parties authorise their competition authorities to carry out enforcement activities on conducts that occur in the territory of one party and affect the national markets of the other party. The competition authority of the party where the anticompetitive effects are felt has the power to investigate into the conduct and engage in the necessary enforcement acts, such as holding meeting, compelling evidence and executing orders in the other country. Australia and New Zealand have reached a considerable level of cooperation and convergence. Their competition authorities are entitled to demand information from companies and individuals of the other country. Their courts have the power to issue orders to nationals of the other party and if they do not comply with the order, they will be fined by the acting authority. The Australia New Zealand Closer Economic Relations Agreement is a successful example of cooperation in the field of competition law. However, the reasons for its success mostly depend on the fact that Australia and New Zealand are countries with several elements in common: they have similar substantive laws, an analogous level of economic development and a common culture. Furthermore, the government authorities and the business circles of each country have a high a degree of confidence in the other country's judiciary and administrative bodies and vice versa. For these reasons the successful replication of the Australia New Zealand Closer Economic Relations Agreement model between two countries that do not have such close similarities seems quite improbable.

B. *Asian Regional Agreements*

The Association of Southeast Asian Nations (ASEAN) was established in 1967 with the objective, among other things, to establish a single market area where goods, services, investment and capital can freely circulate. ASEAN member states grew aware of the importance of competition law to ensure the correct working of single market. So at the 2003 Forum on Fair Competition Law and Policy they agreed on the need to develop legal and economic expertise in order to facilitate the enactment of national competition laws. Training and education were identified as essential steps towards the fulfilment of this goal. Today a number of ASEAN member states has adopted national competition laws, while discussions for the incorporation of competition rules into the ASEAN legal framework are still ongoing. Another Asian organisation the activities of which concern competition law is the Asian Pacific

Economic Cooperation (APEC). This intergovernmental economic forum which aims at reducing trade barriers and promoting investments without requiring its members to adopt legally binding obligations. In the field of competition law the APEC mission is the promote of an understanding of regional competition policies and laws as well as the identification of areas for technical cooperation between its members.

C. *African Regional Agreements*

The Common Market for Eastern and Southern Africa (COMESA) was established in 1994, replacing a former Preferential Trade Area, by countries from Eastern and Southern African. Its final objective is the creation of a single economic space, a key element of which is competition law, which is expected to strengthen market mechanisms. With regard to competition law, the goal of COMESA is to harmonise national competition policies, to avoid inconsistencies and ensure a consistent regional economic environment. COMESA is planning to set up a institutional framework for the administration of competition law, consisting of the COMESA Competition Board, acting as a regional competition authority, and of the COMESA Court to which the decisions of the Competition Board may be appealed.

Another African organisation which may adopt soon competition policy is the Southern African Development Community (SADC). The SADC was established in 1982 with the Treaty of Windhoek through which the participating countries agreed to transform the previous Southern African Development Cooperation Conference into the SADC. The SADC pursues regional economic integration through the establishment of a free trade area. The reduction of trade tariffs and the ongoing implementation of trade liberalisation programmes make it necessary the development of regional competition policy for the regulation of restrictive business practices and the protection consumers. However, due to the divergent views of its member states concerning competition law, the SADC has so far followed a soft approach. It only focuses on model legislation and regional aspects of competition policy and law.

D. *American Regional Agreements*

The competition rules incorporated in the North American Free Trade Agreement (NAFTA) signed by the US, Canada and Mexico are contained in Chapter 15. Article 1501 imposes on member states the obligation to adopt and maintain measures which proscribe restrictive business practices. Member states are also required to cooperate on issues of competition law enforcement policy, including mutual legal assistance, notification, consultation and exchange of information relating to the enforcement of competition laws and policies in the free trade area. However, due to the fact that it is only a free trade area, the NAFTA fails to reach the same level of harmonisation and cooperation as the EC. Contrary to the EC, the NAFTA has not introduced either a regional competition authority or dispute settlement mechanisms.

The 1991 Treaty of Asuncion signed by Argentina, Brazil, Paraguay and Uruguay established a trade union among them- the MERCOSUR. With the Protocolo de la Defensa de la Competencia signed at Fortaleza in 1996 the member states of the MERCOSUR agreed on a set of competition rules to be incorporated into the legal framework of this organisation. This set is quite similar to EC competition law as it prohibits two different categories of restrictive business practices, anticompetitive agreements and abuses of dominant position. The Protocolo has designed a two-tiered regime for the administration of the competition rules: a national and a supranational level. At national level, national competition authorities decide whether a given restrictive business practices is relevant for MERCOSUR. If it is so, it may submit the case to the MERCOSUR authorities: the MERCOSUR Trade Commission is responsible for investigation and evaluation of cases, whereas the Committee for the Defense of Competition has adjudicative powers. However, this regime is not operative since only two member states- Brasil and Paraguay- have so far ratified the Protocolo.

Also the agenda of the Free Trade Area of the Americas (FTAA) includes competition law. The FTAA seeks the conclusion of a hemispheric agreement open to every American country. This agreement should set up a free trade area and attain the gradual elimination of barriers to trade and investment. With those goals in mind, the FTAA has created the Negotiation Group on Competition Policy which has been mandated to prepare a competition chapter of the future hemispheric agreement. The competition rules of the proposed agreement should lead to the adoption of national and regional measures that prohibit restrictive business practices. They should also promote the adoption of mechanisms which can guarantee the development of competition policy and the sound enforcement of competition rules.

In 1973 seven Caribbean countries established the Caribbean Community (CARICOM), an integral part of which is a single market. Rules which governs the Caribbean single market also include competition law. In particular, chapter eight of the Treaty of Chaguaramas provides for the legal basis of CARICOM competition law.[91] A Competition Commission is created with the task to prosecute and adjudicate the restrictive business practices with cross-borders effects. The restrictive business practices which are prohibited by the Treaty include agreements between firms, abuse of dominant position and any other practice the effect or object of which is to frustrate the benefits expected from the creation of the single market.

VI. *European Regional Agreements*

The EC concluded several bilateral agreements in pursuance of regional trade integration objectives that include competition law provisions. These agreements have achieved the commendable result of promoting the enactment of competition laws in the EC's neighbouring countries. These agreements can be divided into three types: Europe Agreements, Partnership and Cooperation Agreements and the Euro-Mediterranean Partnership Agreements.

A. *Europe Agreements*

The Europe Agreements are a new type of Association Agreement that the EC has signed with Central and Eastern European countries. The goal of the Europe Agreements is to promote a closer integration between the Central Eastern European countries and the EC. Many reasons may be invoked to explain the need to establish stronger links with these countries, ranging from geographic proximity to common values. The European Council held in Copenhagen in 1993 recognised that the accession of Central and Eastern European countries was the common objective of the EC and the associated countries. The Copenhagen European Council also laid down the necessary preconditions that candidate countries have to fulfil for accession. As for the economic conditions, candidate countries shall have a functioning market economy and have to be capable of dealing with competitive pressure and market forces within the EC. These general conditions have been refined with specific regard to competition law and three particular requirements have been indicated: accession countries must have the necessary legislative framework concerning competition and state aid provisions; an adequate administrative capacity and a credible enforcement record of the acquis communautaire in competition policy.

As for the anti-competitive conducts that should be regulated by the parties, the Europe Agreements identify three different types of restrictive business practices, the definition of which reflects the concepts of restrictive agreements, abuse of dominant position and state aid laid down by the EC Treaty. The assessment of whether such business practices produce anti-competitive effects in the markets of the parties is carried out according to the incompatibility test. These practices are incompatible with the proper functioning of the agreement when they may affect trade between the EC and the associated country. Furthermore, the practices are assessed on the basis of the criteria developed for the application of Articles 81, 82 and 87 EC Treaty. Finally, the Association Council adopts within the deadline of three years from the entry into force of the agreement the necessary measures to implement the provisions described above.

The Europe Agreements influence the design of competition laws of the Central and Eastern European countries. The agreements prescribe the approximation obligation as an essential condition for the integration of the associated countries into the EC. Thereby, the associated country "shall endeavour to ensure that its legislation shall be gradually made compatible with that of the EC". In light of the approximation clause Central and Eastern European countries are expected to harmonise, and those countries joining the EC in 2004 have already harmonised, their existing and future legislation with the EC law.

B. *Partnership and Cooperation Agreements*

Partnership and Cooperation Agreements are signed by the EC and by the countries which have emerged from the fragmentation of the former Soviet Union. The aim of these agreements is the strengthening of bilateral relations with the view to foster security, stability and prosperity across Europe. These agreements seek to establish a deeper level of integration that goes further than mere cooperation and technical assistance. On the other hand, the level of integration the Partnership and Cooperation Agreements try to achieve is lower than that of the Europe Agreements, as the accession of these countries was ruled out from the outset. Thus the Partnership and Cooperation Agreements include only a few loose competition rules, the most important of which is that the parties must have and apply competition laws in order to remedy or eliminate the restrictive business practices that may affect trade between the EC and the associated country. The relevant restrictive practices are not identified by the classical EC three-pronged scheme. Instead, these agreements identify two general categories: restrictions put into practice by firms and restrictions caused by state intervention, such as the granting of aids. It is important to say that these agreements have no specific provisions on merger control and only contain an embryonic approximation clause.

C. *Euro-Mediterranean Partnership Agreements*

The Euro-Mediterranean Partnership Agreements are cooperation agreements entered into by the EC and the countries of the Mediterranean basin. The goal of these agreements is to establish a free trade area in the Mediterranean region in which to ensure the free circulation of goods, the improvement of the quality of life and the strengthening of the social cohesion of the population.

The Euro-Mediterranean Partnership Agreements follows the EC three-pronged scheme for the identification of relevant restrictive business practices, which are as follows: agreements between undertakings, abuse of dominant position and state aid. These practices are incompatible with the proper functioning of the Agreements when trade between the EC and the associated countries is affected. The legality of these restrictive practices must be appraised consistently with EC secondary law and case law. A five-year transition period is laid down, by which the Association Council shall take the appropriate measures for the implementation of the relevant provisions. The Euro-Mediterranean Partnership Agreements do not lay down any approximation clause, though some provisions of these agreements refer to cooperation mechanism which should prompt the associated countries to bring their domestic legislation closer to that of the EC. Finally, they provide a safeguard clause, which enables one party to take the necessary unilateral measures in case a restrictive business practice is not adequately addressed by the other party or it may cause serious harm to its interests.

The Euro-Mediterranean Partnership Agreements, like the Partnership and Cooperation Agreements, do not contain any specific provision regarding merger control. On the other hand, they include a state aid regime, based on a non-reciprocal mechanism, which relaxes the application of state aid provisions in favour of associated countries. The EC is aware that the economic systems of those countries is still under the control of public authorities and is publicly funded. A gradual application and enforcement of state aid rules is not only sensitive towards the exigencies of the associated countries, but also advisable in order to allow a smooth transition towards a market economy. Finally, the Association Council has quite a disappointing record for the adoption of the implementing measures of the provisions included in the agreements, which are necessary because the agreements have no direct effects in the legal systems of the associated countries.

VII. *Competition rules of European Regional Agreements and regulation of transnational restrictive business practices*

A. *Pursuance of different level of harmonisation*

The competition law provisions included in the European Regional Agreements (Association Agreements) essentially have a supporting role in ensuring a closer economic integration between the EC and the associated countries. They prevent the raising of private barriers that may be an obstacle to the trade liberalisation measures adopted by the parties and they foster the development of a market economy in the associated countries. The Association Agreements pursue a harmonisation strategy that should lead to a standardised regional competition policy across Europe and neighbouring areas as part of the regulatory competition with US. This may create a block of neighbouring countries with similar competition laws which may support EC position within international trade fora.

Importantly, the Association Agreements seek harmonisation to differing levels of intensity depending on the different degree of integration that they aim to establish. As the Europe Agreements set the conditions for the accession of the associated countries to the EC, logically they impose the highest level of legal integration. As has been clarified by the Commission in its White Paper, in order to meet accession conditions candidate countries have to enact competition law and ensure effective enforcement mechanisms. The approximation clause imposes on these countries a binding obligation to make their national laws compliant with EC competition legislation. The approximation clause seems to suggest to candidate countries a convenient path to discharging the obligation to adopt competition law in the sense that their national competition laws should be designed in accordance with EC law. These countries, therefore, rely on a ready-made and already time-tested competition law instead of adopting completely new competition laws.

A less stringent approximation clause applies to countries that have concluded a Partnership and Cooperation Agreement. A high degree of legislative convergence, at the same level as that imposed on candidate countries, would be too onerous a burden for these countries which are not seeking accession for the time being. Similar comments apply to the Euro-Mediterranean Partnership Agreements. Under these agreements the approximation clause should not be construed as imposing on the associated countries the obligations to harmonise their national legal systems with EC law. More precisely, these countries should only bring their national competition laws closer to the general principle of EC law.

The restrictive business practices identified by the association agreements do not include mergers. A merger affecting the markets of the EC and the associated countries is reviewed according to the national law of the jurisdictions where it produces its effects. Considering the wide jurisdictional criteria laid down by EC Regulation 139/2004, a merger that has been executed in an associated country and has produced economic effects within EC territory is likely to be subject to EC jurisdiction. It can be argued that the Association Agreements do not resolve the problem of unilateralism and do not eliminate the risk of multi-jurisdictional review of trans-national mergers.[25]

---

[25] WGITCP, Communication from the European Commission and its Member States, WT/WGTCP/W/222, 19 November 2002. Stefan Amarasinha, 'East is East and West is West and the Twain Shall Never Meet "or Shall They"?' [2003] Fordham Corporate Law Institute 603, 604. Philip Marsden, Competition Policy at the WTO, Not the End, But the End of the Beginning', CLI, November 2002, 6. Mitsua Matsushita, 'Reflections on Competition Policy/Law in the Framework of the WTO' [1997] Fordham Corporate Law Institute 31, 43. However, a much more convenient approach to evaluate the impact of mergers on trade is the ex post control, namely rules that sanction the abuse of dominant position. See chapters three and four. For instance, countries may favour the merger between two domestic firms with the aim of giving birth to national champions that will be able to successfully compete in international markets or with the aim to save a national firm from bankruptcy with the following loss of jobs. Robert Anderson and Peter Holmes, 'Competition Policy and the Future of the Multinational Trading System' [2002] Journal of International Economic Law 531,559. Merit Janow, 'Observations on Two Multilateral Venues: The International Competition Network

The Association Agreements also provide for safeguard measures in case the relevant restrictive business practices are not effectively regulated by one of the parties. This may occur when the implementing rules fail to effectively deal with the practice; or when, in absence of the implementing rules, the practices cause or threaten to cause serious prejudice to the interest of the other party or a material injury to its domestic industry. The adoption of these measures is, however, conditioned to procedural guarantees. The complaining party is required to consult the Association Committee and only after consultation, or after 30 working days from the referral to the Committee, it may take the appropriate measure. On the other hand, the Partnership and Cooperation Agreements provide a more favourable regime as to the adoption of safeguard measures by abolishing the procedural requirement of the preventive referral to the Association Committee. Indeed, under these agreements, the parties retain the right to apply adequate measures in cases of distortions to trade. As a result, they are still free to resort to unilateral measures in order to regulate restrictive business practices that may harm their interests.

B. *Objectives of Association Agreements*

It seems that the primary objective of the Association Agreements is to encourage the associated countries to enact competition laws that emulate EC competition law. Some scholars have cast doubts on the validity of this policy, since this might reduce the freedom of the associated countries to mould competition law provisions according to the shape that best meets their exigencies. EC competition law is the expression of a mature market economy and, as such, focuses principally on the maximization of economic efficiency. But the Central Eastern European Countries, at least at the time of the negotiations of the Europe Agreements, were still transition economies and their national competition laws should have aimed at promoting contestable markets within their economy. Similar negative remarks can be levelled against the Euro-Mediterranean Partnership Agreements. The EC does not impose on these associated countries a binding approximation obligation to adopt EC competition law, but it proposes a loose regulatory convergence, which requires the implementation of the general principles of EC competition law. Yet, in the adoption of the general principles into their national systems the associated countries may incur similar problems as those caused by a deeper regulatory convergence without enjoying the ensuing benefits.

(ICN) and the WTO' [2002] Fordham Corporate Law Institute 47, 69. Jean-Francois Bellis, 'Anti-Competitive Practices and the WTO: The Elusive Search for New World Trade Rules' in Marco Bronckers and Reinhard Quick (eds.) New Directions in International Economic Law (Kluwer Law International, The Hague/London 2000). Abbot Lipsky, 'Competition and the WTO: Beyond Cancun' [2003] Fordham Corporate Law Institute 657, 661.

Indeed, they have to establish an effective institutional framework for competition law and promote the awareness of competition law across firms and consumers. On the other hand, they may not rely on a set of efficient competition rules such as those of the EC Treaty.

VIII. *A critical review of competition rules of European Association Agreements and of Regional Trade Agreements*

The contribution of Association Agreements towards the internationalisation of competition law seems to be rather weak. The Europe Agreements attained the highest level of legislative convergence. However it can be said that this convergence cannot be easily replicated in other contexts because of the strong links between the approximation obligation clause and the objective of accession. The degree of harmonisation reached by the Partnership and Cooperation Agreements and by Euro-Mediterranean Partnership Agreement is limited to the recognition of some widely-framed categories of restrictive business practices that the parties commit to regulate. On the procedural level, the degree of coordination of the enforcement activities ensured by the Association Agreements does not go further than technical assistance and the exchange of non-confidential information. They do not provide any mechanism for resolving conflicts between parties, apart from the preventive consultative procedure within the Association Committee. Therefore, the parties are still able to apply unilateral measures. Arguably, the weak confidence of the EC in the effective enforcement of competition law in the associated countries can be advanced as an explanation for so timid an approach.

With respect to the European Association Agreements the close economic links existing between the parties play a pivotal role in the negotiation and conclusion of the agreements. The decision of the associated countries to enter into the agreements proposed by the EC may have been influenced by the prospect of accession or of strengthening their economic links with the EC. This has weakened their bargaining position with regard to the contents of the agreements at issue. Similar observations can be made with respect to the other regional trade agreements reviewed above. The links between the participating countries may have influenced the process of negotiations of the agreements. The achievements of these agreements have been facilitated by the common values and objectives shared by the member countries. It is uncertain whether such instruments can be successfully replicated between countries which do not have such values and objectives in common. Therefore, regional agreements cannot be seen as an effective model of international cooperation in the field of merger control.

A further reason why regional trade agreements do not appear to be the best model for the regulation of transnational mergers point specifically at their limited territorial reach. These agreements can be successfully deployed for the regulation of regional mergers whose economic effects are felt only within the national markets of the countries that are part to the agreements in question. In this case the acting authorities may rely upon instruments of interagency cooperation provided for by these agreements. But, when a transaction also affects national markets of third countries the attractiveness of regional agreements diminishes. As will be exposed below with regard to bilateral cooperation agreements, the instruments of cooperation contained in regional agreements cannot apply to the relations between competition authorities of the signatory parties and competition authorities of third parties. In this case competition rules laid down by regional agreements are useless.

IX. *A Critical review of the bilateral strategy*

A. *Advantages of bilateral cooperation agreements*

As this chapter has shown, especially with respect to EC/US bilateral cooperation, the most important achievements of the bilateral strategy seem to be the harmonisation of the legal systems of the signatory parties. Regional agreements can be also regarded as valuable instruments to pursue harmonisation programmes, although they require close economic, social and political links existing between the signatory countries.

Bilateral cooperation, and notably the principle of comity, can attenuate the problem of multi-jurisdictional review as outlined by the OECD, which has claimed that positive comity may bring in several benefits. First, it increases the effectiveness of the regulation of illegal conducts and overcomes the limitations that international law imposes on jurisdictions by enabling the harmed country to request the country where the illegal conduct was performed to take the necessary measures. Secondly, it improves efficiency in investigations, which should be carried out by the competition authority which has the best access to the relevant facts. Thirdly, it reduces the need for sharing confidential information as well as other types of information, since the investigations are conducted by the authority closest to the facts. Fourthly, it avoids jurisprudential conflicts in that only the competition law of the requested country applies. Fifthly, due to the voluntary nature of comity, the requested country can fulfil the requests of another country only when this does not harm its national interests. Finally, it ensures protection for other legitimate interests of the requested country, as its competition authority conducts the investigations and is therefore in a position to control the application of its own competition policy.

Legal scholars placed many expectations on positive comity and claimed it would guarantee a closer link between the acting competition authority and the restrictive business practice to be regulated. The latter would be investigated by the competition authorities with the best access to the parties and evidence and who are in the best position to adopt and supervise the required remedies. Another merit of the principle of positive comity is the introduction of a flexible criterion for the allocation of jurisdiction between national competition authorities on transnational restrictive business practices cases.

B. *Disadvantages of bilateral cooperation agreements*

On the other side, it must be said that the bilateral strategy has a number of inconveniences. Cooperation agreements are normally concluded by competition authorities via administrative channels and they therefore fall outside the control of national parliaments. This means there may be a democratic deficit in the process of the formation of these agreements, the risk being that competition authorities might sign cooperation agreements that are incompatible with their own national legal system.

The risk of democratic deficit may be inherent in transgovernmental cooperation. The term of transgovernmentalism refers to the web of relations created by government units of countries. Bilateral cooperation agreements entered into by national competition authorities can be considered as an example of transgovernmentalism. With its ensuing international coordination, transgovernmentalism allows national regulators to deal with international problems more effectively than they would do acting unilaterally. In this respect transgovernmentalism does not mean exercise of regulatory powers independently from national regulators. Indeed, it strengthens the enforcement capabilities of national regulators, especially with respect to the conducts which may escape their regulatory review due to the limitations imposed to their regulatory powers by the principle of sovereignty.

Competition authorities may assume a parochial approach in the application and enforcement of competition law. They are ready to cooperate with foreign competition authorities on the condition that such cooperation is in their mutual interest. It is so when the alleged restrictive business practices have anti-competitive effects in the markets of the requesting and the requested country. It is unlikely that a competition authority may commence proceedings only for the benefit of a foreign jurisdiction. The perspective of facing a political backlash because the prosecutorial decision was based upon "foreign pressure" may dissuade competition law authorities from opening investigations in these cases. This is all the more true in cases in which countries' vital security and economic interests are at stake. In such situations, as proved by Boeing/Mc Donnell Douglas and General Electric/Honeywell, bilateral cooperation is unlikely to work correctly.

Another factor that can weaken the capability of bilateral cooperation agreements to address global competition problems is their voluntary nature.

The conclusion of a cooperation agreement between two countries depends exclusively on their political will. Countries are generally more prepared to set up cooperation schemes with those countries with which they share mutual interests or similar economic conditions or with whom they have common views on competition laws. For example, two importing countries are more likely to conclude a cooperation agreement than one exporting and one importing country. Countries which have similar net trade balances similarly evaluate the attractiveness or inconveniences of cooperation agreements. Such self-interested stance may prevent the chances of developing countries entering into bilateral cooperation schemes with developed countries given that the latter are generally net exporters, while developing countries are generally net importers. On the other hand, developing countries are more likely to conclude bilateral cooperation agreements with those countries with a similar level of economic development. However, the track record of these agreements is rather poor and they appear to be toothless with regard to restrictive business practices carried out by firms located in developed countries.

The majority of bilateral cooperation agreements have been concluded so far by either the EC or the US with a third country. However, this bipolar architecture is waning in favour of the emergence of a multi-polar pattern with an increasing number of bilateral agreements signed by other jurisdictions than the US and the EC. Canada is one of the most dynamic actors in the conclusion of bilateral cooperation agreements. Apart from the above cited agreements with the US and EC, Canada has concluded cooperation agreements with Chile, Costa Rica, Mexico, and the United Kingdom; it also concluded a trilateral cooperation agreement with Australia and New Zealand. Australia, on its part, has concluded bilateral cooperation agreements with, amongst other, South Korea and Taipei and the tripartite cooperation agreement with Taipei and New Zealand may also be cited.

Opponents of the bilateral strategy point out that cooperation mechanisms set up by bilateral cooperation agreements rest on instruments of soft law. As a result, they do not create any legally binding obligations for the signatory countries, which are not obliged to modify their national competition laws, and some argue such a low-profile approach may be conducive to some negative consequences. These agreements pursue the minimum objective of creating a framework within which countries can notify each other at the beginning of enforcement activities which may affect the relevant interests of the other party. They also include arrangements to promote cooperation and coordination between the national competition authorities, mainly upon a voluntarily basis. Bilateral agreements leave the differences in national competition laws mainly untouched, differences giving rise to multiple notifications, different timetables and different substantive tests, which may fuel the risk of conflicting decisions. In addition, they do not provide any dispute settlement mechanisms to resolve controversies between countries on the application and enforcement of their respective national laws. Especially in cases of jurisdictional conflicts the bilateral strategy may be worthless in the face of the resulting tensions between the countries concerned, as it does not contain WTO-style dispute settlement mechanisms to solve such conflicts.

The fact that bilateral agreements do not oblige countries to modify their national laws may have negative consequences on the correct working of the cooperation mechanisms introduced by the bilateral strategy. An example of these consequences is given by the different provisions that in each national legal system protect confidential information. Such differences restrain the ability of competition authorities to share confidential information, which may hamper international cooperation. The 1991 EC/US Agreement does not seem to overcome such limitations. It allows the parties to exchange information concerning the cases under investigation and the application of their respective competition law only within the limits set by Articles VIII and IX. Article IX clarifies that the agreement has to be interpreted consistently with the legal provisions of the US and the EC and its Member States. Under this agreement the protection of confidentiality still prevails over the exchange of confidential information for the benefit of coordination between competition authorities. The authorities cannot share information with one another if it is illegal to do so or if the disclosure of the information is incompatible with important interests of the parties.

The EC and the US competition authorities can share only those pieces of information which their national laws allow them to exchange and in any event they must preserve the confidentiality of the information provided by the other party. As general rule, the data the competition authorities can freely share are the publicly available information and any information submitted to them with a waiver of confidentiality. In order to identify which data benefit from confidentiality protection, it is necessary to distinguish between confidential business information and confidential agency information. The latter type of information is protected by confidentiality in order to ensure the effective handling of the investigations and it can be shared between competition authorities. In contrast confidential business information is covered by professional secrecy and national laws prohibit its disclosure. This type of information includes the data that are submitted to competition authorities during its investigations.

The problem of confidentiality in the field of merger control may be overcome when the merging parties agree to waive their right to confidentiality. This may happen when the merging parties take the view that the advantages of waiving confidentiality rights outweigh the disadvantages of invoking them. Waivers facilitate cooperation between the regulating competition authorities with the ensuing benefits for the merging parties in terms of the reduction of the length of the merger control procedure and the attenuation of the likelihood of a conflicting decision. Nonetheless, merging parties are not always ready to waive their confidentiality rights due to the danger of potential leakages of confidential information to competitors or even to the general public and because of the possibility that the information may be used for other purposes.

Because of the voluntary nature of bilateral cooperation agreements the signatory parties keep their freedom to refuse to cooperate on the regulation of a given restrictive business practice if they are convinced that the request may be in conflict with their best interests. In other terms, one of the advantages of bilateral cooperation agreements is that they do not force countries to carry out enforcement activities which are inconsistent with their economic policy. However, the flipside is that the competition authorities of the parties to the cooperation agreements are free not to extend the benefits of these agreements to firms belonging to third countries. Therefore, these firms may be discriminated against firms from jurisdictions that are parties to bilateral cooperation agreements. It is uncertain whether in this respect bilateral cooperation agreements are compatible with the WTO legal system since it seems to be difficult to reconcile such schemes with one of the main tenets of WTO law: the principle of the most favoured nation.

Further doubts about the effectiveness of bilateral cooperation pertains to the meaning of the principle of comity, which has been narrowly interpreted by the US and the EC. The US Supreme Court and the European Court of Justice, respectively in Hartford Fire and Wood Pulp, ruled that comity applies only to those jurisdictional disputes involving a true conflict. A true conflict only exists when concurrent jurisdictions impose mutually exclusive obligations, as result of which it is impossible to comply with both of them. This requirement may not be easily fulfilled in the field of competition law since, due to the increasing convergence of national competition laws, true conflicts will become very rare.

The promising prospects of positive comity are not matched by its poor enforcement record. Up to date only one formal positive comity request has been made. This was in 1997 when the US Department of Justice invited the European Commission to investigate anticompetitive practices in the market for computerised airline reservation systems. The US Department of Justice feared that the conduct of some EC airlines could prevent computerised airline reservation systems owned by US-based airlines from entering the markets of certain European countries. The European Commission found that Air France provided Amadeus, the reservation system it partly owned, with more accurate information than it provided with SABRE, the reservation system owned by American Airliners. The investigation was closed when Air France offered commitments to ensure equal treatment of every computerized airline reservation system. Professor Mario Monti has praised the satisfactory outcome of this first positive comity request. In his own words, this proves that close cooperation between the US and EC competition authorities enhances the effectiveness of the enforcement of competition law in both jurisdictions.

The last critical remark concerns the practicality of the bilateral strategy. Its narrow scope of application, limited to the firms incorporated in the jurisdictions of signatory parties, renders it unsuitable to effectively address global competition problems. In order to tackle these problems it would be necessary to create a matrix of cooperation agreements between as many national competition authorities as possible. The creation of this matrix calls for long-term commitments as negotiations and conclusions of cooperation agreements may be lengthy and the whole process is costly. Countries have to repeat the negotiations and the drafting of the terms of the agreements with each potential partner. A practical example may be of help. Let us assume that four countries A, B, C and D have jurisdiction over the same transaction and that between them there exist bilateral cooperation agreements. A has concluded a cooperation agreement with B, C and D, B, on its part, has concluded bilateral cooperation agreements respectively with C and D. Finally, the competition authorities of C and D have signed a bilateral cooperation agreement. Thus six different cooperation agreements can in theory apply to regulate the enforcement activities of four different national competition authorities concerning the same transaction. The advisors of the parties to the transaction at issue have to analyse all the applicable cooperation agreements in order to elaborate the strategy to adopt before the competition authorities involved. This is a time-consuming exercise and it does not seem to lower compliance costs.

X. *The bilateral strategy and regulation of transnational mergers*

The bilateral strategy is certainly a step further than the unilateral strategy towards the internationalisation of competition law. Bilateral cooperation agreements are free from those inconveniences that dent the viability of the unilateral application of national competition laws as optimal response to global competition problems. The voluntary nature of bilateral cooperation agreements contributes to soften the legal and political tensions between different jurisdictions which would otherwise affect unilateralism. Bilateral cooperation agreements are voluntarily agreed by the countries and do not legally obligate the parties to cooperate when the requested activity is at variance with their interests. In short, these agreements respect the national sovereignty of countries. Moreover, these agreements provide for a forum within which each party offers consultations, cooperation, coordination and technical assistance to the other party regarding the application and enforcement of competition law. Bilateral cooperation agreements may also bring about benefits at the substantive level, such as convergence between national competition laws.

The countries that have entered into bilateral cooperation agreements, which codify the principle of positive comity principle, avail themselves of a mechanism that can prevent jurisdictional conflicts. In theory, this principle ensures that the competition authorities with the best access to evidence investigate into the alleged restrictive business practices. Yet the expectations placed on this principle have remained unfulfilled since the EC and US competition authorities have so far notified only one positive comity request. More importantly it must be observed that the principle of positive comity cannot be easily applied to merger control, due to the strict statutory deadlines which regulate merger review proceedings.

Having said that, the bilateral strategy is not free from limitations, mainly regarding its capability to effectively regulate transnational restrictive business practices. Bilateral cooperation normally rests on instruments of soft law, which do not impose any legally binding obligations upon the signatory parties. Though these measures do not intrude into the sovereignty of countries, they do not provide effective solutions to the problem of inconsistency in merger control, as shown by this chapter.

Bilateral cooperation agreements can bring about undeniable benefits in favour of the countries that are party to the agreements as well as in favour of their nationals. Yet such benefits cannot normally be extended to third countries and their nationals. Bilateral cooperation arrangements can be likened to a club with a selective admission policy which only countries that have similar degrees of economic development and that have strong economic or political links are allowed to enter. The homogeneity of signatory parties explains the achievements of bilateral cooperation agreements, which have been illustrated in this chapter. However, it is precisely such homogeneity that may render it difficult to successfully replicate the bilateral cooperation between countries not connected by such strong links. Unsurprisingly, the countries that do not meet such criteria are left out by bilateral cooperation agreements and this risk is particularly high for developing countries, which are unlikely to enter into cooperation agreements with developed countries.

In conclusion, the bilateral strategy may provide appropriate remedies to competition problems raised by merger operations whose effects are localised only in the territory of the parties to the cooperation agreements. On the other hand, it is hard to believe that such a strategy can address all the global competition problems raised by transnational mergers. Neither can it effectively deal with the need of firms for rapid investigations and legal certainty. The necessity to identify the cooperation agreement within the scope of application of which a transaction falls may raise the advisory fees and compliance costs the parties incur in.

CHAPTER SIX

MULTILATERAL STRATEGY: INSTRUMENTS OF HARD LAW

I. *Introduction*

The multilateral strategy is another possible option for the internationalisation of competition law. The meaning with which the term multilateral strategy is employed in the context of this book includes all international instruments adopted by more than two countries. This strategy embraces a wide spectrum of ideas and theories ranging from the establishment of a comprehensive institutional framework to the launch of informal fora for the discussion of global competition problems.

The most complex ideas incorporate the creation of an international competition authority and a set of internationally agreed competition rules for the regulation of transnational restrictive business practices. The least complex ideas suggest the establishment of international bodies which publish recommendations and best practice guidelines on competition issues, which nevertheless have no legally binding force. In between these two positions, several ideas advocate the harmonisation of national competition laws. Thus countries should be required to make their laws compliant with a set of minimum competition law standards commonly agreed, and then competition authorities could retain their jurisdiction to appraise mergers according to their national law.

Furthermore, an international authority may be empowered to ascertain whether the parties have fulfilled the obligation to implement the minimum competition standards into their national laws. Other ideas suggest that countries should implement a series of general principles, such as the principle of non-discrimination, without being obliged to amend their national competition laws. An international body may verify whether the participating countries have adopted the principles. The ideas advocating the multilateral strategy use various instruments of differing legal nature: thus some advocate the use of instruments of soft law, which create loose institutional frameworks, and others the use of instruments of hard law, which create more complex institutional frameworks and impose legally binding obligations on countries.

This chapter critically reviews instruments of hard law, from the first pioneering attempts to the latest, more elaborated theories, notably the ideas regarding the incorporation of competition rules into the WTO legal framework. The structure of the chapter is as follows. The second section examines the first efforts to introduce multilateral competition rules, namely the

Havana Charter and the Draft International Antitrust Code prepared by the Munich Group. The third section focuses on the origin of the proposal to incorporate competition rules into the WTO. The fourth and fifth sections review the arguments for and against WTO competition rules. The sixth section describes at length the EC proposal for a WTO multilateral competition agreement. The seventh section explains why the EC proposal was rejected at the Cancun Conference and evaluates the implications of the Cancun fiasco on the prospects of WTO competition rules. The eight section deals with the theory of market access, developed by Professor Fox, as a tool to resolve global competition problems. The ninth section evaluates whether the creation of a set of international legally binding competition rule for the regulation of transnational mergers is a feasible objective. The tenth section draws conclusions.

II. *First attempts to create multilateral competition rules*

A. *The Havana Charter*

After the Second World War the Allied sought to shape a new world economic that was to be administered by three different institutions: the World Bank, the International Monetary Fund and the International Trade Organization. The latter, responsible for trade issues, should have been created by the Havana Charter, which can be regarded as the first endeavour to introduce multilateral rules for the regulation of trans-national restrictive business practices. However, the International Trade Organization never came into existence due to the fact that the US Congress did not ratify the Havana Charter out of the fear of losing national sovereignty.

B. *The Draft International Antitrust Code*

In 1993 the Munich Group published a set of proposals for the regulation of global competition problems. Its most noteworthy proposal was the adoption of an international antitrust code-the Draft International Antitrust Code (the Code). This is a plurilateral agreement that could be administered by the WTO, under the WTO Trade Agreement's Annex 4. The WTO Member States are free to join the agreement. Yet, like the Havana Charter, the Code did not garner the necessary consensus of countries and it has been never implemented.

The Munich Group shelved any plans to attain the substantive harmonisation or unification of national competition laws and opted for the "convention approach". This consists of a set of internationally applicable competition law rules, which become relevant in cases of transnational restrictive business practices. The Code recognises that national competition laws are still the applicable law; so, when a competition authority is called to assess a transnational restrictive business practice it applies its national competition law but it has to ensure that the national rules conform to the principles of the Code. An international competition authority monitors the compliance of countries with the Code.

As for merger control, the Code proposes a two-pronged substantive test, according to which a merger shall be blocked provided that it creates or increases the market power of the merging parties separately or jointly and it impedes effective competition in the relevant market. The test resembles the original EC market dominance test and it is drafted in an open-textured manner with the view of accommodating the different legal backgrounds and different needs of the national competition authorities which were expected to apply the Code at that time.

The original intentions of the drafters were ambitious: building a supranational framework for the regulation of transnational restrictive business practices to include international rules and an international authority. In the view of its proponents, an international authority is intuitively the optimal solution for the regulation of business practices, whose restrictive effects span across several national markets. The decisions of such a body should be free from parochialism, while its exclusive competence should remove the risk of inconsistency which is inherent in multi-jurisdictional review. Finally, the Code must also be praised for its pragmatic approach since it does not restrain national sovereignty and does not it force countries to modify their national competition laws.

Notwithstanding that, the Code has attracted criticisms mainly due to the ambiguity and vagueness of its provisions. It was feared that the wide responsibilities given to the international antitrust authority, combined with the ambiguous wording of the Code, could create an unaccountable and rigid bureaucracy with the ensuing risk of abuse. Further critiques focus on the practicability of the Code, since countries may have different views concerning the goals of competition law, which, fatally, may reduce the chances of the Code of being accepted and adopted by countries. Moreover, the implementation of the Code within national legal systems would entail material modifications to the way national competition law is enforced. The competence of an international antitrust authority to monitor the application of national competition law made by national competition authorities and courts would place unacceptable restrictions on the discretionary powers of national competition law enforcers. Finally, the idea to codifying a set of internationally applicable competition rules is not only politically unfeasible, but also not advantageous as it would also "strait-jacket nations into a single set of rules."[11]

The risk is that "the minimum standards of the Draft Code could ossify over time and become the maximum standards at both the national and international levels". Arguably, the Code was too visionary for its time. Its adoption and implementation would have incurred high political costs for the countries involved in terms of yielding portions of their national sovereignty to international institutions, when the majority of countries were not yet ready to accept that.

III. *The first steps of the proposal for WTO competition rules: From the Van Miert Report to Singapore*

In 1995 former EC Competition Commissioner Karel Van Miert assigned to a "Group of Experts" the task of examining the relationship between trade and competition policy. The proposition of the Group of Experts was a "Plurilateral Agreement on Competition and Trade" with which the signatory parties would commit to promote cooperation amongst their national competition authorities. The proposed agreement also includes a set of substantive minimum rules for trans-national cases which the parties must implement in their respective national competition laws. Finally, it provides for the establishment of an international institutional framework to monitor the compliance of countries.

Upon the basis of the work of the Group of Experts, former EC Commissioners Van Miert and Brittan proposed incorporating a set of competition minimum standards into the WTO framework through the conclusion of an agreement. The rationale underlying this proposal was to mirror within the WTO framework the relationship between trade liberalisation and competition policy already existing within the EC single market. The EC proposal was tabled and thoroughly discussed at the WTO Ministerial Conference of Singapore in December 1996. The EC suggested that the WTO negotiations agenda should include four issues: investment, competition policy, transparency in government procurements and trade facilitation. The resulting Ministerial Declaration set up three working groups, which focused respectively on the following issues: a) trade and investment; b) trade and competition policy; c) transparency in government procurement.

IV. *Arguments for WTO multilateral competition rules*

The proponents of the WTO multilateral rules on competition are, in particular, the EC, Japan, Korea and Canada. Several reasons justify the election of the WTO as the suitable institution through which to adopt international competition rules. First, it ensures an integrated approach for the enforcement of competition and trade laws. Such an approach would reap the greatest benefits from the links existing between trade and competition laws and would attenuate the risk of trade concessions agreed under the WTO being nullified by market access barriers erected by private operators. Secondly, the WTO already has a credible and efficient dispute resolution mechanism, which could be used to resolve conflicts in the field of international competition. Thirdly, it could also guarantee a certain margin of flexibility as to the implementation of the proposed agreement. This could be concluded under Annex 4 of the Agreement establishing the WTO, which provides for a legal basis for the gradual implementation of the agreement. Initially, only the more developed and experienced countries would conclude the agreement; afterwards they would be joined by the developing countries. Finally, by virtue of its wide membership basis, the WTO is the optimal forum to weigh up and reconcile the different interests and concerns of developing and developed countries.

The advocates of the embodiment of competition law in the WTO draw further support from the presence of some specific competition rules within the WTO legal framework. It is possible to cite, for instance, Articles VIII and IX of the GATS; the Reference Paper on Regulatory Principles regarding basic Telecommunications services; Articles 8 and 40 of TRIPS. It can also be said that competition law considerations have already surfaced in some cases litigated before the WTO Dispute Settlement Bodies. Kodak-Fuji was the first case in which the WTO Panel was confronted with competition law issues. The Japanese firm Fuji had put into practice a distribution system which impeded its rivals from selling their products in Japan, having contractually bound its distributors to sell exclusively Fuji products. Kodak, convinced that such agreements had been encouraged by the Japanese government, persuaded the US government to bring the matter before the WTO with the allegation that Japan had contravened its WTO obligations. The US complaints were eventually rejected, as the US could not demonstrate that the contested measures affected the competition between Japanese and US firms and nor that denied to US the benefits to which they were entitled under the WTO agreements. Furthermore, the US did not prove a sufficient causal link between the exclusive distribution network and the conduct of the Japanese government.

The WTO Dispute Settlement Bodies also applied competition considerations in the Mexico-Telecommunications case. In this case the US lamented that the International Long Distance Rules adopted by Mexico were inconsistent with the obligations arising from the telecommunications reference paper. It contested the rules concerning the tariff calculation applied by the Mexican companies that received incoming calls from abroad. It also questioned the rules concerning the distribution among Mexican operators of the revenues generated by incoming calls from abroad. The most noteworthy aspect of Mexico-Telecommunications is the line of reasoning followed by the WTO panellists to assess the conduct of Mexico. For the first time ever the WTO Panel applied a typical competition law approach: it defined the relevant market and then proceeded by establishing whether the conduct of the major suppliers amounted to anti-competitive practices. WTO law is an invaluable tool for exporting firms wishing to remove markets access blocks put in place by private firms located in importing countries with the support of their local authorities. However, any enthusiasm for the advantages of the WTO being given competence over competition law matters should be contrasted with the factors that greatly undermine the possibility of invoking WTO rules to resolve conflicts between private parties. Referring a competition law matter to the WTO Dispute Settlement Body requires the involvement of governmental authorities in the contested restrictive business practice, as well as the agreement of the complaining firm's government to raise the issue before the WTO.

V. *Arguments against WTO multilateral competition rules*

The opponents to the EC proposal have identified two types of problem raised by the inclusion of competition law in the WTO law: those affecting the law making process and those affecting the application of rules.

A. *Law making problems*

The law making problems refer to all the legal and political factors that provide obstacles to the drafting and the enactment of WTO competition rules. As far back as 1996 Joel Klein, a former Assistant Attorney General at the US Department of Justice, warned against the risks inherent in the incorporation of competition law into the WTO and expressed his preferences for the bilateral strategy. He considered the wide membership base of the WTO as a source of concern rather than an advantage because within the WTO each Member State champions a number of divergent national interests which need to be balanced during negotiations. The numerous Member States of the WTO are unlikely to reach an agreement on sound competition law. Negotiators, in order to win a consensus, may opt for the lowest common denominator approach as to the drafting of the competition law. The consequences of this choice might legitimise a set of weak rules which are ineffective to deal with global competition problems. Such rules may not be of interest to those countries which have already enacted competition laws because their national laws are likely to be more sophisticated than the proposed multilateral rules.

Douglas Melamed, who was Assistant Attorney General at the US Department of Justice, has suggested a further element that may hamper the formation of WTO competition rules. He has examined the different goals which countries assign to competition law and policy. For instance, developing countries may be more interested in competition rules that pursue the objective of promoting economic development rather than those which promote the maximisation of consumer welfare or those which ensure a level playing field for all competitors. Furthermore, different objectives may result in different methodologies of analysing competition problems and different criteria for decision-making. All this complicates the task of the negotiators who have to draft competition rules to meet the different exigencies of the different Member States involved. Once again, the risk is that these problems may be addressed using the lowest common denominator approach.

At the political level several factors may lower the chances of the conclusion of a WTO competition law agreement. Countries may not be ready to undertake legally binding commitments imposed by multilateral instruments. Indeed, they find it less problematic joining international schemes that do not impose any legal obligations to cooperate and that allow countries to retain the freedom not to cooperate when the requested cooperation is not in their interests. Other scholars focus on the costs that Member States might incur in discharging the implementation obligations. Such costs have different sources: in part, they are agency costs and are generated by the monitoring of the enforcement activities concerning the harmonised rules; in part, they are caused by the implementation of the multilateral competition rules given that countries have to amend their existing national competition laws and make them compliant with the agreement. Other costs concern the loss of innovation brought about by the crystallisation of competition law following the adoption of the multilateral rules. The amendment of these rules can be a difficult and burdensome task, as they are incorporated into a formal international agreement and the consent of each signatory party is therefore required. For this reason it is feared that the existence of WTO competition rules may stifle progress in the field of competition law.

B. *Misapplication problems*

Misapplication problems refer to those factors which may impede the proper application and enforcement of the proposed WTO competition rules, the most important of which concerns the capability of WTO staff to properly apply competition law. As has been rightly observed, trade and competition law have a different scope of application. The WTO rules only apply to restrictive practices implemented by governments, while competition law applies to those practices executed by private firms. A trade organisation such as the WTO is administered by staff who, while well-versed in trade law and policy, may not be so competent in the regulation of private transnational restrictive business practices. Though trade and competition law have similar objectives, such as the opening up of markets and the enhancing of economic efficiency, their practical application may lead to diverging results. Trade and competition law officials may indeed assess the same restrictive business practices differently. An agreement between a manufacturer and a dealer, under which the latter is legally obliged not to deal with products made by the manufacturers' rivals may be regarded as illegal by trade officials, since this practice is thought to impede the market access of foreign products. Conversely, competition law enforcers may find that transaction legal, as the agreement may create efficiencies by increasing the welfare of consumers. The risk is that the WTO when applying competition rules might sacrifice a pro-competitive practice at the altar of the goal of trade liberalisation.

It is also possible to say that trade and competition law rules are differently drafted. Competition law rules are worded widely in almost constitutional terms with the purpose of facilitating the adaptation of competition law to the ever-changing market conditions or to new economic theories. On the other hand, WTO rules are drafted in a more detailed manner in order to meet the expectations of a large number of countries, which do not have the same interpretative methods, with respect to the benefits arising from the WTO agreements. If the WTO were to have any responsibilities on competition law matters it would have to enjoy wide discretionary powers, akin to lawmaking powers, in the interpretation of these rules. So broad a discretion, together with a lack a familiarity with competition issues, reinforces the worries of those who fear that WTO might misapply competition law by prohibiting practices that hinder market access even if they have pro-competitive effects. In this respect, doubts have been cast on the capability of the WTO panellists to carry out complex fact-intensive investigations that are typical in the enforcement of competition law.

Such considerations introduce the issue of the role of the WTO Dispute Settlement Understanding in the application of the proposed competition rules. In theory, two different tasks may be assigned to this instrument. According to the least far-reaching option, the WTO should verify the compliance of Member State with the obligations agreed in the proposed agreement. This scheme would allay the risk of abuse of confidential information as well as the worries concerning the capability of the WTO panellists to properly decide competition law cases, but it would have a minimal impact on international trade. The second, more ambitious, option entrusts the WTO with the competence to review individual decisions on the basis of the WTO competition rules. However, this may be perceived as an unacceptable intrusion of the WTO into the sovereignty of countries, most notably into their prosecutorial discretion and judicial decision-making powers concerning the application of national competition laws.[36] Firms also fear that their confidential business information may not be adequately protected in procedures before the WTO bodies.

The incorporation of multilateral competition rules in the WTO raises the question of how to reconcile two apparently contradictory conditions: the commitments that the WTO legal framework would impose on Member

States and the discretionary powers of national competition authorities. The proposed multilateral rules may create a number of legally binding obligations for Member States, which may curb the discretionary powers of national competition authorities in their decision of whether to prosecute a restrictive business practice or not. Such a decision may be justified by a number of plausible reasons. For example, a competition authority may not prosecute every restrictive business practice, rather only those practices which cause the most restrictive effects. The justification of this may be the policy of concentrating all available resources on the prosecution of the most serious competition injuries. But at this point a neutral observer may raise many questions. Could the negative decisions not to prosecute be regarded as an infringement of the WTO obligations? If it were so, how could the infringed rule be enforced with respect to the infringing Member State? Would the WTO Dispute Settlement Bodies be able to understand properly the competition law and policy of that Member State?

The possible replies to the above questions seem unconvincing. The WTO Dispute Settlement Bodies could replace the idle national competition authority and proceed with the appraisal of the restrictive business practices. However, as noted above, this solution would constitute a significant intrusion into national sovereignty and, as such, it could hardly be accepted by countries, as indicated by previous fruitless efforts at introducing similar mechanisms described in this chapter. On the other hand, typical WTO sanctions for non-compliant Member States are equally unpersuasive since such measures are unable to preserve or restore the competitive structure of the national markets affected by the restrictive business practice.

Finally, opponents of having WTO competition rules focused on the interpretation and application of the rules that are part of the WTO legal framework. These rules are normally interpreted and applied in quite an adversarial and confrontational manner. Thus exporting countries would be pitted against importing countries, with the former contesting the legitimacy of the restrictive practices adopted by the latter. It is therefore difficult to predict whether and to what extent the creation of WTO competition rules may have a positive effects on international cooperation and on the harmonisation of the legal systems of the Member States. Rather, it seems to be likely to put on a strain on the relationships between national competition authorities and put in jeopardy the prospects of cooperation between them.

All the criticisms levelled against the EC proposal can be summarised with the words of the International Competition Policy Advisory Committee. In its final report it stated that bilateral cooperation is ineffective to deal with global competition issues; but at the same time, it was sceptical about the incorporation of competition law into the WTO. It explained that "not all restraints are anti-competitive and not all competition problems that are global in nature are by definition matters of relevance for international trade policy." Hence, it concluded that WTO activities regarding the interface between trade and competition policy should focus on those conducts that hamper the ability of firms to access foreign markets. Only the regulation of the market access problem is consistent with the trade liberalisation mission of the WTO.

VI. *On the road towards the Cancun Conference*

The Ministerial Declaration adopted at the Doha Ministerial Conference renovated and strengthened the mandate of the Working Group on the Interaction between Trade and Competition Policy. Accordingly, the Doha Declaration enlists a series of key issues to be discussed by the Working Group. These issues are the identification of core principles, the prosecution of hardcore cartels, voluntary cooperation and capacity building programmes. It is important to highlight that amongst these issues there is no reference to merger control.

Regarding the Cancun Ministerial Conference the EC refined and finalised its proposal. First, the EC adopted a low-profile stance and suggested the creation of a set of common core principles. With this stance, it did not aim at the ambitious, but politically unfeasible, objective of the harmonisation of national competition laws, nor did it seek to restrain the freedom of countries to design their own national competition laws. It suggested rather that countries should only be obliged to apply competition law in conformity with common principles, which incorporate fundamental values regarding trade and competition policy.

Such principles are the principle of non-discrimination, the principle of transparency and the principle of procedural fairness. The main purpose of the principle of non-discrimination is to ensure that legal rules and general regulations and guidelines that are part of national competition laws are not discriminatorily applied on the grounds of nationality. The EC distinguishes between de facto discrimination and de jure discrimination, but only the latter would be caught by the principle of non-discrimination. Such restrictive approach may be justified with the difficulties to prove a conduct of de facto discrimination, which requires a careful analysis of the facts of the case. Moreover, the adoption of the criterion of the de facto discrimination would place the individual decisions of national competition authorities under the review of the WTO Dispute Settlement Bodies. The issue of non-national discrimination is even more controversial in merger cases. A competition authority can differently assess a merger depending on whether the transaction concerns only national firms or also foreign firms. A competition authority may approve a merger between national firms if the anti-competitive effects are compensated by the economic efficiencies generated by the transaction to the benefit of domestic producers and/or consumers.

But, it may disallow a merger operation concerning foreign firms if part or whole of the expected efficiencies accrue to the benefits of foreign producers. This may amount to an infringement of the principle of non-discrimination and make the Member States concerned responsible for breaching the WTO obligations.

The only category of restrictive business practice to which the EC proposition refers is hardcore cartels. The majority of Member States of the WTO agreed on the necessity of prosecuting these practices, since cartels whose anti-competitive effects reach over several national markets cause damage to developing and developed countries alike. Therefore, the creation of multinational rules seems to be an appropriate response to deal with the problems raised by hardcore cartels. The proposed agreement would have the effect of obliging Member States to adopt appropriate measures in order to fight hardcore cartels. However, some developing countries have voiced their concerns over the costs they would incur in adopting such measures. The EC, aware of the problems of the least experienced countries, has accordingly put forward the principle of flexibility and progressivity as guiding criteria for the implementation of the agreement. These principles should be interpreted in the sense that the developing countries cannot reasonably be expected to have in force a legal and institutional framework for the enforcement of competition law immediately after the conclusion of the WTO agreement.

As for other category of restrictive business practices, the EC acknowledges that further study is necessary in order to propose a common approach on them that can be agreed by the WTO Member States. In the field of merger control the need for multilateral rules is not as urgent as the need to prosecute hardcore cartels. The link between the market power created through mergers and the restrictive effects on foreign trade is less direct than in the case of international cartels. It can be quite difficult to predict with reasonable certainty whether the conduct of the merged entity would hamper the access of foreign firms to its national market. Moreover, there exists a strong connection between mergers and national industrial structure in that merger control is an instrument through which countries pursue their objectives of industrial policy. Understandably, countries are not willing to relinquish their sovereignty to the benefit of the WTO on this field. Thus the EC has dropped any reference to merger control, at least for the time being.

The EC proposal also seeks to establish cooperation schemes between the Member States. Political considerations have forced the EC to propose voluntary cooperation arrangements. Member States would retain the discretionary power to refuse to cooperate with another Member State when the requested cooperation is not in its interests. Moreover, the EC does not intend to change national laws regarding the protection of confidential information and oblige countries to mutually exchange confidential data. As a whole, the EC proposal is not a great advancement for the cooperation between national competition authorities. The EC also recommends the adoption of technical assistance and capacity-building programmes for developing countries. Such programmes are expected to support the efforts of the developing countries toward the enactment of competition law and the establishment of efficient competition authorities. The role of the WTO would be that of a facilitator for the provisions of these programmes by other organisations.

The EC has a cautious approach towards the role of the WTO Dispute Settlement Understanding. Even if the proposed agreement were incorporated into the WTO, the EC clarifies that the individual decisions of the national competition law enforcers on the legality of restrictive business practices would not be subjected to the legality review of the WTO Dispute Settlement Understanding. Since the power of the WTO Dispute Settlement Bodies to review such decisions would be perceived by countries as a limitation of national sovereignty, the WTO should only ascertain whether the Member States complied with the obligations of the agreement. It must also be said that the fact that the monitoring function is conferred on the WTO reinforces the credibility and the authority of these principles.

The model of governance of international markets pursued by the EC proposal is more ambitious than the mere regulation of market access. Its objectives are the promotion of sound and efficient national competition laws and authorities as well as the strengthening of international cooperation. In any event, strong national competition laws and authorities should certainly regulate those restrictive business practices fettering market access. The EC proposal should also avoid the risk of misapplication of competition rules, which occurs when they are invoked to protect market access instead of to preserve the competitive structure of markets. Finally, the proposal restricts national sovereignty as little as possible. It does not aim at the harmonisation or unification of competition laws nor does it adopt competition minimum standards that the countries have to implement. It only lays down a number of common principles with which Member States have to conform their national competition laws.

Nevertheless, the EC proposal has been criticised in some quarters. Some competition law scholars contest the practical relevance of the proposed multilateral rules. They may be useless for those countries with an open economy and may not meet the specific needs of developing countries. The width of the commitments on the Member States is also unconvincing. The only obligation regarding substantive law is to enact appropriate measures to combat hard-core cartels. The laudable intention of the EC was not to burden the Member States, especially the developing countries, with the need to have competition laws consistent with the multilateral rules. However, nothing would refrain those countries, yet without competition law, from enacting a set of fully-fledged competition rules embracing the hardcore cartels and all the other categories of restrictive business practices. In sum, the EC proposal might prompt developing countries to adopt comprehensive competition laws, even though the EC ruled out that this was the effect of its proposal.

The majority of the countries might lack the necessary institutional framework to ensure the sound enforcement of competition law. Moreover, the increase in the number of new competition laws may have an unsolicited impact on businesses. Firms will have to confront more regulatory regimes, which would raise compliance costs. The benefits expected from the adoption of WTO competition rules may be set off by the inherent risks.

Similarly, the practicality of the common core of principles is questionable. The express recognition of the principle of non-discrimination made by Article III of the GATT renders the stipulation of this principle in the WTO competition agreement redundant. The scope of the principle of non-discrimination is wider in the context of the GATT than in the context of the EC proposal. The principle of non discrimination, in the meaning assigned by the EC proposition, can be regarded as met when a country applies its national competition law to all firms without any discrimination on the grounds of nationality, even if its national competition authority exercises its regulatory powers in a discriminatory manner. Therefore the distinction between de jure discrimination and de facto discrimination is untenable.

The principle of transparency would result in excessive burdens on national competition authorities, especially on the ill-equipped ones of the developing countries. As far as the principle of due process is concerned, the different legal systems of Member States can make it difficult to reach a definition of this principle that can be acceptable to every Member State. Tentatively, this principle should include the obligation to reason and publish individual competition decisions; the obligation to apply national competition law even-handedly; and the obligation to provide strong enough remedies to address the anticompetitive problems. However, the recognition of the right of a concerned firm to a formal meeting would overburden many national competition authorities. Concerns have also been voiced about the capacity-building mission conferred on the WTO. This would be alien to the traditional responsibilities and currently capabilities of this institution, which would then need new staff, expertise and support.

VII. *The failure of the Cancun Conference: Is it the end of WTO competition rules?*

The EC's efforts were ultimately frustrated at the Ministerial Conference held in Cancun in December 2003. The talks amongst the representatives of Member States collapsed and the Mexican chairman of the conference called for the end of negotiations. The unfortunate conclusion of the Cancun Conference adds further reservations on the suitability of the WTO to deal with global competition problems. The EC proposal appeared well balanced and capable of meeting the interests of different countries. It imposed on the Member States the legal obligation to adopt appropriate measures to fight hardcore cartels, which are universally thought to seriously distort the trade flows across international markets. It offered developing countries technical assistance and capacity building programmes to help them fulfil the obligations arising from the agreement. Understanding the reason for the Cancun fiasco can shed some lights on whether the incorporation of competition law into the WTO is still a feasible option.

The WTO negotiations process is based on the single negotiation package approach. At each round of talks the Member States discuss a number of trade issues. Negotiators through a number of mutual concessions try to reach a common position that conciliates the exigencies of each Member State. The ultimate outcome of the WTO trade talks mainly depends on the individual bargaining power of Member States. The negotiations are ended either when the Member States agree on all the issues on the agenda or when the consensus from Member States on them is unlikely

At the Cancun Conference the trade representatives commenced discussing the so-called Singapore issues along with other trade issues. The negotiations came to a deadlock when the developing countries evaluated the undertakings offered by the developed countries on the liberalisation of agricultural products as insufficient. Developing countries took the view that such concessions were insufficient to compensate the costs they would have incurred in the implementation of the proposed multilateral rules. Accordingly, the developing countries decide to object to the Singapore issues altogether.

Cancun seems to prove that the incorporation of competition law into the WTO depends on political considerations and bargaining. During the negotiation process countries tied competition law issues with a plethora of trade issues unrelated to competition law. The key factor for the conclusion of the WTO competition agreement was how much the Member States in favour of multilateral competition rules were prepared to give to the other Member States in exchange for their consensus. Generally, Member States weigh the commitments against the gains following the adoption of every multilateral measure within the WTO framework. On that occasion the developing countries evaluated the balance of costs and benefits as negative for them. One of the reasons for their negative evaluation was that developing countries were disappointed by the weakness of the proposed cooperation framework. The proposal did not contain any binding obligations on the Member States to cooperate. It was based on a voluntary scheme in order to win over the consensus of the developed countries which feared otherwise they would have been inundated with requests of cooperation from developing countries. But a voluntary cooperation framework is not significant progress compared to cooperation arrangements already established by the bilateral cooperation agreements.

It is true that the WTO agreement would have given the cooperation framework a multilateral dimension. But, it is also true that the voluntary status of the cooperation would have enabled national competition authorities to have the last word on every cooperation request. This scheme was not appealing to the developing countries. Why should they embark on the costly, time-consuming process of strengthening or building ex novo national competition laws if the developed countries did not make any relevant trade concessions or did not even ensure their unconditional availability to cooperate? Being unconvinced by the concessions coming from the EC and the other proponents, the logical step for the developing countries was to withdraw from the negotiations.

When the negotiations were about to collapse the EC, as an extreme attempt to reach at least a more limited liberalising trade agreement, dropped the proposition of the competition law agreement. The strategic implications of this move may be quite far-reaching. Until Cancun the necessity of discussing a WTO competition law agreement was universally agreed by all the WTO Member States. It might be difficult for the EC to propose again the competition policy issue in the agenda of the WTO negotiations afterwards. The developing countries were not the only Member States to have worries about the proposed agreement. Probably many countries even amongst them EC Member States, were not particularly enticed by the prospect of losing part of their sovereign powers to the benefit of the WTO institutions, especially in an area, such as competition law, in which the WTO is still inexperienced. So in many capitals the failure of the Cancun Conference was not hailed as a completely negative event.

VIII. *An alternative approach for the creation of multilateral competition rules: The theory of market access proposed by Professor Fox*

The theory of market access developed by an authoritative American competition law scholar, professor Eleanor Fox is another idea resting on multilateral instruments which has been proposed with the purpose of advancing the internationalisation of competition law.

A. *Interaction between competition and trade law*

Before embarking on a discussion of this theory, it would be more convenient to firstly clarify the relationship between competition and trade law. The scope of application of competition law is constituted by reference to restrictive business practices carried out by private firms, whereas trade law applies to trade barriers erected by governments which block or hinder the access of foreign products to national markets. Moreover, it should be noted that competition law is enacted via a law-making process. The relevant provisions are approved by the competent national legislative bodies upon the basis of considerations that normally affect exclusively the domestic interests of the country concerned. On the other hand, the process leading to the creation of trade law rules is mainly influenced by international relations: countries adopt trade rules in order to fulfil the commitments they have undertaken under international agreements. Finally, trade law is more attentive to the protection of the interests of local producers, whereas competition law gives more weight to the welfare of consumers.

Nonetheless, the trade liberalisation process has highlighted the necessity of a close connection between trade and competition law. The danger is that the government barriers foreclosing markets access, which countries have committed to abolish, may be replaced by trade obstacles put in place by private firms. All this would impede countries, firms and consumers from securing the benefits expected by the trade liberalisation process. Such an unfortunate outcome, it is thought, could be avoided by strengthening the interaction between trade and competition law. Indeed, competition and trade law have complementary functions. They have the same broad objective, which is the improvement of the conditions of consumers via the promotion of economic efficiency and the opening up of markets, although they employ different methods to pursue the same objective. Competition law protects consumers from anti-competitive conducts of private firms which enjoy a relevant market power. Trade law, on the other side, protects consumers from higher prices resulting from the distorting effects on trade flow caused by public barriers to trade. Competition law, therefore, should apply with the purpose of preventing private restrictive business practices from replacing the public barriers to free trade, already eliminated by the instruments of trade law.

B. *The set of proposed international principles for regulation of transnational restrictive business practices*

The theory of Professor Fox revolves around a core of "linking principles of a constitutional dimension". The principles, like a EC "framework directive", set out a number of objectives that the countries have to pursue. They also influence the contents of national competition laws by indicating the restrictive business practices that create the most serious threats to international trade and which should therefore be prohibited. The relevant practices are those that block or hamper market access. The theoretical basis for the prohibition of such restrictive practices lies in a principle of international competition law, whose content is equivalent to the principle of trade law which ensures market access to firms. The purpose of the competition law principle is the protection of market access from private restrictive practices. Its status is uncertain and it seems that it should not be regarded as being part of public international law.

Professor Fox argued that the proposed constitutional principles should be incorporated into a multilateral agreement, the Trade-Related Aspects of

Antitrust Measures. The first principle is that countries should have national competition laws and should enforce them. National competition laws, at their best, should regulate cartels, monopolies, abuses of dominant position and possibly mergers. However, the principle can be considered as met when the countries comply with the minimal condition of the enactment of rules banning restriction of market access in accordance with the WTO. Countries should also enforce their national competition laws without any discrimination on the grounds of nationality. They should evaluate not only the national impacts but also the global impacts of the restrictive business practices. The aim of these principles is to expunge any parochialism from the assessment of these practices conducted by national competition authorities.

The proposed agreement should also include the principle of transparency, which rules that the scope of application of statutory provisions and any non-competition criteria for the appraisal of the restrictive business practices should be clearly stated. The principles also incorporate a rule of reason that invites countries to refrain from ordering unreasonably extraterritorial remedies. Another principle states that countries, the interests of which are harmed by conducts carried out beyond their national borders, can complain to the competition authority of the place where the conduct was performed. Any country indeed has jurisdiction over the restrictive business practices that can injure their citizens. Where restrictive business practices harm the exporting activities of a country but the practices and the harmed consumers are located in the territory of the importing country, it is the law of the latter that applies. However, in order to protect the interests of the harmed country, two conditions are laid down for the application of the law of the importing countries. First, the importing country must have competition law in force and secondly, the law must not be applied in a parochial way. The importing countries should also provide an accessible litigation system as well as safeguards of due process. Should the law of the importing countries not meet these conditions the harmed countries or persons are allowed to resort to their own national courts and authorities. The establishment of a dispute resolution system, administered by the WTO, is recommended. The WTO would ensure sufficient credibility to the enforcement mechanism of the principles and should dissipate the risks of parochial application of the principles on the part of the national competition authorities. However, its task should be constrained to the monitoring of compliance of participating countries with the multilateral obligations.

C. *Some critical thoughts on the theory of market access*

The propositions developed by Professor Fox present some analogies with the EC proposal. Neither seeks the harmonisation of national competition laws, but call for the crafting of a core of common principles of a constitutional nature, with which the enforcement activities of national competition laws have to comply. In addition, both are willing to give to the WTO the power to ascertain whether countries fulfil their commitments.

On the other hand, the theory of Professor Fox departs from the EC proposal with respect to the identification of the relevant restrictive business practices. If the EC advocates the idea that the multilateral agreement should oblige countries to regulate only hardcore cartels, the proposition of Professor Fox is that the scope of multilateral rules should be restrained to the practices that block market access. This position seems to be too favourable for the interests of developed countries, while it is so not advantageous for developing countries. The chances of firms of developed countries gaining access to the markets of developing countries thanks to the multilateral rules are greater than the chances of the firms of developing countries exporting their products into the developed countries. Critics focus on the neo-liberal views underlying the proposal of Professor Fox and argue that competition is not a value worth protection per se; it is rather a tool to pursue the objective of the liberalisation of trade, which is the only fundamental value that deserves protection. Should such multilateral rules be brought into the WTO framework, the WTO would lose its legitimacy, especially before the developing countries. These might view the proposed principles as favouring exclusively the interests of the developed countries.

The theory of Professor Fox does not look more convincing than the EC proposal. The likelihood that the multilateral framework proposed by this authoritative scholar will ever come into force is slim due to its scarce appeal on developing countries. In this respect, it is sufficient to say that the principle of market access is not matched by any specific concession to developing countries. Thus, if the EC proposal, though more sympathetic toward the needs of developing countries, failed to secure the necessary consensus of the Member States of the WTO, the proposal of Professor Fox would be even more unlikely to be successful. The limited range of the relevant restrictive business practices is a further weakness of this theory. Countries would thereby only be obliged to regulate those practices that unreasonably impair market access. These would include abuses of dominant position, cartels with boycotts and vertical restraints. On the other hand, it may be difficult to qualify export cartels and merger operations as business practices restricting market access.

In sum, the principle of market access does not appear to be an appropriate tool to regulate transnational mergers since its nature is different from that of merger control. The former attaches greater attention to behavioural considerations and address the question of whether the conduct of firms hinders the access of foreign firms to national markets. The latter focuses on structural considerations and examines the impact of mergers on the competition structure of markets. It may be difficult to establish whether the merged entity would use its increased market power to execute practices restricting market access in post-merger markets. The causal link between the consummation of a merger and the carrying out of the restrictive practices is weak. Banning a merger because the merged entity may commit practices restricting market access is a highly speculative decision and should be corroborated by strong evidence.

Other commentators have argued that barriers other than high market shares of the dominant firms can impede new competitors from entering a market. For example, in the case of non-liberalised markets, regulatory barriers may discourage the entry of new competitors in that market. It is also important to bear in mind the social and political dimension of merger operations. The administration of merger control is closely connected with social and industrial policies as well as with the commercial identity and economic independency of a country. The firms that fall under the scope of the jurisdiction of a given competition authority may pay taxes or create jobs or trade in the domestic markets of the regulating authority. The principle of market access would place the competition authorities in a difficult position: they should weigh the interests of the merging parties, already present in the market, with the interest of firms that are only potential competitors which are not yet in the market.

The above observations can be summarised by the proposition that the rather weak connection between the restriction of market access and the market power gained by the merged entity undermines the capability of the principle of market access of efficiently regulating the anti-competitive effects of transnational mergers. These transactions could be more effectively regulated in other venues than the WTO. Accordingly, Professor Fox advocates the establishment of the World Competition Forum, as an informal forum, open to the participation of the representatives of national competition authorities, business and consumers. The forum would discuss common competition problems and build a consensus towards the internationalisation of competition law. An agreement on multinational merger control should be negotiated and eventually concluded under the auspices of the World Competition Forum. Thus, Professor Fox seems to suggest that it is preferable to set up an international merger control regime through informal fora which normally do not impose any legally binding obligations on the participants. This proposition leads us to the idea of internationalisation of competition law through multilateral instruments of soft law which will be discussed at length in the next chapter.

IX. *Multilateral instruments of hard law as regulatory tools for transnational mergers: Prospects and problems*

A. *Unwillingness of countries to cede sovereignty to international bodies*

The review of the multilateral instruments of hard law has cast some light on the most serious problems of this approach. Historically, countries have been highly sensitive to any initiative which would force them to hand over part of their national sovereignty to supranational institutions. This is all the more true with respect to developed countries. These countries already have in place mature competition laws with their own specific objectives, interpretative criteria and methods of analysis. It is understandable that these countries are rather unwilling to give their support to an international comprehensive competition law code, which is administered by a supranational body with extensive investigative and adjudicative powers. This general rule has no exception in the field of merger control; indeed, it is even stronger since merger control and national industrial policies are closely intertwined. Accordingly, countries are hardly prepared to bestow part of their responsibilities in merger control to international bodies.

An example of this jealous attitude of countries is given by the history of EC Regulation 4069/89. It was only after that Philip Morris and Continental Can exposed the inconveniences and gaps in the recourse to Articles 81 and 82 EC Treaty to regulate merger operations that the EC started discussing an ad hoc instrument for the appraisal of mergers. It should be remembered that EC Regulation 4069/89 was adopted only after long negotiations. All this does not look encouraging for the incorporation of competition law within the WTO. If the enactment of EC Regulation 4069/89 took so long, in spite of the strong political and economic links existing between the EC Member States and in spite of the objective of a closer integration pursued by them, the questions that logically arise are: Is it really feasible that a considerable number of countries, still divided by different views on the objectives and contents of competition law, can ever agree on a set of multilateral competition rules? Is that something which can be reached in a short period of time? Or, instead, is it a goal that can be attained only in the distant future when, as a result of further educational and trust-building activities, different sets of national competition law and policies are more similar?

It is not easy to answer these questions. A backward glance at the ideas reviewed over the present chapter seems to suggest that there is still a long way to go before arriving to an international merger control regime. The Havana Charter and the Draft International Antitrust Code intended to reach the substantive harmonisation of national competition laws, though to a different degree of intensity. They also aimed at establishing a supranational framework for monitoring the compliance of the participating countries with the agreed obligations. However, both of them looked too visionary or ambitious. They were perceived as severely restricting national sovereignty. Such restrictions concern not only the law-making aspect, that is to say, the freedom of countries to adopt the type of competition law rules they would prefer; but also the way of enforcement of the competition law rules already in force.

The EC proposal seems to recognise these problems and, accordingly, it was shaped in the least threatening terms for national sovereignty. The EC gave up its plans for the harmonisation of national competition law in favour of the identification of a core of common principles to be implemented in country's national systems. The EC sensibly indicated that the only relevant category of restrictive business practice is international hardcore cartels. Indeed, it is only in respect of the necessity to prosecute hardcore cartels that a sufficient international consensus has been gained, while countries are still divided on the best approach to regulate mergers and other restrictive business practices. For that reason multilateral rules on merger control have been postponed to when a higher degree of convergence amongst countries can be reached. Finally, the EC tried to limit the impact of the WTO Dispute Settlement Body on the competence of national competition authorities and national judicial authorities regarding the enforcement of their respective competition laws.

Despite all those efforts the EC proposal met with the same fate of the Havana Charter and the Draft International Antitrust Code. At the Cancun Conference it was rejected because the concessions offered by the Member States that supported it were insufficient, in the view of the other Member States, to compensate for the commitments and the costs that would have been necessary for the implementation of the agreement. The unfortunate result of the EC proposal strengthens the doubts of those who are unconvinced by the choice of the WTO for the adoption of multilateral competition rules. The WTO Member States rejected the EC proposal, which respected national sovereignty at the expense, perhaps, of a more courageous approach towards global competition problems. In addition, the EC proposal was sympathetic towards the problems and difficulties that developing countries would have encountered in the implementation of the agreement. Nevertheless, the EC proposal was entangled with the negotiations concerning non- competition trade issues and was eventually rejected by the WTO Member States. But if such a proposal was not approved will the WTO Member States ever be capable of agreeing on a set of effective multilateral competition rules?

B. *Aversion to undertake legally binding commitments*

The second major problem affecting the instruments of hard law is the unpreparedness of countries to undertake legally binding commitments. This attitude normally induces the proponents of multilateral agreements to include only, or mainly, non compulsory mechanisms in their proposals. For instance, the EC proposal included a voluntary framework for cooperation amongst the national competition authorities of the participating countries. Such a minimal stance is not a relevant progress for the internationalisation of competition law. From the quantitative viewpoint the EC proposal certainly improved the cooperation between national competition authorities already achieved by the bilateral cooperation agreements by converting it into a multilateral dimension. The benefits of cooperation would have been enjoyed by every party to the multilateral agreement. However, from the qualitative viewpoint the EC proposal did not greatly innovate the current state of the international application of competition laws. Under the bilateral and multilateral arrangements alike the participating countries keep the power to refuse to cooperate when the requested cooperation is not in their best interests.

Thus, developed countries may refuse to fulfil the cooperation requests addressed by developing countries. In other words, the cooperation requests of developing countries would be still at the mercy of the discretionary considerations of developed countries. But those that most need the collaboration of the more experienced competition authorities of developed countries, especially at the initial implementation stage of agreement are precisely the competition authorities of developing countries. In sum, the proposed multilateral rules do not eliminate the risk that developing countries may be completely excluded from the benefits of international cooperation.

C. *The risk of "race to the bottom"*

Some institutional peculiarities of the WTO, such as the negotiations process and the wide membership base, combined with the resistance of countries to any loss of national sovereignty, may negatively affect the process of creation of WTO competition law rules. The wide membership base of the WTO is, at the same time, both the blessing and the curse of the attempts to enlarge the responsibilities of the WTO to competition law matters. On the one hand, within the framework of the WTO it is possible to set up cooperation mechanisms which are available to a large number of countries. On the other hand, because of its wide membership, it may be difficult to persuade several countries, with different political backgrounds and different levels of economic development, to adopt a set of multilateral competition law rules.

As anticipated by Joel Klein since 1996, the consensus of so many countries might be reached at the expense of the efficient enforcement of competition law. The lowest denominator approach may be a convenient path to gain the consensus of all the countries participating in the negotiations. The flipside of the multilateral strategy is the creation of generic rules, which impose no or few legally binding obligations on the participating country. These rules, though not threatening the national sovereignty of countries, can be of little practical relevance to address global competition problems, especially if compared with the solutions that are already provided by the more sophisticated national competition laws. For the countries that already have mature competition laws the adoption of multinational rules would herald a regression rather than advancement in the enforcement of competition law.

The fears floated by Joel Klein seem to be confirmed by the history of the EC proposal. If it had been approved by the WTO Member States, it would have secured some notable results. First, it would have been the first ever instrument of hard law in the field of international competition law to enter in force. In this respect, it would have constituted the foundations of future mechanisms for the international enforcement of competition laws. Secondly, it would have also ensured other relevant achievements, such as the institutionalisation, at least on paper, of the international cooperation between competition authorities and the international commitment to fight hardcore cartels.

That said, the proposed multilateral rules were drafted in so loose a manner to reduce as much as possible the risk that the agreement would be conceived by the WTO Member States as an unacceptable loss of their sovereignty. This race to the bottom was perhaps inevitable in order to obtain the necessary consensus of the WTO Member States. However, the proposal would not have introduced significant innovation in the field of competition law. The core of common principles embodies rules and values that are already recognised in international trade practice. In some instances, such as in the case of the principle of non discrimination, the agreement would have been a backwards step to what has already been achieved within the WTO's legal texts. As for which restrictive business practices the Member States would have to regulate, the agreement mentioned only hardcore cartels. The existing divergent views on merger control counselled the EC against the inclusion of mergers control in the agreement. Indeed any reference to mergers would have fuelled an intense debate that would have further reduced the chances of approval of the agreement. Finally, the proposal did not resolve the major problems that already affect bilateral cooperation agreements. Thus, the fulfilment of the cooperation request would still depend on the discretionary evaluations of the requested country.

These comments may be extended to the Havana Charter and the Draft International Antitrust Code. The problems faced by the latter are similar to the problems faced by the EC proposal. The usual dilemma is: Is it possible to adopt a set of internationally applicable effective and legally binding competition rules that does not lead to a significant loss of national sovereignty? The fate of the Havana Charter, the Draft International Antitrust Code and the EC proposal would suggest that this is not an easy objective to achieve, at least in the short term. It remains to be seen whether the adoption of multilateral instruments of soft law are more effective.

X. *Conclusion*

This chapter has discussed at length the different proposals which have been put forward with the purpose of creating multilateral instruments of hard law in order to regulate transnational restrictive business practices. Much attention has been given to the ill-fated attempt of the EC to introduce a set of competition rules in the WTO legal framework. None of the proposals reviewed in this chapter have been adopted. The unwillingness of countries to cede their regulatory powers on economic activities to international bodies may explain the reason why these proposals were so unenthusiastically received. In this respect, it should be noted that even those proposals which were crafted in such a fashion to threaten as little as possible national sovereignty, even at the detriment of their capability to effectively deal with global competition problems, failed to obtain approval of countries. Since the adoption and implementation of a set of multilateral instruments of hard law seems to be, at least in the short-term, rather improbable, it remains to be seen whether countries are more willing to agree on multilateral instruments of soft law.

CHAPTER SEVEN

MULTILATERAL STRATEGY: INSTRUMENTS OF SOFT LAW

I. *Introduction*

The present chapter deals with the ideas that pursue the internationalisation of competition law through multilateral instruments of soft law. These instruments do not create any legally binding obligations and can be regarded as mere policy recommendations. Their implementation into national legal systems therefore depends on the voluntary decisions of countries. The crucial question is whether the instruments, though deprived of any legally binding force, are capable of effectively addressing global competition problems.

The structure of the chapter is as follows. The second and third sections give an account of the activities respectively of the UNCTAD and the OECD regarding merger control. The fourth section introduces the reader to the International Competition Network. The fifth section describes the informal cooperation initiatives in the field of financial services. The sixth section tries to identify which lessons the competition law community can draw from the informal international initiatives in the field of financial services. More precisely, it is argued that any initiative for the internationalisation of competition law should be consistent with the concepts of legitimacy and efficiency. The seventh section proposes the creation of an international framework for the regulation of trans-national mergers. The eighth section sets the boundaries of the application of this international framework by defining the concept of trans-national mergers. The ninth section clarifies the concepts of legitimacy and efficiency. The tenth section identifies the international competition principles that should be incorporated into the proposed international framework. The eleventh section deals with the issue of the harmonisation of substantive competition rules. The twelfth section examines the extrinsic dimension of efficiency. The thirteenth section summarises the reasons which support the creation of an international framework for the regulation of transnational mergers. The fourteenth section draws conclusions.

II. *The UNCTAD Set*

A. *Goals and contents*

The mission of UNCTAD is to eliminate those restrictive business practices that hamper the liberalisation of international trade and which harm, in particular, the interests of developing countries. In 1980 it published the Set of Multilaterally Agreed Principles and Rules for the Control of Restrictive Business Practices. The competition rules included in the Set are arranged according to a two-tiered system. The first group of rules is the "Principles and Rules for States at National, Regional and Sub-Regional Levels". These rules apply to countries and require them to enact appropriate regulations and procedures so as to eliminate conduct that restrains market access and unduly restrains competition. The second group of rules, the "Principles and Rules for Enterprises Including Trans-National Corporations", applies to private businesses and sets out the obligations multinational enterprises should comply with as well as the practices these firms are banned from carrying out in the countries where they operate.

The restrictive business practices are defined as "acts or behaviours of enterprises which, through an abuse or acquisition and abuse of a dominant position of market power, limit access to markets or otherwise unduly restrain competition, having or being likely to have adverse effects on international trade, particularly that of developing countries, and on the economic development of these countries, or which through formal, informal, written or unwritten agreements or arrangements among enterprises, have the same impact". Mergers and other transactions which entail acquisition of control are caught by the Set only when they imply an abuse of dominant market power. The UNCTAD has also established the International Group of Experts with responsibilities in the field of international competition law. Its functions are merely consultative; it does not adjudicates on the conduct or behaviour of Governments or individual firms.

B. *The UNCTAD Set and regulation of transnational restrictive business practices*

In spite of some critical voices regarding its lack of binding force, it has been argued that the soft law nature of the Set does not necessarily undermine its effectiveness to deal with global competition problems. The Set has gained political legitimacy following the approval of a substantial number of countries, and moral legitimacy through its attempts at eliminating restrictive business practices in developing countries. Accordingly, countries should be motivated to implement the Set even though it does not have any legally binding force.

Nonetheless, up to now the Set has had a poor practical relevance. The developed countries, which already have efficient competition law, are unlikely to cede to the UNCTAD a portion of their regulatory powers. Leaving aside the issue of its soft law nature, another factor which may explain, perhaps more convincingly, the poor relevance of the Set is the limited interests represented by UNCTAD. This organisation attaches more importance to the interests of developing countries to the detriment of the interests of developed countries.

Therefore, these countries do not consider the works of the UNCTAD as fitting their interests and needs; thereby, their willingness to comply with the Set is rather low.

III. *The initiatives of the OECD*

A. *Instruments adopted by the OECD*

The OECD is an international organisation committed to democracy and a market economy. It pursues a model of global economic governance based on instruments of soft law and firmly champions the advantages that countries can derive from competition law, such as economic growth, improved economic efficiency and an increase in employment.

With these objectives in mind, the OECD has launched several initiatives in the field of competition law. It established the Competition Committee, which is made up of the representatives of the competition authorities of the Member States. The mission of this body is to examine procedural and substantive competition issues and provide governments with policy analysis and advice on the best regulation of market forces for the promotion of global economic efficiency and prosperity.

The OECD has also published the Guidelines for Multinational Enterprises on competition law and policy. They instruct multinational enterprises on how they should behave in the countries in which they operate. The Guidelines state that these firms should refrain from carrying out restrictive business practices that would affect competition and that they should comply with all the relevant applicable competition laws. Firms should take into consideration the national competition laws of all those countries where the anti-competitive effects of their conducts are felt and cooperate with the competition authorities of the countries concerned.

In 1999 the OECD issued a report on the notification of transnational mergers. In this document, with the aim of keeping compliance costs down in cases of multi-jurisdictional review, the OECD proposed the adoption of a standard notification form that the parties could use to notify mergers. The form should contain a common core of information regarding the parties and the main aspects of the merger that are of interest to competition authorities. However, this proposal has been coldly received by the competition law and business community. Finally, the OECD has established the Global Forum on Competition so as to strengthen and deepen cooperation relations with non-OECD countries. The Global Forum enables all its participants to share their experiences on the most interesting competition issues, including international cooperation in transnational mergers investigations.

B. *Evaluation of the OECD activities*

The OECD seeks the approximation of national competition laws and the coordination of the enforcement activities of competition authorities with instruments of soft law rather than with formal international agreements. This idea looks promising on paper in that it fosters mutual trust and peer identification amongst national competition authorities. As a result, the competition authority of one country would be more disposed to accept the decisions of the competition authority of another country. It also lowers the risk of friction between competition authorities in cases of inconsistent views on the legality of a given restrictive business practice. Mutual trust should induce the competition authorities concerned to consider such divergent views as a manifestation of different but legitimate policies, rather than of a manifestation of parochialism. Furthermore, the OECD may facilitate multi-jurisdictional investigations, in particular through the coordination of the activities of a greater number of national competition authorities, which should strengthen the enforcement capabilities of competition authorities.

However, such advantages have to be balanced against the institutional weaknesses of the OECD. Since this organisation is commonly perceived as the voice of the developed countries its initiatives are not usually appealing to developing countries. The recent enlargement of its membership base may have attenuated this common perception; nevertheless, the OECD still have to clarify its relationship with other emerging economy markets. The OECD is viewed as a second-class institution which is more inclined to talk than act and which is burdened by unwieldy bureaucracy. Because of these shortcomings the OECD may not be influential enough to persuade countries to adopt its recommendations and suggestions regarding global competition problems.

IV. *The International Competition Network*

A. *The origin of the ICN*

The Final Report of the ICPAC has acknowledged that the unilateral strategy is not the appropriate response to global competition problems. More cooperation amongst national competition authorities as well as a wide matrix of cooperation agreements would be necessary. The ICPAC was quite sceptical as to the incorporation of competition law into the WTO and considered that the establishment of an informal forum-the Global Competition Initiative-would be preferable. Membership of the Global Competition Initiative should be open to develop and developing countries. This body should promote consultation, dialogue and consensus building regarding global competition problems. Its ultimate objective should be to further greater convergence of national competition laws and favour the emergence of a common understanding of competition law issues. Professor Fox also advocates the idea of an informal forum by proposing the creation of a World Competition Forum, where representatives from competition authorities and from business and consumers organisations can discuss common competition law problems other than market access.

The idea of an informal initiative for the internationalisation of competition law quickly gained ground and the International Competition Network (hereinafter ICN)[1] has been established. Its first meeting was held in Naples in September 2002, while successive meetings were convened in Merida, Mexico in 2003; Seoul, South Korea in 2004, in Bonn, Germany in 2005, in Cape Town, South Africa, in 2006. Since its first annual conference in Naples the ICN has turned out to be a successful venture. For the first time a large number of competition authorities agreed to establish a forum within which to share experiences and views on global competition problems. This is astonishing, especially in an era when only a few multilateral initiatives have succeeded in coming to life. The ICN is committed to discussing competition enforcement and policy issues of common interest and to formulating proposals for procedural and substantive convergence in accordance with a results-oriented agenda. It has already prepared several guiding principles and recommended practices and is also active in the field of merger control, where it has dealt with some aspects of multi-jurisdictional mergers, such as review procedures, analytical frameworks and investigative techniques.

B. *The ICN: A successful venture*

The reasons for the success of the ICN can be attributed to its peculiar characteristics, which distinguish it from other multilateral initiatives. Firstly, it has a wide membership base, made up of the national competition authorities of more than 75 jurisdictions as of March 2006. Its membership base is really heterogeneous: participants are from developed and developing countries and come from each of the continents. Because of its greater inclusiveness the ICN seems to be more suitable than the UNCTAD and the OECD to

[1] According to its own mission statement of October 2001, the ICN: "(...) it is the only International body devoted exlusively to competition issues. Memebrs are not States or governments, but competition autohorities, bodies entrusted with the enforcement of competition laws. Membership is voluntary and curently 90 such agencies are ICN members. There is no permanent secretariat, and no headquatertes, which leads to the ICN often being descrive as a virtual forum. The ICN co-operates closely with and seeks input from existing International Organisations and is assisted by experts from outside competition autorities, for example form the legal and economic professions, consumer organisations, academis, etc. (...)". See also: E.C. Petersmann, "Reforming the world trading system", Oxford University Press, (2005).

address global competition problems and to formulate policy recommendations that can accommodate the array of different national interests.

The structure and internal procedures of the ICN are also important elements. The ICN is not a brick and mortar organisation with a permanent secretariat, but rather is a virtual network of competition law authorities and practitioners. It has a loose organisational structure which includes only the steering group and the working groups. The steering group consists of 15 representatives of the member competition authorities. Each member normally serves a two-year long term, but it is possible to serve additional terms. The main function of the steering group is to identify projects and then draft working plans for each project. The identified projects are subject to the approval of the ICN and are then carried out by the competent working group.

The project-oriented, consensus-based and soft law nature of its activities are other advantages of the ICN. It focuses only on those specific projects in which the member competition authorities have shown an interest. After the instruments are approved by the ICN the participating countries have no legal obligation to implement these instruments, which means that the ICN does not create any challenge to national sovereignty. Finally, the objective of the ICN is a closer convergence among national competition laws and the facilitation of the exchange of information between national competition authorities, rather than the full harmonisation of national competition law. Its instruments are drafted in a flexible manner and only contain a set of best practices or principles, which are often followed by national competition authorities. A further aspect of the ICN which lends it an advantage over the WTO is that all the participants to the ICN activities are expert on competition law. So, the evaluations of the ICN experts are unlikely to be influenced by any sympathy towards trade law considerations as it may be the case with the WTO officials.

V. *Soft law international cooperation in the financial services sector*

It may be worth examining the informal initiatives adopted to deal with the problems created by globalisation in fields other than competition law, namely in the financial services sector. The development of new financial products and new technologies have blurred national boundaries in the provision of financial services. More and more finance houses are providing financial services in different national markets from those in which they are established. This may have important implications regarding the regulation of cross-border financial activities, which are not dissimilar from the problems affecting the regulation of transnational mergers. The major problem is the gap between the international dimension of financial services and the national reach of regulatory regimes. The regulation of financial markets has not evolved at the same pace as markets and its scope of application is constrained to the territory of enacting countries. As a result, a financial house providing cross-border financial services is subjected to the concurrent jurisdictions of each country in which it trades. Applicable national regulatory regimes may also have a different degree of sophistication and different approaches for the evaluation of the various risks.

Financial services regulation seems to have different influence on regulated firms than merger control. The latter come into relevance only when two or more firms decide to merge and it consists of a prognostic assessment of the planned transaction. Financial services regulation, instead, prescribes a set of organisational requirements, such as capital adequacy and other prudential standards. These requirements have to be met by financial firms in order to obtain the necessary authorisation for starting their activities. They have also to comply with them throughout their operations. Financial regulation also lays down rules of conduct financial firms have to abide by while dealing with clients and other operators.

So, a financial firm whose activities affect several national markets may have to face several national regulatory regimes. The approaches of each of these regimes towards similar issues may differ, which may lead to the risk of inconsistency. Analogous problems may arise in case of trans-boundary propagation of the negative effects of a crisis of a financial firm. This situation may harm the interests of investors of investors located in different jurisdictions. The financial regulators of the countries where such negative effects are felt may wish to exert jurisdiction on the firm with the risk, as seen above, of inconsistent decisions. Thus, in order to resolve such problems the international coordination and cooperation between national financial regulators is necessary.

A. *The Basle Committee*

The Basle Committee is an informal forum in which central bankers take part and deal with the regulation of cross-borders banking activities. Its objective is to encourage cooperation and convergence in the prudential supervision of the international banking sector. The instruments through which the Basle Committee pursues its institutional aims are soft law measures, such as supervisory standards, guidelines and principles of best practices. This method should encourage convergence towards common approaches and common standards, without imposing on the participating countries the harmonisation of their national standards.

The Basle Committee has evolved into the de facto international banking regulatory body, with its decisions and recommendations having acquired an undisputed authority and having been adopted by the participating countries. Amongst its most important achievements, it is possible to cite the 1997

Core Principles which codify the international standards on banking supervision by laying down minimum substantive standards and setting criteria for the allocation of supervisory responsibilities between the host country and the home country. The 1998 Accord is also important as it adopted a new set of rules on capital adequacy which replaces the accord originally concluded in 1988. These rules can be regarded as a remarkable example of convergence and constitute the international standards in the field of capital adequacy. Though they do not have any legally binding, they have been implemented in many countries, even in those that are not members of the Group of Tens. The success of the Basle Committee can be imputed to the informality and independence of its initiatives, which are unbiased by any political considerations and are supported by considerable competence and technical expertise in banking and financial matters.

B. *The IOSCO*

The IOSCO (International Organization of Securities Commissions) was established by securities market regulators in 1983 when a former pan-American association was transformed by its members into an international body. Today, about 180 securities regulators have joined IOSCO. Its members regulate almost 90% of the world's securities market, which makes the IOSCO the most important international forum in securities markets. In brief, its mission includes: a) Promoting cooperation between the member securities agencies so as to develop high standards of regulation which can maintain efficient sound markets; b) Exchanging experiences with the aim of promoting the development of domestic markets; c) Establishing standards of effective surveillance of international securities transactions; d) Encouraging mutual assistance between members with the objective of ensuring the integrity of markets through a rigorous application of standards and effective enforcement against offences. Its most important achievements are the Principles and Objective of Securities Regulation, which indicate the best practices financial houses should follow in the provision of services affecting different jurisdictions. Another important instrument is the multilateral memorandum of understanding, the aim of which is to facilitate enforcement and exchange of information amongst national securities regulators. With the Assessment Methodology of 2003 the IOSCO explains how to assess whether the Principles have been implemented in national systems. As a whole, the IOSCO has not reached the same degree of coordination and convergence as the Basle Committee. Its principles have been adopted by a lower number of countries and have a minor influence on businesses. Generally, securities regulation is less interventionist and more concerned with the protection of investors than banking regulation. This may explain why countries are not as keen to implement IOSCO instruments as they are with regard to the statements of the Basle Committee.

C. *The IAIS*

The International Association of Insurance Supervisors (IAIS) was established in 1994. Its current membership base includes 180 insurance regulators from over 120 jurisdictions, which amounts to 97% of the world's insurance premium. The main tasks of the IAIS are as follows: a) Promoting cooperation among insurance regulators; b) Setting international standards for insurance supervision and regulation; c) Training officials from member insurance supervisors; d) Coordinating regulators active in other financial services sectors. Its most important attainments are the Recommendations Concerning Mutual Assistance, Cooperation and Sharing Information and the Model Principles for Insurance Supervisions. The former embodies a number of non-binding principles that national supervisors should adopt to facilitate coordination and the exchange of information. The purpose of the latter is to enhance the supervision of insurance companies operating in international markets by developing cooperation among national regulators. All in all, the IAIS has accomplished an inferior level of international coordination compared with that achieved by the IOSCO.

D. *Other relevant initiatives*

Other examples of multilateral informal initiatives are the Joint Forum on Financial Conglomerates and the Financial Stability Forum. The former was established in 1996 by the Basle Committee, the IOSCO and the IAIS. Its task is to facilitate the exchange of information between supervisors; to deepen supervisory coordination and to encourage the developments of principles that can ensure a more effective supervision of financial conglomerates. The Financial Stability Forum was established by the Group of the Twenties to promote stability and correct functioning of international financial markets. It also seeks to reduce the risk that financial crises propagate from one national market to another. The forum has set up a framework that enables national financial regulators to coordinate activities and exchange information. These initiatives are important in advancing international convergence, coordination and the information-sharing process between national regulators.[2]

---

[2] For instance, the US merger control law initially requires a less amount of data because the US competition authorities can obtain additional information through Second Requests. Instead, the EC requires more initial information in order to give to the Commission as much information as possible on the transaction since the beginning of the procedure. See chapter three; OECD, Report by the Committee on Competition Law and Policy, Notification of Transnational Mergers, OECD Journal of Competition Law and Policy, Volume 1, no. 3 26, 27. Jurisdictions which use the HHI test may require the merging parties to provide information on market shares that are tailored to the peculiarities of the HHI test. Wilson, above n. 3, chapter 1, 296.

VI. *Lessons from international cooperation in the financial services sector*

The account of the informal initiatives in the financial services sector shows the results that instruments of soft law can achieve as to the cooperation between national regulators. The creation of a genuine supranational body with real decision-making powers was also proposed in this field. A World Financial Authority was considered by its proponents as the best solution to resolve the problems created by the globalisation of the financial industry. Since the regulatory issues faced by national supervisors often have a transnational dimension, it would therefore be advisable to confer regulatory powers to a supranational body. However, this idea, as already demonstrated by this book with respect to similar proposals in the field of competition law, is unfeasible. Arguably, the problems caused by globalisation could be better addressed with instruments of soft law, which have some advantages over the instruments of hard law, especially in terms of pragmatism and flexibility.

Instruments of hard law may lack flexibility due to the fact that the process of negotiating a formal international treaty is time-consuming and cumbersome. When the signatory parties decide to modify the agreement they have to apply a similar procedure, which requires the consensus of all the participating countries. On the contrary, instruments of soft law, not being incorporated into formal international agreements, may be adopted and modified without the need to comply with such procedures. The pragmatism of the instruments of soft law derives from the mutual trust built up between the participating countries through regular meetings, the technical expertise of the delegates and the small size of the working groups.

Instruments of soft law also have some shortcomings. Because of their lack of binding force it can be difficult to predict whether, when and how they will be implemented. However, these problems also affect formal international agreements. Indeed, the resort to such legal instruments for a creation of a set of international principles does not always guarantee that these principles will be implemented in all countries. Countries are legally obliged to implement an international agreement only after that they sign and ratify that agreement. But before that it is difficult to predict how many countries will decide to sign the agreement and adopt the principles and how, eventually, they will implement the principles within their national systems.

These problems are all the more serious with respect to instruments of soft law, given that they are normally drafted by the standard-setting supranational body as broad principles rather than as a formal legal text. It is only when they are implemented by national authorities that these instruments are further refined and transposed into national regulation or legislation. This means that the more countries which participate in the drafting of these instruments, the more unlikely these countries are to implement the international principles in the same manner. Thus, the level of legal certainty regarding the instruments of soft law is rather lower if compared with that of international treaties due to the higher risk of inconsistent implementation. The issue of the legal certainty of these instruments may be further aggrieved when national courts apply these principles in the absence of guidance from supranational bodies.

These problems, however, are not insurmountable; they can be resolved by a "sticks and carrots" policy. Such a policy requires that a number of incentives, which can be labelled as either official or market incentives, should be offered to countries with the aim of encouraging them to transpose the principles into their national systems. The official incentives include any measure that is applied by the official sector upon the condition that national systems meet specific targets in the implementation of principles. For example, the access to more favourable conditions in International Monetary Fund funding may be granted to countries that implement the relevant international principles. Market incentives refer to the decisions taken by investors on the assessment of the risks inherent in making investments in a given country. One of the factors that investors take into consideration is the adherence of that country to international financial standards. On the basis of this assessment investors decide which treatment to apply to that country with regard to credit risk ratings and other issues regarding lending or investments. These incentives should be complemented by mechanisms to verify the compliance of countries with the international principles, such as self-assessments made by national authorities and external assessment made by peer reviews or specialised teams of international institutions.

VII. *Building a feasible international framework for regulation of transnational mergers*

The question now is whether it is possible to replicate in the field of competition law, and more specifically in merger control, the mechanisms of international cooperation and coordination set up in the financial services sector. This author is convinced that the creation of an international framework based on the instruments of soft law for the regulation of transnational mergers is a feasible objective. Its constitutive elements should comprise the enforcement of merger control entrusted to national competition authorities and a weak harmonisation policy recommending only the implementation of a set of non-binding international competition principles. Among these, conflict-of-jurisdiction rules are of particular importance, since they can attenuate or eliminate the problem of multi-jurisdictional review from the beginnings.

Such an approach, though modest, should be preferred to more comprehensive and complex ideas requiring the creation of supranational authorities and stronger harmonisation policies. The previous chapters have already demonstrated that countries are still unprepared to relinquish the whole or part of their regulatory powers in merger control. The idea of a comprehensive harmonisation of national competition laws, including the adoption of a single worldwide substantive test for the appraisal of mergers, seems impossible. The differences between national competition laws make it improbable that the necessary consensus from all countries would be gained. Moreover, since merger control is based on the examination of facts, inconsistent decisions may be explained with regard to divergent market conditions rather than with regard to divergent national competition laws.

VIII. *The definition of "transnational" mergers*

Before discussing the proposed international framework, it would be helpful to clarify the meaning of the term "transnational" mergers. This is instrumental in setting the boundaries of the scope of application of the proposed framework. How many national markets a merger should affect before being considered as transnational? Are two markets sufficient? Or should the merger produce its effects in a wider range of markets?

Intuitively, a merger whose effects are felt in the national markets of more than two countries should be caught by the scope of application of the international merger control framework (IMCF). In this event the IMCF would enable all the regulating competition authorities involved to exchange their views and data and coordinate their enforcement activities. However, it is less clear whether the IMCF should apply to mergers affecting only two national markets. The resort to the IMCF for the regulation of such transactions may appear redundant given that the two national competition authorities concerned might cooperate and coordinate their activities through bilateral agreements.

Yet up to now the most notorious cases in which competition authorities have split on the appraisal of the same merger operations have been those affecting two national markets. It can be said that from a qualitative viewpoint the problems raised by a merger affecting only two national markets are similar to those caused by a merger affecting several national markets. Both raise the same issues in terms of overlapping jurisdictions, conflicting decisions, lack of legal certainty and increasing compliance costs. Where the two situations differ is on the quantitative level, where the higher number of national competition authorities concerned magnifies the above lamented problems, resulting in higher compliance costs and higher risks of inconsistencies.

Therefore, the minimum requirement for a merger operation in order to fall within scope of application of the IMCF should be that it affects at least two national markets. A similar position is also embraced by the OECD, according to which transnational mergers include transactions that fall under the merger review of more than one jurisdiction. A criterion of subsidiarity would be helpful to further clarify how the IMCF would apply to mergers affecting only two national markets. As a general rule, the IMCF would apply to these transactions except when two conditions are met. Firstly, when the countries affected by the merger have concluded a bilateral cooperation agreement. Secondly, when this agreement guarantees the same level of minimal standards as the IMCF regarding inter-agency cooperation and coordination of enforcement activities. In this case, the two competition authorities concerned should be free to rely on their bilateral cooperation agreement.

This proposal appears to be well balanced. International competition principles are generally applicable to every merger operation whose effects are felt in more than one national market. It also rules out the automatic application of the principles to mergers affecting only two national markets when there exists a bilateral cooperation agreement between these two countries. The resort to the principles is superfluous when the only two countries affected by the merger have entered into a bilateral cooperation agreement, which establishes an equally close cooperation and coordination scheme.

IX. *The concepts of legitimacy and efficiency*

The major problem with every idea for the internationalisation of competition law which rests on instruments of soft law, such as the proposed IMCF, is that these instruments may not be adopted by countries because they lack legally binding force. Nonetheless, this author believes that the chances of the instruments of soft law being implemented will be increased if they are consistent with the concepts of efficiency and legitimacy.

The concept of legitimacy refers to the procedure for the drafting of the instrument of soft law. Such procedures comply with the concept of legitimacy if they are open to every interested country; if the instruments are agreed by all countries on an equal basis and if their adoption is not perceived as the attempt of some countries to impose their views on other countries. The concept of efficiency touches on two different dimensions. The first one, the so-called intrinsic dimension of efficiency, pertains to the contents of the instruments, which should raise a sufficiently strong interest in the countries to make them want to adopt the instruments. Accordingly, the instruments have to provide appropriate and feasible solutions to global competition problems and they should not threaten national sovereignty. The second dimension of efficiency, the so-called extrinsic dimension, includes all those measures the function of which is to provide countries with incentives to implement the instrument of soft law in their national systems of countries.

Apparently, not every international organisation working in the field of competition law fulfils these requirements: neither the OECD, which does not meet the concept of legitimacy due to the limited number of countries associated to this organisation; nor the UNCTAD, which does not meet the concept of efficiency as its initiatives are mostly tailored for the priorities of developing countries. On the other hand, the ICN seems to satisfy these requirements. Its decision-making procedures have an open nature; moreover, they are consensus-based and results-oriented. The member countries of the ICN are free to choose which projects the working groups will carry out and are equally free not to adopt the following results. Another decisive element is the wide and heterogeneous membership base of the ICN, which includes developed and developing countries alike. Participation in the Steering Group is open to the representatives from all members for the time period of two years. Since the Steering Group has 15 elective components, every 8–10 years each member competition authority has one representative in this body. Any member competition authority may take part in the works of the Steering Group, even those from the developing countries, as suggested by the fact that Mexico had the presidency of the Steering Group in 2003. All these elements refute the allegations that the documents of the ICN are the outcome of a top-down process, through which a few countries force many other countries to embrace their positions on determined issues. Instead, they are approved with the consent of the countries concerned, consistently with the concept of legitimacy. The activities of the ICN seem to also be compliant with the concept of efficiency. It has developed a set of international and, above all, with the Recommended Practices.These codify the best practices on several merger control procedural issues in the form of principles, followed by comments voluntary competition principles for the regulation of transnational mergers with the Guideline Principles.

X. *The International Competition Principles*

A set of international competition principles regulating the merger control process should be one of the constitutive elements of the proposed framework. The initiatives of the ICN, notably the principles codified in the Recommended Practices for Merger Notification Procedure, are compliant with the concepts of legitimacy and efficiency. Accordingly, this author believes that the principles developed by the ICN, with the necessary adjustments that will be illustrated below, should be incorporated in the proposed framework as a set of international competition principles.

A. *Conflict-of-jurisdiction rules*

The first practical problem the principles have to address is that of overlapping jurisdictions and the ensuing risk of conflicting decisions. When a merger operation affects different national markets it is essential to identify the competition authorities which have jurisdiction over the transaction. The drafting of plausible criteria for the allocation of jurisdiction is arguably more important than the harmonisation of substantive rules with respect to the resolution of the problems associated with multi-jurisdictional review. Reaching a satisfactory level of harmonisation on the substantive merger control rules may be difficult due to the divergences between national competition laws. The negative consequences of multi-jurisdictional review which are more likely to affect the merging parties are usually imputable to procedural rules rather than substantive rules. They have to file different notification forms, regulated by different rules, to different competition authorities, which raises the transaction costs for the parties. On the other hand, the risk of conflicting decisions due to different substantive standards may not be so immediate a problem, as proved by the fact that up to now competition authorities have taken inconsistent decisions on the appraisal of merger operations only on a few occasions. Moreover, such a risk may also depend on other factors such as the market conditions and the goals underlying different national competition laws.

The plain identification of one or a small number of national competition authorities which have jurisdiction over any given merger would be helpful in eliminating or attenuating the problems of multi-jurisdictional review. One possible option would be to entrust a supranational body with the task of determining the competent competition authority. However, the establishment of a supranational body with such powers is not easily acceptable to some countries. The alternative is a more flexible approach, epitomised by the model of the conflict-of-laws rules. These rules allocate jurisdiction on the basis on the degree of intensity of the contacts between the countries concerned and the situation to be regulated, the country with the closest contact to the situation having jurisdiction over it.

This position was adopted by the ICN in the Recommended Practices, which state that a competition authority should review a merger only if an appropriate nexus is established between its jurisdiction and the transaction.[75] The principle of appropriate nexus restrains the discretion of national lawmakers as to the crafting of the merger notification thresholds. These thresholds have to incorporate an adequate level of materiality with respect to the nexus with the acting jurisdiction. The purpose of this principle is to ensure that only those mergers that are likely to produce appreciable effects on competition in a given country will fall within the jurisdiction of that country. The condition of an appropriate nexus is satisfied if the activities of at least two merging parties or of the acquired business are located in the territory of the acting jurisdiction, which should be established by reference to the amount of sales and assets of the merging parties localised in that jurisdiction.

The intention of the ICN is to restrain the willingness of competition authorities to expand the scope of their regulatory powers in order to enable themselves to assess even those transactions with minimal effects on their national markets. According to the propositions of the ICN, a competition authority should exert its regulatory powers only over those merger operations that are likely to have significant, direct and immediate economic effects within its jurisdiction. Such effects are felt when the activities of the merging parties or the activities of the acquired business are located in the territory of the jurisdiction concerned and only when such activities, as determined by the value of sales and assets, exceed the statutory financial thresholds. It is only when these conditions are met that a material territorial link between the merger and a national jurisdiction can be established.

The limitation of the scope of application of merger control to those transactions with relevant effects in the national markets of the regulating authorities has its merits. It should curb the territorial reach of merger control, which should contribute towards the elimination of the problem of overlapping jurisdictions. It should also relieve firms from the burden of multi-jurisdictional notification with a consequent reduction in compliance costs as well as an increase in legal certainty. Yet this approach does not provide the absolute guarantee of the elimination of the problem of multi-jurisdictional reviews. It is still possible that more than one jurisdiction may have an appropriate nexus to a merger and, consequently, have legitimate jurisdiction over that transaction.

An alternative solution would be the lead regulator approach followed in the financial services sector. Through the principle of the home-country regulator jurisdiction is allocated to only one authority, which is that belonging to the territory where the firm to be regulated is incorporated; and only minor regulatory tasks are conferred on the host-country regulator. However, it is uncertain whether the host country/home country regulators paradigm can be applied in the field of competition law. The degree of convergence in the supervisory standards attained in the field of financial services has still to be achieved in competition law. Moreover, the ultimate decision on mergers is also influenced by the structural conditions of the markets concerned and by the policy goals pursued by the relevant competition authorities. These are unlikely to renounce their powers and simple rely upon the assessments made by the authority designed as lead regulator. This would require a considerable level of mutual trust between competition authorities as well as a significant convergence in substantive standards and competition policy goals, which do not exist yet. Those who advocate applying the lead regulator principle to competition law point out that the theory should be accompanied by a mechanism to settle the conflicting views of competition authorities concerning the identification of the lead regulator. They propose that the competition authorities and the merging parties should have the right to bring the matter before a supranational specialised body, whose decisions should be binding. However, this book has already shown the unfeasibility of the establishment of a supranational body with such adjudicative powers.

The principle of the appropriate nexus is therefore preferable to the theory of the lead regulator. This principle, however, needs to be further refined in order to improve its reliability as a tool for the designation of the competent authority. The cosmopolitan principles developed by Professor Fox may reinforce the practicality of this approach. It is therefore possible to rely on principle no. 5, which states "Nations should refrain form ordering relief that is unreasonably extraterritorial". A rule of proportionality may be inferred from this statement: a country, whose interests are not significantly affected by the merger, should abstain from ordering relief which is broader than necessary to remedy the anti-competitive effects produced within its the territory. The purpose of the rule is to place reasonable restraint on enforcement jurisdiction in merger control. Countries that are not primarily affected by a merger are only allowed to address the aspects of the merger operation affecting their national markets while they are expected to minimise the possible consequences of their regulatory intervention with regard to the other aspects of the transaction. The second relevant principle developed by Professor Fox is aimed at preventing conflicting views of the competition authorities on the appraisal of mergers. This principle suggests that a country may not block a merger which has been already been approved by the jurisdiction in which the merger has a greater impact. Other cosmopolitan principles may help strengthen the mutual trust of countries regarding their respective enforcement activities. Thus, it is possible to cite principle no. 2, which says "Nations should enforce their laws without discrimination as to nationality" and principle no.3, which states "national law enforcement should account for global impacts not just national impacts". Such principles may be thought to give more credibility to the criterion of the appropriate nexus.

Further support can be drawn from the Guiding Principles for Merger Notification and Review drafted by the ICN. They confirm the principle of non-discrimination on the basis of nationality and embrace the principle of transparency. Countries should abide by the principle of transparency in various respects, such as with regard to policies, practices and procedures, the identity of its decision-makers, its substantive standards of reviews and the basis of any adverse enforcement decision on the merits. More transparency regarding these elements should increase consistency, predictability and fairness. Compliance with these principles should dissipate the worries of the other jurisdictions concerned that the evaluations of the regulating competition authority may be affected by parochial considerations and thus should reinforce mutual trust.

The functioning of the principle of the appropriate nexus may also be strengthened by a mechanism to settle disputes between countries regarding jurisdiction. The IMCF should therefore include a settlement mechanism in case after the application of the principle more than one country still believes it has jurisdiction over a merger. This mechanism should first provide for a consultative procedure between the countries concerned in order to promote a negotiated solution of allocation of jurisdiction. If the conflict is still unresolved the competition authorities claiming jurisdictions over the same merger should have the option of referring the matter to arbitrators. The following decisions of the arbitrators should be binding upon countries. National sovereignty would be preserved by giving countries the right to oppose the decisions of the arbitrators when these concern national interests of particular significance. For example, a national competition authority may retain its jurisdiction on those transactions affecting sensitive sectors, such as defence or energy industries.

The principle of appropriate nexus echoes the principle of comity. As has been indicated before, vagueness and lack of legally binding force impede the latter from being an effective instrument to regulate jurisdictional conflicts. However, the principle of the appropriate nexus appears to be capable of overcoming such limitations. The fact that it is incorporated into a comprehensive framework should convince countries to abide by this principle, despite its lack of binding force.

B. *Principles regarding mergers notification*

The merger notification thresholds usually mirror local sensitivities and the size of national economies, which may vary dramatically from country to country. For these reasons the standardisation of the notification thresholds seems to be undesirable. A high common threshold may be accepted to competition authorities of countries with larger economies. But, it may be objected by countries with smaller economies because high thresholds may impede them from reviewing transactions, which have significant effects in their national markets, despite not reaching high financial figures.

Thus, the ICN opts for setting out only general criteria for the crafting of thresholds. First, notification thresholds should be clear and understandable The ICN recommends that the thresholds should be drafted in such a manner that merging parties can easily determine when they have to notify a merger. Accordingly, the notification thresholds should be based on objective and quantifiable criteria such as assets and sales volumes. On the contrary, they should not be based on market shares since these are subjective criteria, not easily administrable by merging parties and competition authorities. This is a very important point, as many competition laws adopt market share thresholds.

Another aspect of merger control procedure in which convergence is desirable is the events that determine the obligation to notify a merger. The previous chapters have shown that national competition laws are divided and have a wide spectrum of different solutions, ranging from the signing of a letter of intent to the conclusion of a definitive agreement. The different triggering events with the ensuing lack of synchronisation between merger control procedures may frustrate the efforts to establish effective coordination and cooperation among competition authorities. Convergence of notification triggering events is also essential in order to harmonise other aspects of merger control procedure.

The ICN suggests that "parties should notify proposed mergers upon certification of a good faith intent to consummate the proposed transaction". Interestingly, the ICN does not require the conclusion of a legally binding merger agreement as a pre-condition for the notification obligation, rather a declaration certifying the qualified intention of the parties to execute the transaction is sufficient to trigger the responsibility to notify. Thereby, the ICN widens the range of triggering events of the notification obligation and anticipates the starting point of the merger control procedures to be before the conclusion of a formal agreement. A greater convergence in the timing of notification should be welcomed by competition authorities and business. It should remove the restrains on the capacity of competition authorities to coordinate their respective investigations imposed by the different competition laws. It should also satisfy the need of the merging parties for legal certainty and speed in merger review. The harmonisation of the timing of the notification, along with the harmonisation of the timetable of the merger review, would enable the merging parties to determine when they can execute the merger without breaching any statutory waiting periods.

C. *Principles regarding review period*

A more effective coordination of the enforcement activities also requires the harmonisation of the review period. The proposition of the Recommended Practices, that, "Merger reviews should be completed within a reasonable period of time", can be regarded as a first step towards this objective. However, this is an open-textured statement that needs to be better articulated. The timetable of merger control procedures should be framed in such way as to accommodate the exigencies of competition authorities and the merging parties. The former calls for sufficient time to analyse all the legal and economic issues raised by mergers. The latter would rather a tight timetable in order to obtain the decision on the legality of the merger within the shortest possible time.

The ICN suggests that merger review should be concluded within a period of a time that is determinable by the merging parties and indicates some general criteria regarding the length of merger control procedures. In the jurisdictions where the merging parties cannot execute the merger until the competition authority completes the appraisal of the transaction, the initial statutory investigation period should not exceed six weeks. Further waiting periods, needed for more detailed investigations, should not go beyond six months. The merging parties should be free to consummate the merger after the expiration of the statutory waiting period unless the competition authority applies for an extension of the investigative period. Identical time frames are also recommended for non-suspensive jurisdictions. The Recommended Practices do not indicate the implications of the notification of the merger on the ability of the parties to consummate the transaction. The question of whether the notification does or does not create an obligation not to execute the merger is left to the discretion of national lawmakers. In conclusion, the ICN seems to favour the rigid EC time frame instead of the more flexible US model.

D. *Principles regarding notification form*

The harmonisation of notification forms is one of the most delicate issues in merger control procedure. National competition laws may require the merging parties to submit different types and amounts of information in the statutory notification form. This heralds negative consequences for firms since it is precisely the different information which the merging parties have to submit that contributes to raise in the compliance costs. The harmonisation of notification forms is thus highly desirable, yet it is complicated by some legal obstacles, as the national regimes of notification forms reflect the procedural and substantive rules of their respective merger control laws.

The ICN adopts a low profile and business-friendly approach. It does not take any position regarding the dilemma of whether to adopt the US or the EC model. The only guidance provided by the ICN concerns the types of information that the merging parties should initially have to provide with the notification form. These consist of the minimal core of information that is necessary to initiate the merger review, which should enable the acting competition authority to ascertain whether it has jurisdiction on the notified merger and whether the transaction is likely to create competition problems. A more precise insight into the content of these data is given by the OECD's Report on Notification of Transnational Mergers. This document lists the data that should be provided with the notification form: the identification of the merging parties; the description of the transaction itself; the description of the activities carried out by the parties in the territory of the notified competition authority. Finally, the merging parties should produce the final version of the documents incorporating the transaction agreement and their most recent annual reports.[3]

The objective of the ICN to reduce the burden of the initial notification requirements imposed upon merging parties and keep compliance costs down emerges from other excerpts of the Recommended Practices. For example, the initial notification requirements should not impose unnecessary burdens on the parties to those merger operations which do not raise any significant competition problems. In addition, countries should not require extensive translations of supporting documents.

As far as the content of the initial notification is concerned, the ICN offers several options to countries. They can opt for a system with two alternative notification formats, a long form and a short form; a system with wide initial notification requirements combined with the discretionary power of national competition authorities to waive some pieces of information; or a system with limited initial notifications requirements, coupled with the power of national competition authorities to require additional information.[106] This approach, although it cannot guarantee a complete harmonisation of national laws regulating the content of the initial notification, seems to be quite pragmatic. On the one hand, by offering a range of possible solutions, it does not completely erase national sovereignty on this matter; on the other hand, the fact that countries are nevertheless expected to choose one model from those proposed by the ICN allows them to reach a minimal harmonisation of the contents of the notification form.

As a whole, the principles on the notification requirements seem to be well thought out and weigh all the different interests at stake. They try to reduce the compliance costs for firms and take into consideration the needs of competition authorities to obtain from the outset sufficient information to enable them to take basic decisions on the merger review. Finally, it does not reduce national sovereignty as countries still enjoy certain flexibility as to the regulation of the initial notification requirements.

However, it would be advisable to add to the list of data contained in the Recommended Practices an indication of the national competition authorities to which the merger has been notified. The European Competition Authorities network,[4] aware of the importance of these data, has prepared a standard

[3] OECD, Report by the Committee on Competition Law and Policy, Notification of Trans-national Mergers, Appendix: Framework for a Notification and Report Form for Concentrations, D, OECD Journal of Competition Law and Policy, Volume 1, no. 3.

[4] The Commission and the competition autohorities of the member States have put in place a European Competition Network. It will allow for greater cooperation and provides for an allocation of cases according to the principle of the best placed authority. The Commission will remain at the center of the ECN. It will, as the guardian of the Treaty, ensure that decisions taken by national authorities are consistent and that the antitrust rules are applied in a uniform manner. Several mechanisms of co-operation with the national authorities designated

form notice, which should be used in case mergers are notified to more than two national competition authorities. The competition authority, which is informed by the merging parties that the same transaction is already or will be notified to other competition authorities, should send the standard notice

by the member States are provided tramit the Regulation 1/2003 which was in force for just over 40 years: "(…) when national competition authorities apply national competition law to agreements within the meaning of EC Art. 81 (1) which may affect interstate trade, they must also apply EC Art. 81 (1); the same applies for abuses of a dominant position (…) 2. National competition authorities may not take decisions which would run counter to decisions already adopted by the Commission; 3. The Commission must transmit to the competition authorities of the member States copies of the most important documents it has collected with a view of finding and ordering an infringement to be terminated, ordering interim measures, accepting binding commitments, deciding the competition rules do not apply or whithdraw the benefit of a block exemption; 4. The national competition authorities must inform the Commission in writing before commencing the first formal investigate measure; 5. The national competition authorities must note later that 30 days before the adoption of a decision concerning infringements, undertakings or withdrawal of the benefit of a block exemption, inform the Commission (…) 6. The national competition authorities may consult the Commission on any case involving the application of community law; 7. The initiating by the Commision of proceedings shall relieve the national authorities of their competence to apply the community competition rules; 8. The Commission and national competition authorities may exchange and use in evidence any matter of fact or of law, including confidential information; 9. The Commission may reject a complaint on the ground that a national authority is dealing with the case; 10. A for the national Courts it is explictly provided that they have the power to apply art. 81 and 82 of the Treaty (…)". The role of the Commission as the above Regulation provides for procedures to be followed by the Commission is concentrated to: "(…) 1. Acting on a complaint form a Member State or a natural or legal person who can show a legitimate interest, or on its own initiative that there is an infringement ad require untertakings or associations of undertakings to end such an infringement (…) 2. Order interim measures in case of urgency due to the risk of serious and irreparable damage to competition in the basis of prima facie, finding of infringement (…) 3. Make commitments offered by undertaking binding. This is an interesting novelty since it allows the Commission to end a procedure without having to decide whether or not the community competition rules were infringed (…) 4. Find that the prohinition is not applicable in case the community public interest relating to the application of the prohibitions so requires; 5. To interview any natural or legal person who consents to be interviewed for the purpose of collecting information relating to the subject matter of an investigation; 6. To obtain all necessary information form Governments and national authorities and form undertakings, either by simple request or by decision (…) 7. To undertake inspections of understaning. To this end officials authorised by the Commission to conduct an inspection are empowered to: a) enter any premises land or means of transport; c) to examine books and business record irrespective of the medium on which they are stored; c) to take copies of or extracts form the books and business record; d) to seal any business premises and books or record for the exstend necessary for the inspection; e) to ask for oral explanations on the spot (…) 8. To impose fines and penalties. For the calculation of fines see Guidelines on the method of setting fines and combination of the value of the sales to which the infringement relates and of the duration of the infringement is regarded by the Commission as an appropriate proxy to reflect the economic importance of the infringement as well as the relative weight of each undertaking involved (…) 9. Notice on immunity form fines and reduction of fines in cartel cases (…) 10. Impose, by decision, periodic penalty peyments not exceeding five per cent of the daly turnover in order to comel undertakings to a) put an end to an infringement; b) comply with a decision irdering interim measures; c) comply with a biding commitment; d) supply complete and correct information and e) submit to an inspection (…)". See also: Case 792/79R Camera Care v. Commission (1980) ECR 119 at 131 (1980 CMLR, 180 to the other competition authorities. The purpose of the notice is to inform the recipient authority about the fact of the notification. In addition, the notice also includes the identity of the parent or group of companies of the firm concerned; the relevant economic and geographical markets; the date of notification and the provisional deadline. The IMCF should adopt a standard notice similar to that of the European Competition Authorities network. The data to be supplied with the standard notice should enable the competition authorities concerned to learn which other jurisdictions are involved in the review of the transaction, the date on which the merger control procedures started and the affected markets. Intuitively, the availability of such data should facilitate the cooperation between competition authorities and the coordination of their enforcement activities.[5]

E. *Other procedural principles*

The Recommended Practices set out a series of standards with which national merger reviews should comply. These standards pertain to different aspects of merger control proceedings, such as the rules of conducts in merger investigation, transparency and procedural fairness. Effectiveness, efficiency, transparency and predictability are all constitutive elements of a sound merger control regime, and merger investigations should be conducted consistently with these fundamental values. The ICN also recommends that national competition laws should ensure the opportunity of dialogue between the competition authorities and the merging parties by enabling them to meet at key points of the investigation. Finally, when the investigation period is not subject to definitive deadlines, national competition laws should set out that investigations have to be completed without undue delay.

The Recommended Practices attach a considerable importance to the concept of transparency. This concept is defined as the ability of the public to see and understand how the merger review works. However, transparency should not infringe the national provisions that protect confidential information. The preservation of confidentiality is a very controversial issue in merger control since it pits the interests of competition authorities to obtain relevant information for their investigations against the proprietary interests of the merging parties. The latter are normally reluctant to communicate to competition authorities sensitive and confidential data lest such data might be leaked or be used for non-institutional purposes. Nonetheless, the disclosure of sensitive data may be in the interests of the merging parties in that it can speed up the merger review process.

---

[5] Alec Burnside and Helen Crossley, 'Co-operative Mechanisms within the EU: A Blueprint for Future Co-operation at the International Level?' [2004] International Trade Law & Regulation 25, 25.

Confidential information should enjoy appropriate confidentiality protection either under statutory provisions or under policies and procedures adopted by competition authorities. Competition authorities should commit to using the confidential data they receive only for the purpose of merger review and ensure procedural fairness for merging parties. The Recommended Practices also set the conditions of the disclosure of confidential information. The exchange of information must be authorised by international treaties, agreements or protocols if they provide for reciprocal protection of confidentiality. Information can also be exchanged in response to requests for judicial assistance from foreign competition authorities, if the disclosure is authorised by national legislation and the requesting competition authorities ensures confidentiality protection. Finally, the exchange is also allowed with the consent of the submitting party.

The ICN principles on confidentiality can be arranged into two different groups. The first one covers a number of principles, which are a sort of benchmark for the protection of confidential information, with which national rules should conform. The second group sets the conditions under which competition authorities should be allowed to exchange information. The exchange is possible only when authorised by international instruments or by national regulation or when it is approved by the parties concerned. Seemingly, the ICN does not bring in any substantial innovations compared with what is already laid down in bilateral cooperation agreements. The only worthy advancements of the ICN work is the codification and clarification of the practices and principles currently followed by countries.

The possibility of exchanging information is an essential pre-condition for cooperation and coordination among competition authorities. Cooperation and coordination can be at the mercy of merging parties if the exchange of information depends on the decision of those parties to waive their confidentiality rights. Therefore, it may be appropriate to propose more audacious rules on the exchange of information. In this respect, some scholars advocate the relaxation of national confidentiality laws in order to allow exchanges of information with appropriate safeguards. Those safeguards might be the principles developed by the ICN in the Recommended Practices, which ensure a minimal, but highly meticulous, level for the protection of confidential information that every participating country should incorporate into its national systems. Moreover, an ad hoc clause could be included in the notification form, whose effect is to waive the confidentiality rights of the parties over the data contained in the notification forms, unless the parties expressly declare their intentions to invoke their confidentiality rights. This clause would codify what happens in practice, as the merging parties normally renounce their confidentiality rights in order to speed up the merger review.

Procedural fairness is a multifaceted concept that embraces many aspects of the merger control procedure. First, it refers to the position of the merging parties and of third parties throughout the merger control procedure. As an expression of the principle of "audi alteram parte", competition authorities, before adopting the final decision on the merits of the merger, should give the merging parties sufficient and timely information on the facts and on the competition problems on which the decision will be based. The disclosure obligation should enable the merging parties to present their defensive arguments against the competitive problems raised by the competition authority. Equally, the merger review process should allow third parties to express their views on the notified merger. Procedural fairness also demands that national competition authorities put into practice a system of safeguards in order to make certain that the merger review is carried out in a fair, consistent and efficient manner.

The last procedural fairness requirements concern the ability of merging parties to oppose the final adverse decision of the regulating competition authority on the merits of the merger. More precisely, the merging parties should have the right to contest the decision in the shape of a judicial review before a separate adjudicative body. The ICN is aware of the fact that a long-lasting judicial review on the merger is of no help for the merging parties. Therefore countries should commit to setting for such judicial review with the aim of ensuring the completion of the review within a period of time when the merger is still viable for the merging parties.

The Recommended Practices also deal with the issue of coordination between competition authorities. It states that "competition agencies should seek to coordinate their review of mergers that may raise competitive issues of common concern". The goals of coordination are far-reaching: promoting efficient review of mergers; eliminating conflicting decisions; reducing duplications and unnecessary burdens for merging parties and national competition authorities. These objectives should be pursued in accordance with the limitations set by the ICN, which replicates the traditional restraints imposed on the coordination between competition authorities under international law. Thus, if a national competition authority receives a coordination request it is not obliged by the Recommended Practices to fulfil such a request.

F. *Principles regarding remedies*

The Recommended Practices also include a number of principles on remedies, the purpose of which is to provide a transparent and efficient framework for the administration of these measures. The ICN clarifies that remedies have to properly address the alleged anti-competitive effects of mergers. The principle of transparency requires that information concerning, amongst other things, the type of remedies accepted by the competition authorities, and the deadlines by which the remedies have to be proposed, should be readily available to the parties. Furthermore, national merger control laws should give competition authorities and merging parties sufficient time to discuss and evaluate remedies. The ICN also states that remedies should be easily administrable and effective. This means that, on the one hand, the competition authorities should clearly set out the commitments undertaken by the parties; on the other hand, the remedies should enable the prospective purchaser of the assets divested by the parties to be a viable and long-term competitor in the market affected by the merger. Finally, the competition authorities should have the power to monitor the compliance of the parties with the agreed terms of the remedies as well as the power to enforce the remedies in case the parties do not comply with them.

G. *Principles regarding powers of competition authorities*

A further group of principles developed by the ICN deals with the powers of competition authorities. These should be given appropriate investigative tools: the power to institute enforcement activities against anti-competitive mergers; and the power to clear, possibly conditionally, those mergers which do not raise competition problems and the power to enforce the conditions imposed on the parties. The competition authorities should have adequate staff, expertise and financial resources to discharge their tasks. With these principles the ICN suggests that countries should confer similar powers on their competition authorities and should supply them with the necessary resources to correctly carry out their institutional activities. Competition authorities should also have sufficient independence for the objective application and enforcement of merger control laws. This principle should dissipate any perceptions that the enforcement activities are motivated by considerations alien to merger control. In other words, its aim is to dispel the concern that parochialism may affect the appraisal of mergers.

H. *Comments on the Recommended Practices*

The Recommended Practices deserve to be acclaimed for several reasons. For the first time a set of common principles and practices for merger control has been codified by an international body. The principles are drafted using a sophisticated and detailed technique and embody the best practices in merger control, which should ensure a high level of protection of competition and of the interests of merging parties. With the implementation of these principles countries should be able to harmonise and rationalise their respective merger control regimes. Amongst the expected achievements, the approximation of national rules on some key points of the merger control process is particularly worth mentioning. This approximation will give countries similar methodologies to address the various problems that normally arise in merger control. It may also create further benefits in terms of promotion of international cooperation and in terms of the elimination of unnecessary transaction costs in cases of multi-jurisdictional review. These observations justify the election of the Recommended Practices as the noyau dur of the set of international competition principles. The advantages expected from the implementation of the principles should outweigh the costs ensuing from the necessary amendments to national regimes. This should give countries an incentive to adopt them, as expected by the ICN which states that "Jurisdictions should consider reforms to their merger control laws and procedures that promote convergence toward recognized best practices".

Interestingly, some jurisdictions have already decided to implement some of the recommendations of the ICN. For example, EC Regulation 139/2004 embraces the principles of the Recommended Practices regarding the regime of the triggering events of the notification obligation. The Brazilian competition authority adopted the principle of appropriate nexus, as a result of which it reconsidered its earlier interpretation of the statutory financial thresholds; these are now calculated exclusively on the basis of the sales and assets located in Brazil. The new approach should restrict Brazilian jurisdiction to mergers that have relevant effects in this country and, therefore, should limit the likelihood of overlapping jurisdictions. Brazil, in accordance to the ICN recommendations, also introduced a fast track procedure for the review of mergers which do not raise serious competitive effects. In addition, consistently with the principle of transparency, the US competition authorities publish a reasoned explanation of the decisions that approve a merger if such decisions set a precedent or differ from earlier policies or practices.

XI. *Harmonisation of substantive rules*

A. *Problems associated with harmonisation of substantive rules*

The principles of the Recommended Practices focus only on the procedural aspects of merger control. This choice resembles the EC's cautious stance in its proposed WTO agreement on competition law. The complexity of the harmonisation of substantive aspect of merger control laws and the difficulty of gaining the necessary consensus of countries may explain this choice. The comparative study of the national merger control laws has shown that there exist three different substantive tests for the appraisal of mergers, other than the new EC significant impediment of competition test: the market dominance test, the substantial lessening of competition test and the public interest test.

Each of these tests may lead to inconsistent decisions in the review of mergers. As seen above, the anti-competitive unilateral effects attributable to mergers in non-collusive oligopolistic markets are caught by the substantial lessening of competition test, but they are not caught by the market dominance test.[139] Moreover, the public interest test allows competition authorities to take into account industrial policy considerations and other factors that are not strictly related to competition law. These factors embrace heterogeneous elements such as restrictions on foreign ownership and control, the promotion of national champions, regional employment policy and policies regarding the black economic empowerment.

One may think that the harmonisation of substantive tests should result in the elimination of inconsistency, but this idea is ill-founded. It does not consider that the objectives of competition law play an equally important role in merger control. The alignment in competition law objectives would be more fruitful; yet it does not seem to be feasible. The obstacles created by the unwillingness of countries to accept the limitations to their national sovereignty imposed by the harmonisation of substantive rules are equally likely to materialise with regard to the harmonisation of the objectives of competition law. This may attract an even stronger opposition from countries, due to proximity of the competition law objectives to national industrial and economic policies.

Legally speaking, the harmonisation of the substantive rules would also have important negative consequences. Several countries might be forced to shift from their current substantive test to a brand new one with a probable increase in legal uncertainty since the case law developed under the old merger control regime might be deprived of any relevance. The costs that countries may sustain in implementation of new tests are high and perhaps not completely compensated for the expected gains.

Standardisation is also redundant in addressing the problem of parochialism in merger control. Competition authorities may administer merger control regime with the purpose of favouring the creation of "national champions" with the necessary size to compete successfully with foreign rivals. But the ensuing costs of this process are externalised, being passed on to foreign consumers and competitors. This parochial approach can be addressed more effectively with the prohibition of discrimination on grounds of nationality rather than with the harmonisation of substantive rules. The principle of non-discrimination is one of the basic tenets of international trade law. It is included in Article III of GATT. It is also incorporated in many proposals for the internationalisation of competition law, such as the Draft International Antitrust Code or the proposed WTO Agreement on Competition Law. It is also one of the Guiding Principles For Merger Notification and Review prepared by the ICN. This principle can be ranked among the general principles of merger review, with which every competition authority should comply. It is strongly desirable that this principle is included in the proposed framework as it should prevent national competition authorities from giving preferential treatment to their domestic interests to the detriment of foreign interests. A similar function can be assigned to the principle of the objective application and enforcement of the merger control laws adopted by the ICN.

B. *An innovative approach to harmonisation*

Since the direct harmonisation of the legal provisions regulating the substantive appraisal of mergers is scarcely practicable due to the differences between national competition laws, the approximation of substantive rules ought to be reached through alternative paths. A captivating approach pursues this objective via the harmonisation of merger guidelines. These documents are non-legally binding administrative practices, which are nevertheless important, as competition authorities clarify how they intend to apply the competition laws with the publication of guidelines. For this reason, firms can legitimately expect that competition authorities address a particular issue of merger control in accordance with their views expressed in the guidelines. The fact that guidelines are not legislative instruments signifies that for countries it would be easier to make the necessary amendments for the implementation of internationally agreed approximation plans to these documents rather than to formal pieces of legislation.

The idea of the approximation of guidelines is endorsed by the American Bar Association, which suggests that competition authorities should publish and regularly update Merger Enforcement Guidelines. It also devises some mechanisms to secure a sufficient degree of consistency among the different national guidelines. So during the drafting stage close consultations between competition authorities should take place in order to eliminate unnecessary differences. This could result in beneficial consequences for the international enforcement of competition law, such as the elimination of conflicting decisions and a greater convergence. Similar proposals are also backed by other competition law scholars and by the ICN, although the ICN is still in the exploratory stage. Indeed, only in 2004 the ICN has completed a comprehensive study on the merger guidelines adopted in a selected number of jurisdictions. It has reached the conclusion that, in spite of the different wording of formal laws, different merger guidelines have many aspects in common such as the methodology for market definition and the assessment of unilateral and coordinated effects. Notwithstanding that, there are still some relevant differences, which are due either to the different level of detail in which the guidelines are drafted or to the different treatment of some substantive issues such as efficiencies.

The goal of the ICN is not to create a single model of merger guidelines, but more modestly, is to set out a common core of issues that guidelines should address. With the Merger Guidelines Checklist Project of 2004, the ICN committed to the preparation of a manual for drafting of merger guidelines. It will specify the key issues that should be covered by merger guidelines, which include market definition, unilateral and coordinated effects, barriers to entry and expansion, efficiencies, vertical and conglomerate mergers and mergers remedies. The list is similar to that compiled by the American Bar

Association, which covers the definition of mergers, the jurisdictional thresholds, the market definition, the evaluative criteria, vertical and conglomerate mergers, joint-ventures, defences and exceptions. Furthermore, the guidelines should also describe the possible factors that may be of relevance in the appraisal of mergers which have nothing to do with competition law.

The ICN submitted at the annual meeting of Bonn its Preliminary Draft of Merger Guidelines Workbook for further discussion. This paper sets out the eight core topics that should be covered by Merger Guidelines, which are as follows: market definition, market structure and concentration, unilateral effects, coordinated effects, market entry and expansion, efficiencies, failing firms and vertical mergers. For each of these topics the ICN prepared a worksheet, whose purpose is to provide analytical guidance on the methodologies competition authorities should follow to assess mergers and interpret the data collected.

At first sight, the idea of harmonising only non-binding instruments may be rather a low profile one, especially if compared with other more ambitious, but ill-fated, proposals for the internationalisation of competition law. However, it is quite a pragmatic approach with some undeniable advantages, the most important of which is that countries are not required to amend their national competition laws in order to implement these instruments in their respective national systems. Indeed, it is sufficient to make policy papers, such as guidelines, consistent with the recommendation of the ICN. Moreover, this approach develops a set of common methodologies to which competition authorities can refer for the appraisal of mergers and might result, possibly, in future convergence among national laws.

The issue of how to bring closer the different objectives of competition laws still remain unanswered. The harmonisation of procedural and substantive merger control laws might activate a process which could bring about a deeper interaction between national competition authorities and a closer convergence in merger control. These future developments could create a favourable climate for countries to consider approximating the objectives regarding competition law. Such objectives are not unchangeable as suggested by the history of US merger control law. In the 1960s the US courts ascribed to it the objective of preventing the formation of large firms which might undermine the economic viability of smaller firms. The situation radically changed with the advent of the Chicago School when the objective of competition law was re-formulated so as to maximise of economic efficiency and consumer welfare.

XII. *The extrinsic dimension of efficiency*

The extrinsic dimension of efficiency encompasses those measures, whose purpose is to provide countries with sufficiently strong incentives to persuade them to adopt the proposed IMCF. These measures cannot be regarded as international competition principles, though they are functionally connected with them, as they aim at strengthening the credibility of principles and increasing their chances of being transposed into national systems. The principle of conditionality, the assistance programmes and the peer review systems can all be cited as possible incentives.

A. *The principle of conditionality*

In international economic law the principle of conditionality sets the conditions under which countries have access to the lending facilities supplied by the International Monetary Fund and other official institutions. Funds are granted provided that borrowing countries comply with internationally agreed standards concerning the governance of economic and financial activities. The International Monetary Fund frequently sets out the conditionality requirements by demanding the applicant to commit to economic policies aimed at the removal of structural impediments to healthy economic growth, such as services and trade liberalisation or the strengthening of financial markets. The relevant conditions might also include a set of internationally recognised standards related to the application and the enforcement of competition law. In this regard, it should be borne in mind that the International Monetary Fund and the World Bank have already addressed competition law issues. It is possible to advance the idea that the international competition standards should be the principles codified by the ICN.

This proposal, however, is not free from problems that may undermine its feasibility. Firstly, the principle of conditionality is among the most controversial issues in international economic law. Initially the conditions imposed by the International Monetary Fund were limited to macroeconomic targets. Then with the increasing recourse to stand-by arrangements the conditions became more and more detailed and extensive. Some are unconvinced by so broad a recourse to conditionality, their criticism being directed at the idea of conditionality as such and at some specific prescriptions. Conditionality may interfere with the internal affairs of the borrowing countries by limiting their sovereignty and may also disregard the political and social situations of these countries.

The principle of conditionality can only apply to those countries seeking to borrow from the international financial institutions. This does not appear to be a serious obstacle given that developing countries are more likely than developed countries to resort to official funding and they are also rather sceptical with regard to the internationalisation of competition law. Cynically, the principle of conditionality could force those countries to adopt the international competition principles as a requirement for access to funds. But, as anticipated above, the conditions imposed by the lender may be so stringent as to interfere with the domestic policies of the borrowers. In this case the principle of conditionality may be felt as an intrusion of supranational bodies into the sovereignty of the borrower and it would be exposed to the same critiques already examined with regard to the instruments of hard law.

B. *Technical assistance and capacity building programmes*

Technical assistance and capacity building programmes seem to be more promising. A fundamental requirement for sound and effective implementation and enforcement of competition law is the presence of an efficient institutional framework; however, the fulfilment of this condition may be problematical for developing countries. The ICN is aware of these difficulties and recognises the importance of external assistance. Since the first Annual Conference in Naples it started examining which obstacles the developing countries have to overcome for the implementation of competition laws as well as what type of assistance should be provided to them. It is important to bear in mind that, as these programmes are specifically tailored to the needs of developing countries, they may make the activities of the ICN more attractive to them.

Technical assistance consists of the transfer of skills and know how from one national competition authority to another. Capacity building is the process of building, at regional or national level, sustainable competition law frameworks. Both are necessary for the establishment of a reliable competition law regime, which requires a number of sophisticated skills and expertise. The ICN has begun educative work and has collected information from the various competition authorities on the assistance programmes conducted by them. The goal of this exercise is to assess the advantages and disadvantages of the assistance programmes and to recommend which measures should be taken in order to improve them. The creation of a database containing the skills and expertise that the competition authorities of developed countries are ready to pass on to the competition authorities of developing countries has been suggested. This should facilitate the contacts between the competition authorities of developed and developing countries and the launch of assistance programmes. A survey conducted in 2003 by the World Bank, which sent a questionnaire to 48 competition authorities of emerging and transition countries, assessed the training needs of competition authorities. This survey may provide guidance to the ICN on the contents and training methods of the assistance programmes.

C. *Peer review systems*

A peer review system would be an essential companion in the setting of non-binding international competition principles. It could certainly strengthen the likelihood that the principles are implemented by the participating countries. Unlike instruments of hard law, instruments of soft law normally do not envisage any adjudicatory body to verify the compliance of the participating countries. Compliance may be nevertheless secured through informal, non-legally binding mechanisms. One of them may be the transparent self-assessment by the participating countries. The findings of this exercise should then be published in order to enable every party concerned to know the degree of compliance of each country.

The same function may be carried out by the peer review, which is already used in the financial services sector. IOSCO, for example, has launched a multi-step initiative for the purpose of widening the adherence of national supervisors to financial international standards. Firstly, it identifies those countries that are unable to guarantee adequate levels of protection and that are unwilling to collaborate. Secondly, it starts dialogue with those national supervisors so as to assess their willingness and capability to collaborate and to offer them technical assistance. Finally, it evaluates the progress made by the national supervisors in the implementation of the IOSCO principles.

In the field of competition law a peer review is adopted by the OECD, which reviews the competition law and the enforcement of that law in various countries. This exercise provides precious insights into the competition law of the examined country and fosters transparency and mutual trust. The ICN also puts into practice a peer review and sends out questionnaires to competition authorities and members of the competition law community so as to evaluate the progress of countries in the implementation of the principles and to identify which are the impediments to further convergence. A hint at a peer review system is also given by the Recommended Practices, which invites countries to periodically review merger control laws and procedures in order to improve the merger review process.

This author strongly advocates the incorporation of a peer review system into the proposed international framework. Ideally, it should be executed by periodical audits of national laws in order to establish whether countries are complying with the international competition principles. If a country does not observe the principles the only applicable sanction is a public objection to that country. This system should give countries convincing incentives to implement the international principles and it increases the degree of transparency regarding national competition law regimes. It enables all countries to know which of them are not implementing the principles and to take consequential measures. Thus, the countries that have not adopted the principles may be barred from enjoying the benefits resulting from participation.

The compliant countries may reject the cooperation requests coming from non-compliant countries and may also refuse to start, or decide to withdraw from, an ongoing assistance programme with a non-compliant country. In order to get the most out of peer review, it should not be limited to monitoring whether countries have transposed the principles into their national systems; but it should also assess whether the competition authorities effectively observe and apply the principles. The adoption of the principles would be worthless if they were not applied or were applied in a lax manner.

Peer review increases transparency by showing whether and how countries are implementing the principles. This may be instrumental in the correct working of another type of extrinsic incentives, that of market incentives. These refer to the links between the competition law of one country and the decision of firms to take up economic activities in that country. A country which intends to attract more investments should provide a legal environment capable of meeting the needs of business. In this regard, a sound merger control law should be consistent with the principles drafted by the ICN.

The Recommended Practices indicate how to design merger control laws more responsively to the needs of firms. They attempt to reduce the number of the potentially overlapping jurisdictions; they lay down the principle of non-discrimination, thanks to which foreign firms should not be discriminated in favour of national firms; the merger review process should be conducted by the regulating authority transparently and efficiently and should impose less burdens on the merging parties as possible; merger review should be completed within a reasonable period of time and be consistent with the criteria of procedural fairness.

In sum, the position of firms in a country that has implemented these principles is better than the position of a firm in a country that has not. A country that is genuinely committed to trade liberalisation and which plans to increase the flow of investment into its territory should make its national competition law compliant with such principles. If it does not so, firms may decide against making investments or starting business operations in that country. The ultimate negative consequences will be suffered by consumers, whose choices may be restricted by the presence of a smaller number of firms trading in that market.

XIII. *Arguments for the creation of the International Framework for Merger Control: A summary*

This author supports the creation of an international framework for the regulation of transnational mergers based on instruments of soft law. The noyau dur of the framework are the principles developed by the ICN with the necessary adjustments. These principles have a voluntary, non-legally binding nature. They do not pose any threat to the integrity of national sovereignty. But such advantages have to be confronted with what is their fundamental problem: how to convince countries to implement principles that do not create any legal obligations on them. This problem may be resolved by offering countries sufficiently convincing incentives to adopt these principles, such as the concepts of legitimacy and efficiency.

The concept of legitimacy requires that the drafting of principles is based on wide consensus across the international community. This condition is fulfilled when the procedures for the drafting of the principles allow the participation of a substantial number of developed and developing countries on an equal basis. The ICN complies with the concept of legitimacy since its procedures have a strong participatory nature and its instruments are based on the consensus of developed and developing countries.

The concept of efficiency refers to the necessity that the proposed framework includes viable solutions to the problems of multi-jurisdictional merger reviews without threatening national sovereignty. This concept includes both intrinsic measures, such as the contents of the international principles and extrinsic measures that can strengthen the resolve of countries to adhere to the IMCF. Ideally, intrinsic efficiency should take into consideration the interests of competition authorities in the efficient enforcement of merger control as well as the interests of firms in legal certainty and less compliance costs. The principles included in the Recommended Practices seem able to accommodate such exigencies. For example, principles which fit the interest of firms are those concerning procedural fairness, transparency and the protection of confidential information. Instead, the principle of the appropriate nexus for the allocation of jurisdiction on transnational mergers and all the principles that promote convergence on the key points of the merger control procedure should be of interest to competition authorities. Convergence on procedural issues is indispensable to secure deeper cooperation and coordination among national competition authorities and strengthen their enforcement capability with regard to transnational mergers.

Harmonisation of the substantive merger control laws has turned to be more difficult. Up until the Seoul Annual Meeting, the ICN had only started an exploratory work on the feasibility of the harmonisation of national merger control guidelines. This approach has its merits as it is easier to obtain the support of countries for multilateral instruments which require them to modify informal policy papers, such as merger guidelines, rather than modify formal legal rules. Indeed, a complete harmonisation of the substantive rules, inclusive of the objectives of merger control, is neither feasible nor convenient. Leaving aside the difficulty of obtaining the necessary consensus of countries, the harmonisation of substantive rules probably would not completely remove the risk of conflicting decision, due to the discretion still kept by competition authorities in the evaluation of the alleged anti-competitive effects of mergers. The harmonisation of the merger guidelines is then a more pragmatic approach, which is more likely to be supported and implemented by countries. At the same time, it may contribute towards more consistency in the regulation of transnational mergers by equipping national competition authorities with common methodologies for the examination of the competitive problems raised by these operations.

Amongst the extrinsic measures, the assistance programmes and the peer review programmes deserve a particular mention. The latter should especially be tailored to the needs of developing countries and they are therefore important in obtaining the support of these countries for the IMCF. The importance of peer review can be appreciated from different standpoints. Firstly, it improves market transparency by enabling competition authorities and firms to learn whether and how a country is implementing the international principles. Secondly, the results of the peer review are necessary step in the process of taking disciplinary actions against the non-compliant countries. Thereby the competition authorities of the compliant countries may refuse to cooperate with the competition authorities of jurisdiction which have not implemented the principles. In addition, firms may decide against making investments in this country.

XIV. *Conclusion*

The reliance on instruments of soft law in order to regulate transnational mergers presents advantages and disadvantages. On the one hand, the main advantage secured by these instruments rests in their legal nature. Since the instruments of soft law do not have legally binding force instruments they do not threat countries' sovereignty. On the other hand, the soft law nature of these instruments can be perceived as their most serious weakness. Since the instruments of soft law do not impose any legally binding obligations upon countries, it is possible that countries may not comply with these instruments.

However, national financial regulators have created a number of international frameworks which rest upon instruments of soft law with the purpose of coordinating their enforcement activities regarding those conducts affecting several national financial markets. What has been achieved in the financial sector may be replicated in the field of competition law. It has been submitted that an international framework for the regulation of transnational mergers should rest upon instruments of soft law which are consistent with the concepts of legitimacy and efficiency. Legitimacy means that each country concerned can take part to decision-making process leading to the creation of the instruments. Efficiency means that the instruments provide effective solutions to global competition problems. An international framework, which has been designed in accordance to these concepts, should give countries incentives to adhere to it.

The proposed IMCF meets these conditions. Firstly, it embraces the international competition principles crafted by the ICN through decision-making process which are open to each country concerned. Secondly, the above principles provide appropriate solutions to the problems raised by the regulation of transnational mergers. Finally, within the IMCF instruments of soft law are associated with a number of measures, such as peer review and assistance programmes, the purpose of which is to strengthen the efficiency of such instruments.

CONCLUSIONS

The regulation of transnational mergers raises several problems, which, as we saw, do appear to require some careful attention. These problems affect both the parties to a merger operation and the competition authorities and they concern, among other things: risks of inconsistent decisions; high compliance costs; difficulty in collecting evidence and executing remedies abroad; lengthy merger review procedures and the risk of a parochial appraisal of mergers. As previous chapters made it clear, such problems are caused by the fact that transnational mergers produce economic effects in a number of national markets and, accordingly, may be subjected to the merger review in many countries, whose national laws may be different.

The traditional response of countries to the problems raised by transnational mergers is the application of their merger control laws to all transactions that harm their national economic interests under a unilateral strategy. As chapter two demonstrated, however, the unilateral strategy does seem to be an inappropriate approach through which to regulate transnational mergers. Instead of resolving global competition problems, which may result from such transactions, the strategy appears to exacerbate them. Thus, despite the fact that certain competition authorities attach high significance to the strategy, the problems caused by the strategy must be recognised as serious. Firstly, there is the real possibility that different competition authorities may reach conflicting decisions over the legality of the same merger operation. Secondly, multiple filings on the merging parties increase their compliance costs quite significantly. Thirdly, the extraterritorial application of national competition laws, inherent in the unilateral strategy, may cause diplomatic tensions between countries, with the inevitable result that merging parties will find themselves caught up in these tensions. Finally, the unilateral strategy can be said to lack legitimacy as countries tend to apply their competition laws extraterritorially to regulate 'inbound' restrictive business practices, which harm national economic interests, whilst they are less disposed to prosecute 'outbound' restrictive business practices that only harm foreign interests.

It is therefore necessary to re-consider the way national merger control laws are applied and enforced in cases of transnational mergers. As stated above, such operations may harm the economic interests of more than one country; as a result, it is quite logical to expect that more than one national competition authority will assert jurisdiction over the same transaction. Arguably, therefore, the internationalisation of merger control review may provide more an appropriate solution to global competition problems arising in cases of transnational mergers.

Amongst the options that are theoretically available, preference should be given to those ideas that are capable of attracting the interests of a wide variety of countries. Generally speaking, countries tend to favour ideas that ensure effective solutions to global competition problems, which are the least intrusive into their national sovereignty. The most sophisticated of these ideas recommends the creation of a supranational competition authority. This body would appraise transnational mergers against a set of internationally agreed rules. With the creation of such a body, national competition authorities would cede their regulatory competence in favour of the new body. In the past, such ideas inspired the drafting of the 1993 International Antitrust Code and even the formulation of the Draft Havana Charter and have been repeatedly used as a ground for proposals to launch the WTO Competition Law Agreement.[3] The creation of a supranational body is perhaps the best approach to the regulation of transnational mergers. This body would be independent from national jurisdictions and as such it would not be obliged to protect any particular national interest. Accordingly, the supranational body would be in the best possible position to evaluate the economic effects of any given transnational merger in every national market concerned. It would draw conclusions with the eyes of a neutral observer and without the risk of surrendering to parochial considerations. Yet, as the discussion in chapter seven revealed, such an idea is unlikely to win the approval of countries due to their reluctance to cede national sovereignty in favour of a supranational competition authority. From the viewpoint of countries this would mean loss of control of their national policies.

The idea of having uniform rules on merger control is likewise neither plausible nor desirable, as uniformity does not eradicate the risk of inconsistency between the merger decisions of different competition authorities. The appraisal of mergers may be influenced by factors other than those related to the wording of substantive tests, such as the goals of competition law and the specific competitive structures of different national markets. Furthermore, the creation of a uniform set of merger rules requires the consensus of countries, which can be difficult to achieve. National competition laws are the outcome of a plethora of circumstances and experiences. They are so entrenched in the socio-economic fabric of countries that it can actually be difficult to devise a set of 'one-size-fits-all' competition rules.

In the light of the above, it would be advisable to consider other ideas to internationalise merger control, which, though less sophisticated, are more likely to have the required support from countries. In this regard bilateral cooperation agreements look quite promising for a number of reasons. They do pose no serious threats to national sovereignty since they are voluntarily entered into by countries. Moreover, bilateral agreements have lead to considerable results, especially in relation to facilitating cooperation between competition authorities and the harmonisation of competition laws. The cooperation agreements concluded between the US and the EC and between Australia and New Zealand furnish excellent examples in this regard. However, the benefits of bilateral cooperation agreements are limited to the parties themselves. Thus the countries that have not entered into such agreements (and their nationals) are unable to gain any benefit from them. Accordingly, these instruments are not particularly suitable to effectively addressed global competition problems.

Bilateral cooperation agreements should therefore be complemented by multilateral instruments, such as a set of non-legally binding international competition principles which can be applied to a wider range of situations. Such principles do not restrict national sovereignty since they do not impose any legally binding obligations on countries. Yet, with notable exceptions, because of their 'soft law' nature these principles cannot be guaranteed to be adopted by all countries within their domestic legal systems. Such a concern may be dispelled by observing that some of the principles have been already implemented into important jurisdictions.

In the view of this author the global competition problems inherent in the regulation of transnational mergers may be successfully addressed by the establishment of an international merger control framework. This is an attainable objective, provided that some safeguards are adhered to. Most importantly, the IMCF should be developed following a step-by-step approach and upon the basis of instruments of soft law which do not restrict national sovereignty. The multilateral instruments of soft law and the bilateral cooperation agreements should be the constitutive elements of the proposed IMCF. These instruments should first incorporate criteria for the effective allocation of cases amongst those competition authorities asserting jurisdiction over a given merger. The identification of one or a few competition authorities with jurisdiction over any given merger may eliminate the risk of jurisdictional overlapping and avoid problems of legal uncertainty and increases in compliance costs.

This author is aware of the fact that this proposition is not free from problems. It may be observed that the proposed allocation of merger cases may affect the substantive outcome of regulatory review. In this regard, the allocation of merger cases to a given national competition authority is not irrelevant since national regulators may evaluate differently the same competition issues. A solution to this problem may be a safeguard clause which will empower countries to oppose the allocation of merger cases to a national competition authority when sensitive national interests are affected by mergers. Also the degree of harmonisation and interagency collaboration which may be achieved with the implementation of the proposed IMCF may be helpful. This contributes to foster mutual trust among regulators, which should further attenuate the likelihood of inconsistency. Merging parties' interests should be taken into consideration too, since the parties are burdened with the identification of the competent competition authorities and also bear the risk of negative decisions. For this reason the allocation criteria should be draft as much precise and clear as possible. Referral mechanisms, similar to those provided for the EC Regulation 139/2004 may be introduced with the aim of enabling the merging parties to entrust regulatory powers to the competition authorities which appears to be closer to the transaction. So, the merging parties would have say in a matter which, as seen above, may influence the appraisal of their merger.

The IMCF should also aim at the approximation of national merger control laws, especially with regard to procedural rules. The approximation of the substantive national merger control rules, on the other hand, does not seem to be a feasible objective. Therefore, for the time being, it is sufficient that the national competition authorities agree to observe the principle of non-discrimination upon grounds of nationality. Respecting such a principle should ward off parochial considerations from the substantive assessment of mergers.

The IMCF should also include some mechanisms for cooperation and coordination of the enforcement activities between competition authorities, which may be invoked if a merger operation is subjected to multi-jurisdictional review. Such instruments, for instance, may enable the exchange of data and information among the competition authorities concerned or may allow the participation of officials from one competition authority in the activities of another authority.

In light of the above observations, the IMCF should rest on two pillars: the informal pillar, which should consist of a set of international competition law standards; and the formal pillar consisting of a nexus of bilateral cooperation agreements. It is proposed that the informal pillar should be exclusively based on instruments of soft law and should be a sort of lex generalis in the field of international merger control. The ICN should be entrusted with the task of setting the relevant competition standard. As indicated in chapter eight, with its Best Practices the ICN has already demonstrated its capability to produce high-level general standards and principles. The following principles from the Recommended Practices should be incorporated into the informal pillar: a) The principle of the appropriate nexus as a criterion for establishing the jurisdiction of competition authorities in transnational merger cases. The use of the appropriate nexus principle will ensure the existence of effective criteria for the allocation of cases between national competition authorities, which in turn will reduce the likelihood of multi-jurisdictional reviews. Thus, the adoption of the will reduce the number of competition authorities that are potentially able to assert jurisdiction on a merger operation. Finally, the principle of the appropriate nexus should be supported by special statutory exemptions, by virtue of which the notification obligation does not apply to mergers between foreign firms which have no relevant effects within the national territory of a given country; b) Principles that provide for a harmonised regulation of the events triggering the notification obligation, the content of the notification form used by the merging parties and the time limits for the investigations. The harmonisation of these aspects may facilitate the coordination between competition authorities; c) Principles regulating merger control proceedings, such as the principle of non- discrimination on grounds of nationality; the principle of transparency; the principle of fair process and the principle of confidentiality. These principles will lead to the harmonisation of the rules regulating the key stages of the merger control process. The harmonisation should foster mutual trust between national competition authorities and strengthen their willingness to cooperate.

Beyond the inclusion of these principles, the informal pillar should embrace competition law standards concerning the substantive aspects of merger control. The pillar should not pursue the adoption of one single standard substantive test due to the different views of countries in this respect. Rather, it should harmonise the methodologies that competition authorities employ for the purpose of reviewing mergers operations. More specifically, the informal pillar should develop common approaches to issues such as vertical and conglomerate mergers; unilateral and coordinated effects in oligopolistic markets; definition of relevant markets and the treatment of efficiencies. By following the recommendations of the informal pillar competition authorities may reach common or similar approaches in the examination of these issues, which might reduce the risk of inconsistencies. It is suggested the beginnings of the harmonisation process should focus on the adoption of policy guidelines. Only after the harmonisation of the administrative practices of competition authorities, will it be possible to seek the approximation of substantive legal rules.

Finally, it is advisable to support the informal pillar with two additional measures: assistance programmes and peer review. These measures have already examined in chapter eight. The assistance programmes should be tailored to the needs of the developing countries, which would be important in winning their support for the IMCF. The function of the peer review, on the other hand, is to encourage countries to conform with the principles adopted within the informal pillar. It may be used to monitor the compliance by countries with the principles. This will help identify non-compliant countries and possibly expose them to retaliatory measures.

The formal pillar, on the other hand, is to be constituted by a nexus of bilateral cooperation agreements and should be made subject to the principles of public international law. The rules contained in the formal pillar can be considered as the lex specialis of international merger control. More specifically, bilateral cooperation agreements apply only if two conditions are fulfilled. First, the transnational merger to be regulated must produce its effects within the territory of one of the parties to the bilateral cooperation agreement. Second, the bilateral cooperation agreement ensures a degree of cooperation and harmonisation that must be at least equivalent to that of the informal pillar.

The institutional aim of the IMCF would be the promotion of harmonisation and cooperation. It could also promote a competition law awareness culture across the world and, more specifically, promote the importance of adopting international mechanisms for the regulation of transnational mergers. Such educative work ought to be considered within a long-term perspective. The efforts of the ICN and of the other actors committed to promoting the internationalisation of competition law should convince countries that the benefits derived by the establishment of the IMCF compensate for the losses caused by the possible restrictions on national sovereignty. When all the countries concerned endorse this view, the time will be ripe for the introduction of more sophisticated frameworks for the regulation of transnational mergers, based on instruments of hard law, possibly within the WTO framework. Though the IMCF, as proposed in this book, may be perceived as a tentative approach to the regulation of transnational mergers, the adoption of the IMCF does not exclude the possibility of embracing more far-reaching ideas in future. In the meantime, however, while waiting for this moment to come, such an approach may provide the first viable response to the global competition problems in the field of merger control.

At this point readers may ask themselves whether the proposed IMCF is a convincing solution to the problems affecting the regulation of transnational mergers. A reasonable way of testing the validity of the IMCF is the hypothetical assessment of General Electric/Honeywell under the framework. A number of questions may so arise: Had the transaction in question been assessed with the IMCF already in place would the outcome of the regulatory review have been any different? Would it have been possible to prevent the EC and the US competition authorities from taking different views regarding the transaction? Would the IMCF have managed to settle such different views?

Since only the European Commission and the US Department of Justice have exerted jurisdiction over the transaction, the EC/US bilateral cooperation agreement would apply as lex specialis. The EC/US bilateral cooperation agreement was already in force when the transaction was examined. Notwithstanding that, the European Commission and the US Department of Justice did take divergent views regarding the transaction and such divergences remain unaddressed since the EC/US bilateral cooperation agreement does not include any mechanism to settle conflicting views. Thus, had the proposed IMCF been already in place at the time of the appraisal of General Electric/Honeywell, it would not have been able to prevent the European Commission and the US Department of Justice from taking conflicting decisions. Therefore the IMCF would have had no effects on the result of the regulatory review of this transaction.

In chapter four this author has attempted to explain the reasons why the EC and the US competition authorities divided on the appraisal of General Electric/Honeywell. It has been argued that the transaction concerned the goals that the two jurisdictions assign to competition law. Such goals are deeply entrenched in the political cultural and social fabric of countries and this has important implications for merger control. Countries may not easily agree on the harmonisation of competition goals as values and objectives pursued by each of them may be at variance with those pursued by the others. Furthermore, competition goals can also affect merger control as national competition authorities may wish to establish whether a proposed merger is compatible with national competition goals in order to approve it or not. So the European Commission can legitimately block a merger which may close off national markets and impede the correct working of the single market. The South African competition authority can legitimately block a merger which may frustrate the pursuance of the goal of black economic empowerment.

In these hypothetical cases the European Commission and the South African competition authority have exercised their regulatory powers consistently with the goals of their competition laws. Their decisions to block to merger can be regarded as a legitimate exercise of economic sovereignty. Nonetheless, these decisions may be criticised by the other countries affected by the merger, the competition laws of which do not have the same goals. These countries prefer pursue different goals and so disregard the objectives of preservation of single market or of the black economic empowerment.

Divergences regarding competition goals are likely to result in conflicting decisions. The elimination or the attenuation of the risk of inconsistency is an objective which is rather difficult to achieve due to the above reasons. So, it should be accepted that the risk of inconsistency is inherent in the appraisal of transnational mergers and this cannot be easily eliminated neither with the establishment of international fora such as the ICN or the proposed IMCF.

After having excluded that the IMCF would have been helpful for the regulation of General Electric/Honeywell, it can be interesting to evaluate whether the recent innovations in the EC merger control regime illustrated in chapters three and four would have had any effect on the appraisal of this transaction. The EC Courts are now willing to exert a stricter judicial control over the enforcement activities of the Commission; they have also set out the evidentiary standard with which the Commission has to comply. So, in case of conglomerate mergers, which normally have neutral effects on competition, the Commission is expected to supply sufficiently strong evidence to demonstrate that such negative effects may occur. The appointment of a

Chief Economist should improve the level of the economic analysis of the alleged consequences of mergers carried out by the Commission.

It may be then argued that if the Commission had decided the General Electric/Honeywell merger these days it would not have relied upon controversial economic theories such as the theory of conglomerate effects to block the transaction. Bearing in mind the relatively unimportant role played by the horizontal overlaps in the line of reasoning of the Commission in its negative decision of 2001, the Commission would have probably authorise the merger. It must be stressed that the above overhaul of the EC merger control regime is not the outcome of the activities of international fora such the ICN or the proposed IMCF. Rather, the overhaul in question is the outcome of the internal debate within the EC triggered by some judgements of the EC Courts that criticised the way the Commission administered merger control.

In conclusion, as a general rule, the proposed IMCF can be a valuable framework which enables competition authorities to cooperate and coordinate their enforcement activities. It can also favour harmonisation of national rules, especially the procedural ones. National competition authorities can resort to the IMCF for the appraisal of transnational mergers except for a particular situation. Such a situation occurs when national competition authorities have to review a transaction which is liable to affect competition law goals such as General Electric/Honeywell. In this case there is no or little room for reliance upon international instruments for the regulation of transnational mergers. National interests may prevail over third countries' interests and international cooperation with the authorities of the other countries concerned. So, these transnational mergers may be still regulated with the unilateral strategy with the ensuing risk of inconsistent decisions, which in such a scenario sometimes seem to be inescapable. Fortunately, and this is the conclusive remark of the present book, this situation has been so far rather a rare event.

LIST OF ABBREVIATIONS

BYBIL	British Yearbook of International Law
CLI	Competition Law Insight
CML	Rev Common Market Law Review
CMLR	Common Market Law Report
ECLR	European Competition Law Review
ECR	European Courts Report
EIPR	European Intellectual Property Review
EL Rev	European Law Review
ICCLR	International Commercial and Company Law Review
ITLR	International Trade Law Review
JCMS	Journal of Common Market Studies
LIEI	Legal Issues of Economic Integration
OJ	Official Journal of the European Communities
PCIJ	Permanent Court of International Justice
RIDE	Revue International de Droit Économique
RMCLUE	Revue de Marché Commun et de L'Union Européenne
RTD Eur	Revue Trimestrielle de Droit Européenne
YEL	Yearbook of European Law

BIBLIOGRAPHY

Abbamonte G, Rabassa V., *Foreclosure and vertical mergers*, (2001), ECLR, 214.

Abdelgawad Walid, *Jalons de l'internationalisation du droit de la concurrence: vers l'éclosion d'un ordre juridique mondial de la Lex Economica* [2001] Revue Internationale de Droit Economique 161.

Aiginger Karl, McCabe Mark, Mueller Dennis, Weiss Christoph *Do European and American Industrial Organization Economists Differ?* [2001] Review of Industrial Organization 383.

Akbar Yusaf, *The Internationalization of Competition Policy: Implications for International Business* (2000) 42 Thunderbird International Business Review 47.

Akbar Yusuf, *Grabbing Victory from the Jaws of Defeat: Can the GE/Honeywell Merger Facilitate International Antitrust Policy Cooperation?* (2002) 25 World Competition 131.

Akehurst Michael, *Jurisdiction in International Law: Antitrust Law* [1972–73] British Yearbook of International Law 145.

Al Najjari Nasdat, Di Bon Francesca, Cross-border mergers of limited liability companies. Some considerations on fiscal implication, (2007), Fiscalità Internazionale, 215.

Alford Roger, *The Extraterritorial Application of Antitrust Laws: A Postscript on Hartford Fire Insurance Co v California* (1993–94) 34 Virginia Journal of International Law 213.

Alison Jones, Smith Brenda, EC competition law: Text, cases and materials, Oxford University Press, (2007).

Amarasinha Stephan, *East is East and West is West and the Twain Shall Never Meet or Shall They?* [2003] Fordham Corporate Law Institute 603.

Amato Filippo, *International Antitrust: What Future?*, (2001) 24 World Competition 451.

Amato Giuliano, Antitrust and the Bounds of Power, (Hart Publishing Oxford, 1997).

——, Il gusto della libertà. L'Italia e l'Antitrust, (Editori Laterza Bari, 1998).

Anderson Robert and Holmes Peter, *Competition Policy and the Future of the Multinational Trading System* [2002] Journal of International Economic Law 531.

Applebaum Harvey, *The Interface of the Trade Law and the Antitrust Law* (1998) 6 George Mason Law Review 479.

Arhel Pierre, *Droit International de la concurrence* [1997] Revue du Marche Commun et de l'Union Européenne' 492.

——, *Droit international de la concurrence: S'oriente-t-on vers des négociations?* [1999] Revue du Marche Commun et de l'Union Européenne 84.

Atwood James, *Positive Comity. Is It a Positive Step?* [1992] Fordham Corporate Law Institute 79.

Austin Esq. John, *The Role of Supervisory Authorities in Connection with Bank Mergers* <http://www.imf.org/external/np/leg/sem/2002/cdmfl/eng/austin.pdf>.

Baer William, *International Antitrust Policy,* [1998] Fordham Corporate Law Institute 247.

Baetge Dietmar, *Competition Law and Perspectives for Harmonisation* [2004] Uniform Law Review 503.

Bailey D., *Standard of proof in EC merger proceedings: A common law perspective*, (2003), CMLR, 845.

Baker Donald et al., The Harmonization of International Competition Law in the Global Economy, in Leonard Waverman et al. (eds.) Competition Law for Global Economy: Modalities for Cooperation 439 (Routledge, London & New York 1997).

Baker Simon, *Antitrust Merger Review in an Era of Escalating Cross-Border* [2000] Wisconsin International Law Journal 577.

Baker Simon and Ridyard Derek, *Portfolio Power: A Rum Deal* [1999] European Competition Law Review 181.

Baker Simon and Wu Laurence, *Applying the Market Definition Guidelines of the European Communities* [1998] European Competition Law Review 273.

Banks J.D. *The Developments of the Concept of Extraterritoriality under European Merger Law and its Effectiveness under the Merger Regulation following the Boeing/Mc Donnel Douglas* [1998] European Competition Law Review 306.

Bavasso Antonio, *Boeing/Mc Donnel Douglas: Did the Commission Fly Too High?* [1998] European Competition Law Review.

——, *Gencor: A Judicial Review of the Commission Policy and Practice: Many Light and Some Shadows* (1999) 22 World Competition 4, 45.

Bay Matteo and Ruiz Calzado Javier, *Tetra Laval II: the Coming of Age of the Judicial Review of Merger Decisions* (2005) 28 World Competition 433.

Beckler Richard and Kirtland Matthew, *Extraterritorial Application of U.S. Antitrust Law: What Is a "Direct, Substantial, and Reasonably Foreseeable Effect" under the Foreign Trade Antitrust Improvements Act?* [2003] Texas International Law Journal 11.

Bellamy C., Child G., *European community law of competition*, Oxford University Press, 2007.

Bellis Jean Francois, *Anti-Competitive Practices and the WTO: The Elusive Search for the New World Trade Rules*, in Marco Bronckers and Reinhard Quick (eds.) New Directions in International Economic Law, essays in honour of John H. Jackson (Kluwer Law International 2000).

Berg Werner, *The New EC Merger Regulation: A First Assessment of its Practical Impact* (2004) 24 Northwestern Journal of International Law and Business 683.

Berg Werner and Holger Bielesz, *The WTO and Competition: Option and Perspectives* [2003] International Trade Law and Regulation 94.

Bernini Giorgio, *La dimensione internazionale della concorrenza: Prospettiva di regolazione in ambito OMC* <www.agcm.it>.

Bishop B., Caffara C., *Merger control in new markets*, (2001), ECLR, 31.

Bishop S., Walker M., *The economics of EC competition law. Concepts, application and measurement*, Sweet and Maxwell, 2002.

Boeden Thomas and Sharp Benjamin, interview with, Antitrust (Fall 1997), 5.

Boege Ulf and Mueller Edith, *From the Market Dominance Test to the SLC Test: Are There Any Reason for a Change?* [2002] European Competition Law Review 494.

Bourgeois Jacques, *EEC Control over International Merger* [1990] Yearbook Of European Law 108.

Brandeburger Rachel and Janssen Thomas, *European Merger Control: Do the Checks and Balances Need to Be Re-Set* [2001] Fordham Corporate Law Institute 135.

Briggs John and Rosenblatt Howard, *A Bundle of Trouble: The Aftermath of GE/Honeywell* 16 Antitrust 26.

Bright Chris and Schmidt John, *Financial Strength in EC Merger* [2005] European Competition Journal 293.

Broberg M., The European Commissionì's jurisdiction to scutinise mergers, (2003), Kluwer.

Broberg Martin, *The European Commission's Extraterritorial Powers in Merger Control. A Comment on the Court of First Instance's Judgement in Gencor v. Commission* [2000] International Comparative Law Quarterly 172.

Broder D.F., *A guide to US Antitrust law*, (2005), Sweet and Maxwell.

Bronckers Marco and Quick Reinhard (eds.), New Directions in International Economic Law, (Kluwer Law International, The Hague 2000).

Brown Jay and Connery Niamh, *Comparing US and EU Merger Review: Procedures, Principles and* **???**

Brownlie Ian, Principles Of Public International Law, (Clarendon Press Oxford, 1998).

Brunt Maureen, *Australian and New Zealand Competition Law and Policy* [1992] Fordham Corporate Law Institute 131.

Burnside Alec, *GE, Honey, I Sunk the Merger*, [2002] European Competition Law Review 107.

Burnside Alec and Helen Crossley, *Co-operative Mechanisms within the EU: A Blueprint for Future Co-operation at the International Level?* [2004] International Trade Law & Regulation 25.

Burnside Alec and Yves Bottenon, *Networking amongst Competition Agencies*, [2004] International Trade Law & Regulation 1.

Cadot Olivier, Grethier Jean Marie and De Melo Jaime, *Trade and Competition Policy. Where Do We Stand?* (2000) 34 (3) Journal of World Trade 1.

Cambell Thomas, Bilateral monopoly in mergers, (2007), Antitrust law journal, 5.

Camesasca Peter, *The Explicit Efficiency Defence in Merger Control: Does it Make the Difference?* [1999] European Competition Law Review 14.

Campbell Neill and Trebilcock Michael, *Interjurisdictional Conflict in Merger Review* in Leonard Waverman et al. (eds.) Competition Policy in the Global Economy: Modalities for Cooperation (Routledge, London & New York 1997).
Canenbley Cornelis and Rosenthal Michael, *Co-operation Between Antitrust Authorities In- and Outside the EU: What Does it Mean for Multinational Corporations?* part 2 [2005] European Competition Law Review 178.
Carol George, *WTO Panel Condemns Anti-Competitive Behaviour in International Telecom Case: Mexico-Measures Affecting Telecommunications Services—WT/DS204/R* [2004] International Trade and Law Review 106.
Carreau Dominique, Droit International, (Pedone Paris, 2001).
Carstensen, Peter C., Susan B. Farmer, Competition policy and merger analusis in deregulated and newly competitive industries, Edward Elgar Publishing, (2008).
Castaneda Gallardo Gabriel, Mexico Merger Control Law, in William Rowley and Donald Baker (eds.) International Mergers (Sweet and Maxwell, London 2000).
Cheng-Jui Lu Angela, International Airline Alliance: EC Competition Law/US antitrust law and International Air Transport, (Kluwer Law International, The Hague/London, 2003).
Christoforou Theofonis and David Rockwell, *European Community Law: The Territorial Scope of Application of EEC Antitrust Law* (30) Harvard International Law Journal 195.
Cicero Michael J., *Overview: International Merger Control*, Antitrust Magazine (Spring 2001) Vol. 15, No. 2.
Cini Michelle and McGowan Lee, Competition Policy in the European Union, (Mac Millan Press London, 1998).
Cocuzza Claudio and Montini Alessandro, *International Antitrust Co-operation in a Global Economy* [1998] European Competition Law Review 156.
Colangelo Giuseppe, *Il Caso Tetra Laval* [2003] Mercato Concorrenza Regole 126.
Colley L., *From defence to attack? Quantifying efficiency arguments in mergers*, (2004), ECLR, 355. Vesterdorf J.B., *Certain reflection on recent judgments reviewing commission merger control decisions*, in M. Hoskins and W. Robinson (eds.), A true European, Essays for judge David Edward, (2993), Hart publishing, 10.
Condomines Aurelien, *The Prohibition of the General Electric/Honeywell* www.jurismag.net
Connolly William, *Lessons to be Learned: The Conflict in International Antitrust Law Contrasted with Progress in International Financial Law* [2001] Fordham Journal of Corporate and Financial Law 207.
Conrad Christian, *Strategies to Reform the Regulation on International Competition* (2003) 26 World Competition 101.
Cook C.J. and Kerse C.S., EC Merger Control, (Sweet and Maxwell London, 2000).
Cook J., Kerse C., *EC Merger control*, (2005), Sweet and Maxwell.
Cowie Michael and Novotna Monica, *Pre-merger Notification in Central and Eastern Europe* Antitrust (Summer 1998) vol. 12, No. 3, 19.
Craig Paul and De Burca Grainne, EU Law, (Oxford University Press, Oxford, 2002).
Cranston Ross, Principles of Banking Law (Oxford University Press, Oxford, 2002).
Dabbah Maher, EC and UK Competition Law, (Cambridge University Press, Cambridge 2004).
Dabbah Maher, The Internationalization of Antitrust Policy (Cambridge University Press, Cambridge 2004).
Dabbah Maher, Zambia in Dabbah and Lasok (eds.) Merger Control Worldwide (Cambridge University Press, Cambridge 2005).
Dabbah Maher and Lasok Paul (eds.) Merger Control Worldwide (Cambridge University Press Cambridge, 2005).
Dalhuisen Jan, Dalhuisen on Commercial, Financial and Trade Law, (Hart Publishing Oxford, 2004).
Damro Chad, *Multilateral Competition Policy and Transatlantic Compromise* [2004] European Foreign Affair Review 269.
Davidow Joel, *International Implication of U.S. Antitrust in the Government of George W. Bush Era* (2002) World Competition 493.
Davidow Joel and Chiles Lisa, *The United States and the Issue of the Binding or Voluntary Nature of International Codes of Conduct Regarding Restrictive Business Practices* (1978) 72 American Journal of International Law 247.

Demaret Paul, *Extraterritorialité des lois et les relations transatlantique: Une question de droit international ou de diplomatie?* [1985] Revue trimestrielle de Droit Européen 1.

Demetriou Maria and Robertson Aidan, *US Extraterritorial Jurisdiction in Antitrust Matters*, [1995] European Competition Law Review 461.

Dethmers Frances, Dodoo Ninette and Morfey Anna, *Conglomerate Mergers under EC Merger Control* [2005] European Competition Journal 265.

Devellennes Yves and Kiriazis Georgios, *Competition Policy makes it into* **???**

——, *The Creation of an International Competition Network* Competition Policy Newsletter (February 2002) 25.

Di Via Luciano, *Le misure di protezione commerciale nel diritto del commercio internazionale* [2005] Il Diritto del Commercio Internazionale 443.

Dialti Francesco, *Principali differenze e somiglianze tra standards e norme avente valore di legge nel settore della regolamentazione finanziaria* [2005] Il Diritto del Commercio Internazionale 535.

Draetta Ugo, *La giurisdizione internazionale della Commissione in materia di controllo delle concentrazioni* [1999] Il Diritto del Commercio Internazionale 785.

——, *International Law Aspects of Cooperation in Merger Review: Long and Short Term Solutions* [2002] Il Diritto del Commercio Internazionale 3.

——, *Need for Better a Trans-Atlantic Co-operation in the Field of Merger Control* [2002] International Business Law Review 557.

Drautz Gotz, *Unbundling GE/Honeywell: The Assessment of Conglomerate Mergers Under EC Competition Law* (2002) 25 Fordham International Law Journal 885.

——, Bengtsson Claes, Jones Christopher, mergers and acquisitions, Leuven, Claeys and Casteels, (2006).

Drexl Josef, *Trade-Related Restraints of Competition—The Competition Policy Approach* in Roger Zäch (ed.), Towards WTO Competition Rules, (Kluwer Law International The Hague/London 1999).

——, *International Competition Law Policy after Cancun: Placing a Singapore Issue on the WTO Development Agenda* (2004) 27(3) World Competition 419.

Dupuy Pierre Marie, Droit International Public, (Editions Dalloz Paris, 1998)

Eilmansberger T., *How to distinguish good rom bad competition under Article 82. In search of clear and more coherent standards for anti-competitive abuses*, CMLR, (2005), 42.

Ehlerman S., *The contribution of EC competition policy to the single market* (1992) 29, CMLR, 257.

Epstein Julian, *The Other Side of Harmony: Can Trade and Competition Law Work Together in the International Market Place?* (2001–02) 17 American University International Law Review 343.

Evans David and Salinger Michael, *Competition Thinking at the Commission: Lessons from the Aborted General Electric/Honeywell* [2002] George Mason Law Review.

Ezrachi Aziel, *Limitation on the Extraterritorial Reach of the European Merger Regulation* [2001] European Competition Law Review.

Farjat Guy, Editorial, [2001] Revue Internationale de Droit Economique 121.

Farmer Susan Beth, *Introduction: Competition without Borders. Antitrust Law and the Challenge of Globalization* [2003] Dickinson Law Review 725.

Farrid Bektashi, Collective dominance in EC competition law: Role of structural links: Case law analysis under the EC merger regulation, VDM Verlag, (2008).

Faull J., Nikpay A. (eds.), *The EC law of competition*, Oxford University Press, 2007.

Faull Jonathan, *Antitrust and Trade Policy* [1998] Fordham International Law Journal 261.

Fels Allan, Henrick Sharon and Taylor Martyn, Australia, in Maher Dabbah and Paul Lasok (eds.) Merger Control Worldwide (Cambridge University Press, Cambridge 2005) 76.

Ferry John E. *Towards Completing the Charm: The Wood Pulp Judgement* [1989] European Intellectual Property Review 19.

Ferson Young Sandra, *An International Antitrust Dilemma: An Analysis of the Interaction of Antitrust Laws in the United States and in the European Union* [2002] The John Marshall Law Review.

Fiebig Andre, *International Law Limits on the Extraterritorial Application of the European Merger Control Regulation* [1998] European Competition Law Review.

——, *The Extraterritorial Application of the European Merger Control* (1998–99) 5 Columbia Journal of European Law 79.
Fikentscher Wolfgang, *An International Antitrust Code* (1996) 27 International Review of Industrial Property and Copyright Law 755.
Fikentscher Wolfgang, *A Trans-national Antitrust Convention and the Recent European Antitrust Proposals: Exercises in Economic Anthropology* in Clifford Jones and Mitsuo Matsushita (eds.), Competition Policy in the Global Trading System, (Kluwer Law International, The Hague/London 2002).
First Harry, *The Intersection of Trade and Antitrust Remedies*, Antitrust (Fall 1997) 16.
Fowler Olivier, Kenya Merger Control Law, in William Rowley and Donald Baker (eds.) International Mergers (Sweet and Maxwell, London 2000).
——, *Accesso ai mercati, antitrust e sistema commerciale mondiale: In cammino verso misure antitrust connesse agli scambi commerciali* <www.agcm.it>.
Fox Eleanor, 'Extraterritoriality and Antitrust' [1986] Fordham Corporate Law Institute 52.
——, *Toward World Antitrust and Market Access* [1997] American Journal of International Law 16.
——, *International Antitrust: Against Minimum Rules, for Cosmopolitan Principles* (1998) 43 Antitrust Bulletin 3.
——, *International Antitrust: Cosmopolitan Principles for an Open World* [1998] Fordham Corporate Law Institute 271.
——, *Competition Law and the Millennium Round* (1999) 2 Journal of International Economic Law 665.
——, *The Merger Regulation and its Territorial Reach: Gencor Ltd. v. Commission* [1999] European Competition Law Review 337.
——, *National Law, Global Market, and Hartford: Eyes Wide Shut* [2000] Antitrust Law Journal 73.
——, *Global Markets, National Law and the Regulation of Business: A View from the Top* [2001] St. John's Law Journal 383.
——, *Mergers in Global Markets: General Electric/Honeywell and the Future of Market Control* (2002) 23 University of Pennsylvania Journal of Economic Law 457.
——, *US and European Merger Policy. Fault Lines and Bridges. Mergers that Create Incentives for Exclusionary Practices* (2002) 10 George Mason Law Review 471.
——, *What is Harm to Competition? Exclusionary Practices and Anticompetitive* [2002] Antitrust Law Journal 371.
——, *Can We Solve the Antitrust Problems of Globalization By Extraterritoriality and Cooperation? Sufficiency and Legitimacy* [2003] Antitrust Bulletin 355.
——, *International Antitrust and the Doha Dome* (2003) 43 Virginia Journal of International Law 911.
——, *We Protect Competition, not Competitors* (2003) 26 World Competition 149.
Fox Eleanor and Sullivan Laurence, *Antitrust-Retrospective and Prospective: Where Are We Coming From?* (1987) 62 New York University Law Review 936.
Fox Eleanor and Sullivan Lawrence, Cases and Material on Antitrust, (West Publishing Saint Paul Minnesota, 1989).
Friend Mark, *Competition and Industrial Policy: The Long Arm of Community Law* [1989] European Law Review 169.
Frignani Aldo and Michel Waelbroeck, The EEC Competition Law, (Transnational Publishers Inc., Ardsley New York, 1998).
From the Bottom—Moving from Patchwork toward Network [2003] The Antitrust Bulletin 439.
Fullerton Larry and Mazard Camelia, *International Antitrust Co-operation Agreements* (2001) 24 World Competition 405.
Furse M., *Competition law of the UK and EC*, Oxford University Press, 2006.
Furse Mark, *Competition Law and the WTO Report: Japan-Measures Affecting Consumer Photographic Film and Paper* [1999] European Competition Law Review 9.
Gangi Massimiliano, *L'iniziativa dell'Unione Europea per la realizzazione di un accordo multilaterale di regole sulla concorrenza nell'ambito dell'Organizzazione Mondiale del Commercio* [2001] 1 Diritto del Commercio Internazionale 123.

Garcia Bercero Ignacio and Stefan Amarasinha, *Moving the Trade and Competition Debate Forward* [2001] Journal of International Economic Law 481.
Garrick Jason, *International Horizontal Mergers: A Comparison of the European Union and the United States Regulatory Policy and Procedure* (1994) 7 Transnational Lawyer 294.
Gastel Jean Gabriel, *The Extraterritorial Effects of Antitrust Laws* (1983) I 21 Académie de Droit International Recueil des Cours 13.
Gellhorn Ernest, Kovacic William and Calkins Stephen, Antitrust Law and Economics, (Thomson West Saint Paul Minnesota, 2004).
George Carol, *WTO Panel Condemns Anti-Competitive Behaviour in International Telecom Case: Mexico-Measures Affecting Telecommunications Services—WT/DS204/R* [2004] International Trade and Law Review 106.
Géradin Damien and Nicolas Petit, *Competition Policy and the Euro-Mediterranean Policy* [2003] European Foreign Affairs Review 153.
——, *Règles de concurrence et Partenariat Euro-Mediterranéen: Echec ou succès* [2003] Revue International de Droit Economique 47.
Gerber David, *The U.S.-European Conflict Over the Globalization of Antitrust Law: A Legal Experience Perspective* (1999–00) 34 New England Law Review 123.
Ghezzi Federico, *Verso un diritto antitrust comune? Il processo di convergenza delle discipline statunitense e comunitaria in materia di intese* [2002] Rivista delle Società 499.
——, *La disciplina delle concentrazioni e la promozione dei campioni nazionali tra diritto comunitario e normative nazionali antitrust* [2003] Rivista delle Società 1098.
Ghidini Gustavo, *Due culture? Il Ruolo dell'efficienza sulle due sponde dell' Atlantico* [2003] Mercato Concorrenza e Regole 169.
Giannacari Andrea, *Il caso GE/Honeywell*, [2006] Mercato Concorrenza Regole 141.
Gifford Daniel, *Antitrust and Trade Law Issues: Similarities, Differences and Relationship* (1995) 44 De Paul Law Review 1049.
——, *The Draft International Antitrust Code Proposed at Munich: Good Intentions Gone Awry* (1997) 6 Minnesota Journal of Global Trade 1.
Gifford Daniel and Sullivan Lawrence, *Can International Antitrust Be Saved for the Post-Boeing Merger World?* A Proposal to Minimize International Conflict and to Rescue Antitrust from Misuse' (2000) 45 Antitrust Bulletin 55.
Giotakos Dinitris, *General Electric/Honeywell: A Theoretic Bundle Assessing Mergers Across the Atlantic* [2001] University of Pennsylvania Journal of International Economic Law 469.
——, Petit Laurent, Garnier Gaelle and De Luyck Peter *General Electic/Honeywell—An insight into the Commission's investigation and decision* 3 Competition Policy Newsletter (October 2001) 5.
Giovanoli Mario, *Reflections on International Financial Standards as 'Soft Law'*, The London Institute of International Banking, Finance and Development Law, Essays in International Financial & Economic Law, London (2002).
Goldman Calvin and Facey Brian, *Antitrust and Trade Policy: International Business Perspectives* [1998] Fordham Corporate Law Institute 279.
Goldmann Berthold, *Les champs d'application territoriale des lois sur la concurrence* (1969) III Académie de Droit International Recueil des Cours 1.
Gomart Thomas, *Le Partenariat entre l'Union Européenne et la Russie à l'épreuve de l'élargissement* [2004] Revue du Marche Commun et de l'Union Européenne 349.
Gonzalez-Diaz Francisco Enrique, *Recent Development in EC Merger Control Law. The Gencor Judgement* (1999) 29 (3) World Competition 3.
Goyder D., *EC competition law*, Oxford University Press, 2003. A. Jones, B. Sufrin, *EC Competition law: text, cases and materials*, ultimate edition, Oxford University Press.
Goyder Dan, EC Competition Law (Oxford University Press, Oxford 2003).
Graham Edward, *Internationalizing Competition Policy: An Assessment of the Two Main Alternatives* (2004) 48 Antitrust Bulletin 947.
Greene Jenna, *Antitrust Action Moves to Europe. EU Seen as Friendlier Forum for Slowing Down Mega-Deals* 24 (2001) Legal Times vol. no. 14.
Grewlich Alexandre, *Globalisation and Conflict in Competition Law* (2001) 24 World Competition 367.
Griffin Joseph, *The WTO Study of the Interaction Between Trade and Competition Policy: Timely and Controversial* [1997] International Trade & Regulation 39.

——, *Antitrust Aspects of Cross-Borders Merger and Acquisitions* [1998] European Competition Law Review 12.

——, *Reactions to U.S. Assertions of Extraterritorial Jurisdiction* [1998] European Competition Law Review 64.

Gugler Philippe and Krone-German Irenka, *Cycle Millénaire de l'OMC, vers une intégration de règles multilatérales de concurrence?*, [2000] Revue de Droit des Affaires Internationales 159.

Gustafson Lawrence, Collins Brian and McKay Brian, *Criminal Consequences of Anticompetitive Conduct* (2003) 45 South Texas Law Review 89.

Guzman Andrew, *Is International Antitrust Possible* (1998) 73 New York University Law Review 1501.

Ham Allard, *International Cooperation in the Antitrust Field and in Particular the Agreement between the United States of America and the Commission of the European Communities* (1993) Common Market Law Review 571.

Hampton Celia, *EC Merger Control: Summary of a CEPR discussion paper by Tommaso Duso, Damien J. Neven and Lars-Hendrik Roeller* Competition Law Insight (July/August 2003) 18.

——, *Harmonisation of the Thresholds System Is Now Overdue*, Competition Law Insight (10 May 2005) 6.

Harlick Gary and Meyer Michael, *The International Convergence of Competition Policy* (1995) 29 International Lawyer 65.

Haupt Heiko, *Collective Dominance under Article 82 EC and EC Merger Regulation in the Light of the Airtours Judgement* [2002] European Competition Law Review 434.

Hawk Barry and Fuser Henry, European Community Merger Control: A Practitioner's Guide, (Kluwer Law International The Hague, 1996).

Herwig Hoffmann, *Good Governance in EU Merger Control. Due Process and Checks and Balances under Review* [2003] European Competition Law Review 119.

Hewitt Gary, *Portofolio Effects in Conglomerate Mergers*, 4 OECD Journal of Competition Law and Policy 66.

Hillion Christophe, *Partnership and Cooperation Agreements between the European Union and the New Independent States of the Ex-Soviet Union* [1998] European Foreign Affairs Review 399.

Himelfarb Allison, *The International Language of Convergence: Reviving Antitrust Dialogue between the United States and the European Union with a Uniform Understanding of "Extraterritoriality"* (1996) University of Pennsylvania Journal of International Economic Law 909.

Hochstadt Eric, *The Brown Shoe of European Union Competition Law* (2002) 24 Cardozo Law Review 287.

Hoelscher Jens and Stephan Johannes, *Competition Policy in Central Eastern Europe in the Light of the EU Accession* [2004] Journal of Common Market Studies 321.

Hofer Paul and Williams Mark, *Non-Horizontal Mergers* (2007) The European Antitrust Review 6.

Hoffmann Herwig, *Good Governance in EU Merger Control. UE Process and Checks and Balances under Review* [2003] European Competition Law Review 119.

Hovenkamp Herbert, Federal Antitrust Policy, (West Publishing Saint Paul Minnesota, 1994).

Huser Henry and Depoortere Frederic, *Substantive Enforcement in Horizontal Mergers Under the EC Merger Regulation*, 17 Antitrust (Autumn 2002) 44.

Hudec Robert, *A WTO Perspective on Private Anti-Competitive Behaviour in World Markets* (1999–00) 34 New England Law Review 79.

Idot Laurence, *Note à Entreprise de Pâte de Bois c. Commission des Communautés Européennes* [1989] Revue trimestrielle de Droit Européen 341.

——, *L'internationalisation du droit de la concurrence* (2000) 3 La Semaine Juridique-Enteprise et Affaires 27.

——, *Mondialisation, liberté et régulation de la concurrence* [2001] Revue Internationale de Droit Economique 175.

——, *Deux interdictions annulées par le Tribunal: Tempête sur le contrôle des concentrations*, Europe, (December 2002) 12.

Jacquemin Alexis, *International Dimension of EU Competition Policy* (1993) Journal of Common Market Studies 91.

Jalabert-Doury Nathalie, *Concentration et position dominante collective après l'arrêt Airtours: Le point sur le concept, les facteurs et les critères* La Semaine Juridique, Cahiers du Droit de l'Entreprise, (November 2002) 1.

——, *The International Competition Network: Convergence dans le domaine des concentrations?* [2003] Revue de Droit des Affaires Internationales 702.

James Charles, *OECD Roundtable on Portfolio Effects in Conglomerate Mergers. Range Effects: The United States Perspectives* [2001] Fordham Corporate Law Institute 6.

Janow Merit, *Observations on Two Multilateral Venues: The International Competition Network (ICN) and the WTO* [2002] Fordham Corporate Law Institute 47.

Janow Merit and Cynthia Lewis, *International Antitrust and the Global Economy Perspectives on the Final Report and the Recommendations of the International Competition Policy Advisory Committee to the Attorney General and the Assistant Attorney General for Antitrust* (2001) 24(1) World Competition 3.

Jebsen Per and Stevens Robert, *Assumptions Goals and Dominant Undertakings: The Regulation of Competition under Article 86 of the European Union* (1996) 64 Antitrust Law 443.

Jennings R.Y., *Extraterritorial Jurisdiction and the United States Antitrust Law* [1957] British Yearbook of International Law 146.

Jenny Frederic, Globalization Competition and Trade Policy: Convergence, Divergence and Cooperation, in Clifford Jones and Mitsuo Matsushita (eds.) Competition Policy in the Global Trading System (Kluwer International Law The Hague/London, 2002).

——, *Competition Law and Policy: Global Governance Issues* (2003) 26 World Competition 609.

——, *Competition, Trade and Development before and after Cancun* [2003] Fordham Corporate Law Institute 631.

——, *International Cooperation on Competition Policy. Myth, Reality and Perspectives* (2003) 48 Antitrust Bulletin 4.

Jones A., Sufrin B., EC competition law: Text, cases and materials, (2004), Oxford University Press, ch. 12.

Jones Alison and Sufrin Brenda, EC Competition Law: Text, Cases and Materials, (Oxford University Press Oxford, 2004).

Jones Christopher and Gonzalez-Diaz Enriques, The EEC Merger Control Regulation, (Sweet & Maxwell London, 1992).

Jones Clifford, *Toward Global Competition Policy? The Expanding Dialogue on Multilateralism* (2000) 23(2) Journal of World Competition 25.

Jones Clifford and Matsushita Mitsuo (eds.) Competition Policy in the Global Trading System (Kluwer International Law The Hague/London, 2002).

Karpel Amy Ann, *The European Commission Decision on the Boeing-Mc Donnell Douglas Merger and the Need for Greater United States-European Union Cooperation in the Merger Field* (1997–98) 49 The American University Law Review 1029.

Käseberg Thorsten, *Are Merger Control and Article 82 EC in the Same Market?—The Assessment of Mergers Which Facilitate Exclusionary Conduct under EC Merger Control* [2006] European Competition Law Review 409.

Kaszorowska Alina, *International Competition Law in the Context of Global Competition Law* [2000] European Competition Law Review 117.

Kauper Thomas, *Merger Control in the United States and the European Union: Some Observations* (2000) 74 St. John Law Review 305.

Kennedy Kevin, Competition Law and the World Trade Organisation: The Limits of Multilateralism, (Sweet & Maxwell London, 2001).

Kerremans Bart, *What Went in Cancun? A Principal-Agent View on the EU's Rationale towards the Doha Development Round* [2004] European Foreign Affair 363.

Kerse C., *EC merger control*, (2005), Sweet and Maxwell.

Kerse C., Khan N., *EC antitrust procedure*, Sweet and Maxwell, 2005.

Kintner Earl, Federal Antitrust Law, Volume IV, (Anderson Publishing, Cincinnati, 1984)

Kokkoris Ioannis, *The Reform of the European Control Merger Regulation in the Aftermath of the Airtours Case—the Eagerly Expected Debate: SLC v Dominance Test* [2005] European Competition Law Review 37.

Kolasky William J., *GE/Honeywell: Continuing the Transatlantic Dialogue* [2002] University of Pennsylvania Journal of International Economic Law 513.
——, *GE/Honeywell: Narrowing, But Not Closing The Gap* Antitrust, Spring 2006, 69.
Kolasky William J. and Greenfield Leon B., *A View to a Kill* Legal Times, (30 July 2001) Vol. XXIV NO. 31.
Korah V., *EC Competition law and practice*, Hart publishing, 2004.
Korah Valentine, *Gencor v. Commission: Collective Dominance* [1999] European Competitive Law Review 334.
Kovacic William, *Transatlantic Turbulence: The Boeing-Mc Donnell Douglas Merger and International Competition Policy* (2000–01) 68 Antitrust Law 805.
Lampert Thomas, *International Cooperation among Competition Authorities* [1999] European Competition Law Review 214.
Lange Dieter and Sandage John Byron, *The Wood Pulp Decision and its Implications for the Scope of EC Competition* [1989] European Competition Law Review 137.
Lanucara Lucio, *Interaction between Antitrust and International trade: In favour of a WTO Approach* [2001] Il Diritto del Commercio Internazionale 395.
Lastra Rosa Maria, Central Banking and Banking Regulation (Financial Market Group London School of Economics, London, 1996).
Lenaerts Koen and Van Nuffel Piet, Constitutional Law of the European Union, (Sweet Maxwell London 2005).
Ligneul Nicolas *Droit International de la concurrence: plaidoyer pour une approche intégrée et progressive* [1999] Revue du Marché Commun et de l'Union Européenne 458.
Lipsky Abbot, *Competition and the WTO: Beyond Cancun* [2003] Fordham Corporate Law Institute 657.
Lispey R, Chrystal K., *Economics*, Oxford University Press, 2003.
Lowenfeld Andreas, International Economic Law, (Oxford University Press Oxford, 2002).
Luz Kathleen, *The Boeing-Mc Donnell Douglas Merger: Competition Law, Parochialism and the Need for a Globalized Antitrust System* (1999–00) 32 George Washington Journal of International Law & Economics 155.
Maher I., *Competition law and intelelctual property rights: Evolving formalism*, in P. Craig and G. De Bùrga (eds.), *The evolution of EU law*, Oxford University Press, 1999, ch. 16.
Mann F.A. *The Doctrine of Jurisdction in International Law* (1964) 3 Academie de droit International recueil des Courses 13.
——, *The Public International of Restrictive Practices in the European Court of Justice* [1989] International Comparative Law Quarterly 375.
Maresceau Marc and Montaguti Elisabetta, *The Relation between the European Union and the Central and Eastern Europe: A Legal Apprasail*, [1995] Common Market Law Review 1327.
Marsden Philip, *Dealing with International Exclusion. The Right Focus for the WTO Working Group on Trade and Competition Policy*, (1997) 21(2) World Competition 91.
——, *Tune in to the International Competition Network—not the WTO—for Practical Advances in International Antitrust* In Competition (December 2001) 3.
——, *Not the End but the End of the Beginning: Competition Policy at the WTO* Competition Law Insight (November 2002) 6.
——, A Competition Policy for the WTO (Cameron May, London, 2003).
——, *Trade and Competition. Competition after Cancun—A Personal View* Competition Law Insight (October 2003) 22.
——, *Trade and Competition: WTO decides first competition case with disappointing results* Competition Law Insight (May 2004) 3.
Mathijsen S., A *guide to European Union law*, (2007), Sweet and Maxwell.
Matsushita Mitsuo, *Reflections on Competition Law/Policy in the Framework of the WTO* [1997] Fordham Corporate Law Institute 36.
Matsushita Mitsuo, Schoenbaum Thomas and Mavroidis Petros, The World Trade Organization Law, Practice, and Policy (Oxford University Press Oxford, 2003).
Matsushita Mitsuo and Watanabe Eriko, Japan, in Maher Dabbah and Paul Lasok (eds), Merger Control Worldwide (Cambridge University Press, Cambridge 2005).
Mazzoni Alberto, *Globalizzazione, commercio internazionale e giustiziabilità di pretese private fondate su norme internazionali* [2006] Il Diritto del Commercio Internazionale 255.

Mc Guinness John, *The Political Economy of International Antitrust Harmonization* (2003) 45 William and Mary Law Review 549.
McDavid Janet L., *Globalization of Pre-merger Notification and Review: Practical Problems and Solutions* [1999] Fordham Corporate Law Institute 31.
McDavid Janet L. and Nauwelaerts Wim J., *Antitrust Law* The National Law Journal (7 January 2002).
Megliani Mario, *Il caso Microsoft: l'accesso alla rete e le sue implicazioni transnazionali,* [2001] Il Diritto Commerciale Internazionale 43.
——, *La riforma della disciplina comunitaria del controllo delle concentrazioni tra imprese* [2004] Il Diritto del Commercio Internazionale 685.
Melamed Douglas, *International Antitrust in an Age of International Deregulation,* (1997–98) 6 George Mason Law Review 437.
——, *Antitrust Enforcement in a Global Economy* [1998] Fordham Corporate Law Institute 1.
——, *International Cooperation in Competition Law and Policy* [1999] Journal of International Economic Law 427.
Messen Karl, *Antitrust Jurisdiction under International Law,* [1984] American Journal of International Law 783.
Mette Alfter, *Tetra Laval/Sidel and the Future of EC Merger Control,* Lawyers' Europe (Winter 2003) 17.
——, Bishop Simon and Mahr Eric, *New Horizontal Merger Guidelines: Plugging the Gap or Opening the Floodgates?* [2004] Business Law International 385.
Miller Debra and Davidow Joel, *Antitrust and the United States: A Tale of Two Codes,* (1982) 18 Stanford Journal of International Law 347.
Miller Russell Victor, *Australia Merger Control Laws,* in William Rowley and Donald Baker (eds.) International Mergers (Sweet and Maxwell, London 2000).
Miller Todd and Donald Baker, *USA Merger Control Laws* in William Rowley and Donald Baker (eds.) International Mergers (Sweet and Maxwell, London 2000).
Mitchell Andrew, *Broadening the View of Trade Liberalisation: International Competition Law and the WTO* 24 (2001) World Competition 243.
Mollard John, *Asean Overview* The International Financial Law Review Guide to Merger and Acquisition (2004).
Monti Mario, *La dimensione internazionale della politica di concorrenza europea* [2001] Mercato Concorrenza Regole 423.
——, *The External Aspects of EU Competition Policy* [2002] European Foreign Affairs 235.
Montini Massimiliano, *Globalization and International Antitrust Cooperation* <www.unisi.it>.
Motta Massimo, *EC Merger Policy and the Airtours Case* [2000] European Competition Law Review 199.
Muchlinski Peter, Multinational Entreprises and the Law (Blackwell Oxford, 1999).
Muris Timothy, *Competition Agencies in a Market-Based Global Economy* [2002] European Foreign Affairs 241.
Murphy Gavin, *Responding to the Challenges of a Globalised Marketplace* [2002] European Competition Law Review 227.
Nascimbene Bruno, *Aspetti internazionali della politica di concorrenza comunitaria* [2001] Il Diritto del Commercio Internazionale 309.
Neale A.D. and Stephens Mel, International Business and National Jurisdiction, (Claredon Press, Oxford, 1988).
Nollkaemper Andre, *Rethinking States' Rights to Promote Extraterritorial Values* in (F. Weiss, E. Denters and P. de Waart eds.) International Economic with a Human Face (Kluwer Law International The Hague, 1988).
Norton Joseph, *A New International Financial Architecture?—Reflections on the Possible Law-Based Dimension* (1999) 33 International Lawyer 891.
O'Connor Kevin, *Federalist Lessons for International Antitrust Convergence* [2002] Antitrust Law Journal 413.
O'Donaghue Robert and Feddersen Christoph, *Notes on Airtours v. Commission* [2002] Common Market Law Review 1171.
Odudu O., *The boundaries of EC competition law: The scope of article 81,* Oxford University Press, 2006.
Osti Cristoforo and Roberto Pardolesi, *Falsi amici: le concentrazioni in Europa e negli Stati Uniti* [2002] Giurisprudenza Commerciale (I) 153.

Osti Cristoforo and Roberto Pardolesi, *La decisione della Commissione CE sul caso General Electric/Honeywell* [2002] Giurisprudenza Commerciale (II) 311.
Overd Alan, *After the Airtours Appeal* [2002] European Competition Law Review 375.
Owen Deborah and Parisi John, *International Mergers and Joint Ventures: A Federal Trade Commission Perspective* [1990] Fordham Corporate Law Institute 1.
Palser Rebecca, *EU Competition 2002: The Even Full Monti* <www.worldmarketanalysis.com>.
Parisi John, *Enforcement Co-operation among Antitrust Authorities* [1999] European Competition Law Review 133.
Patterson Donna E. and Shapiro Carl, *Trans-Atlantic Divergence in GE/Honeywell: Causes and Lessons* Antitrust Magazine (Fall 2001) 18.
Paul Robert, *The Increasing Maze of International Pre-Acquisition Notification* [2001] International Company and Commercial Law Review 123.
Peck Brian, *Extraterritorial Application of Antitrust Law and the US-EU Dispute over the Boeing and Mac Donnell Douglas Merger: From Comity to Conflict? An Argument for a Binding International Agreement or Antitrust Enforcement and Dispute Resolution* (1998) 35 San Diego Law Review 1163.
Perez Antonio, *International Antitrust at the Crossroads: The End of Antitrust History or the Clash of Competition Policy Civilization* (2001–02) 33 Law and Policy in International Relations 527.
Petersmann E.C., *Reforming the world trading system*, Oxford University Press, (2005).
Petersmann Ernst-Ullrich, *Legal, Economic and Political Objectives of National and International Competition Policies: Constitutional Functions of WTO "Linking Principles" for Trade and Competition* (1997–98) 34 New England Law Review 145.
——, *WTO Core Principles and Trade/Competition Roundtable* [2003] Fordham Corporate Law Institute 669.
Pflanz Matthias *Oracle/Peoplesoft: the Economics of the Review* [2005] European Competition Law Review 123.
Picazo Buyco Tan Fider and Santos, Philippines, in Maher Dabbah and Paul Lasok (eds.) Merger Control Worldwide (Cambridge University Press, Cambridge 2005).
Piilola Anu, *Assessing Theories of Global Governance: A Case Study of International Antitrust* 39 (2003) Stanford Journal of International Law 207.
Pitofsky Robert, *Proposal for a Revised United States Merger Enforcement in a Global Economy* [1993] Georgetown Law Journal 195.
——, *International Antitrust: An FTC Perspective* [1995] Fordham Corporate Law Institute 1.
——, Antitrust Cooperation Global Trade and US Competition Policy, in (Jones and Matsushita eds.) Competition Policy in the Global Trading System, (Kluwer Law International, The Hague/London 2002).
Porter Elliott, *The Gencor Judgement: Collective Dominance, Remedies and Extraterritorial under the Merger Regulation* [1999] European Competition Law Review 638.
Portwood Timothy, Mergers Under EEC Competition Law, (The Athlone Press, London & Atlantic Highlands NJ, 1994).
Power Helen, *The Honeywell monster* The Lawyer (23 July 2001).
Pricewaterhouse Coopers, *A Tax on Mergers? Surveying the Time and Costs to Business of Multi-jurisdictional Merger Review* [2003] Business Law International 275.
Priest George and Romani Franco, *L'antitrust negli Stati Uniti e in Europa. Analisi e psicoanalisi di una divergenza* [2002] Mercato Concorrenza Regole 151.
Prosperi Mangilli Maria Luisa, *Merger Review in a Global Market from the EU-U.S. Perspective: International Co-operation and Harmonization* [2001] Contratto e Impresa/Europa 163
Qureshi Asif, International Economic Law, (Sweet & Maxwell London, 1999).
Ragolle Filip, *Schneider Electric v. Commission: The Court of First Instance; Response to the Green Paper on Merger Review* [2003] European Competition Law Review 176.
Rainelli Michel, *A propos du règlement européen n° 139/2004 relatif au contrôle des concentrations entre entreprises: une vision sceptique de la prise en compte des gains d'efficacité* [2006] Revue International de Droit Economique 45.
Raskid Leo, *Comment: Convergence and Harmonization of Antitrust Principles.*
Renzi Lisa, *The GE/Honeywell: Catalyst in the Transnational Conglomerate Merger Debate (2002) 37 New England Law Review 109.*

Reuland Robert, *Hartford Fire Insurance Co., Comity and Extraterritorial Reach of United States Antitrust Law* (1994) 29 Texas International Law Journal 159.

Reynolds Richard, Sicilian James and Wellmann Philip, *The Extraterritorial Application of the U.S. Antitrust Laws to Criminal Conspiracies* [1998] European Competition Law Review 151.

Ridyard D., *Exlusionary pricing and price discrimination abuses under article 82—An economic analysis*, ECLR, (2006), 286.

Riesenkampff Alexander, *The New EC Merger Control Test under Article 2 of the Merger Control Regulation* (2004) 24 Nortwestern Journal of International Law & Business 715.

Rigamonti Silvia, *I principi della comitas gentium negli Accordi tra Comunità Europee e Stati Uniti in materia di concorrenza* [1997] Il Diritto dell'Unione Europea 835.

Rill James and Metallo Virginia, *The Next Step: Convergence of Procedure and Enforcement* [1992] Fordham Corporate Law Institute 15.

Rill James and Soames Trevor, *Transatlantic Cooperation Paving the Way for Success* [2002] International Business Lawyer 483.

Rishikesh Deepa, *Extraterritorial Versus Sovereignty in International Antitrust Jurisdiction* (1991) 14 (3) World Competition 33.

Rivas Josè, The EU Merger Regulation and the Anatomy of the Merger Task Force, (Kluwer Law International The Hague/London, 1999).

Rodger Barry, *Competition Policy, Liberalism and Globalisation: A European Perspective* (2000) 6 Columbia Journal of European Law 289.

Rodger Barry and Mac Culloch Angus, Competition Law and Policy in the European Community and United Kingdom, (Cavendish Publishing London, 2001).

Rodriguez Armando, *On the Art of Slaying Dragons: The Case against the International Competition,* Competition Law Insight, (February 2003) 16.

Roebling Georg, Ryan Stephen and Sjoeblom Dan, *The International Competition Network (ICN) Two Years on: Concrete Results of a Virtual Network* Competition Policy Newsletter (Autumn 2003) 37.

Rowley William, 'IBA Agrees to Facilitate Global Competition Law Initiative and Cross-Border.

——, *The Internationalisation of Merger Review: Global Solutions Require Both Words and Actions* [2003] Business Law International 183

Rowley William and Campbell Neil, *Implementation of the International Competition Network's Recommended Practices for Merger Review: Final Survey on Practices IV–VII* (2005) 28 World Competition 533.

Rowley William and Donald Baker, *Introduction* in William Rowley and Donald Baker (eds.) International Mergers (Sweet and Maxwell, London 2000).

Ruffner Thomas, *The Failed GE/Honeywell Merger: The Return of Portfolio-Effects* [2003] De Paul Law Review 1285.

Ryngaert Cedric, *Foreign-to-Foreign Claims: the US Supreme Court's Decision (2004) v the English High Court's Decision (2003) in the Vitamins Case* [2004] European Competition Law Review 611.

Sabatini Michele, *Verso un assetto multilaterale di regole sulla concorrenza: The Doha Development Agenda e la creazione dell'ICN* [2002] Il Diritto del Commercio Internazionale 951.

Sabbatini Pierluigi, *Concentrazioni. Le tre sconfitte della Commissione in Tribunale* [2003] Mercato Concorrenza e Regole 159.

Samuels David and Bendell Emily *Rating Enforcement*, (2005) 5 Global Competition Review 2.

Saylor David, Pheasant John and Armengod Hector, *How Litigation May Affect The Mergers and Acquisitions Clearance Process: US and EU Compared* Global Competition Review, The Antitrust Review of Americas (2007).

Schaub Alexander, interview with, Antitrust (Fall 1997) 13.

Schere F, Ross D., *Industrial market structure and eonomic performance*, Houghton Mifflin, 1990.

Schmitz Stefan, *How Dare They? European Merger Control and the European Commission's Blocking of the General Electric/Honeywell Merger* (2002) 23 University of Pennsylvania Journal of International Economic Law 325.

——, *The European Commission's Decision in General Electric/Honeywell and the Question of the Goals of Antitrust Law* (2002) 23 University of Pennsylvania Journal of International Economic Law 539.

Schoenbaum Thomas, *The Theory of Contestable Markets in International Trade. A Rationale for Justifiable Unilateralism to Combat Restrictive Business Practice?* [1996] 3 Journal of World Trade 161.
Seidl-Hohenveldern Ignaz, *The Limit Imposed by International Law on the Application of Cartel Law* (1971) 5 International Lawyer.
Serebrisky Tomas, *What Do We Know about Competition Agencies in Emerging and Transition Countries? Evidence on Workload, Personnel, Property Sectors and Training Needs* (2004) 27 World Competition 651.
Shark Robert, *The Justice Department's Recent Antitrust Enforcement Policy: Toward a "Positive Comity" Solution to International Competition Problems?* (1996) 29 Vanderbilt Journal of Transnational Law 155.
Shaw Malcom, International Law, (University Press Cambridge Cambridge, 1997).
Shelanski Howard, Katz Michael, Mergers and innovation in antitrust, (2007) Antirust Law Journal, 1.
Shenefield John, *Coherence or Confusion: The Future of the Global Antitrust Conversation* (2004) 49 Antitrust Bulletin 385.
Silvestri Massimo, *Le Partenariat Euro-Mediterranéen* [2002] Revue de Marche Commun et de l'Union Européenne 183.
Singh Ajit, *Multilateral Competition Policy and Economic Development. A Developing Country Perspective on the EC Proposals*, UNCTAD Series on Issues in Competition Law and Policy, New York and Geneva 2004.
Slater Malcom, *L'application extraterritorial du droit communautaire* [1986] Cahiers du Droit Européen 309.
Slaughter Anne-Marie, *The Real New Order*, (1997) 76 Foreign Affairs 183.
Slot Piet Jan, *Note on Gencor v. Commission* (2001) 38 Common Market Law Review 1573.
Smets Hilde and Van Cayseele Patrick, *Competing Merger Policies in a Common Agency Framework* [1995] International Review of Law and Economics 15.
Smirne Paolo-Maria, *Antitrust e Joint-Ventures: il punto sull'esperienza italiana e sul modello comunitario* [2003] Giurisprudenza Italiana 1298.
Smith Patricia, *A Long and Winding Road: TRIPS and the Evolution of an International Competition Framework* [1999] Journal of International Economic Law 435.
Snyder David, *Mergers and Acquisitions in the European Community and the United States: A Movement Towards a Uniform Enforcement Body?* (1997–98) 29 Law & Policy in International Business 115.
Soames Trevor and Maudhuit Sylvie, *Changes in EU Merger Control: Part 1* [2005] European Competition Law Review 57.
——, *Changes in EU Merger Control: Part 2* [2005] European Competition Law Review 75.
——, *Changes in EU Merger Control: Part 3* [2005] European Competition Law Review 144.
Sornarajah M., *Towards an International Antitrust Law*, [1982] Indian Journal of International Law 1.
Stark Charles, *International Cooperation in the Pursuit of Cartels* (1997–98) 6 George Mason Law Review 531.
Steiner Josephine and Woods Lorna, Textbook on EC Law (Oxford University Press, Oxford 8th edition).
Stephan Johannes, *Competition Policy in Central Eastern Europe in the Light of the EU Accession* [2004] Journal of Common Market Studies 321.
Stephen D., *Mergers and merger remedies in the EU: Assesing the consequences for competition*, (2007), Cheltenham, UK, Edward Elgar J. Cook.
Stern Brigitte, *Une tentative d'élucidation du concept d'application extraterritoriale* [1986] Revue de Droit Québécoise de Droit International 48.
——, *L'extraterritorialité revisitée: Où il est question de l'affaire Alvarez-Machan, Pâte de Bois et de quelques autres* [1992] Annuaire Français de Droit International 239.
——, *Quelques observations sur les règles internationales relative a l'application extraterritorial du droit* [1986] Annuaire Français de Droit International 7.
Stevens Sarah, *The Increased Aggression of the EC Commission in Extraterritorial Enforcement of the Merger Regulation and its Impact on Transatlantic Cooperation in Antitrust* (2002) Syracuse Journal of International Law & Commerce.
Stewart Taimoon, *The Fate of Competition Policy in Cancun: Politcs or Substance* (2004) 31 Legal Issues of Economic Integration 7.

Stock Eric, *Explaining the Differing US and EU Position on the Boeing/Mc Donnell Douglas Merger—Avoiding Another Near Miss* [1999] University Of Pennsylvania Journal of International Economic Law 825

Stoll Neal and Goldfein Shepard, *A Tale of Two Regulators* [2001] New York Law Journal 226.

Swaine Edward T., *The Local Law of Global Antitrust* (2001–02) 43 William and Mary Law Review 641.

——, *Competition, not Competitors nor Canards: Ways of Criticizing the Commission* (2002) 23 University of Pennsylvania of Journal of International Economic Law 539

Tarullo Daniel, *Competition Policy for Global Market* [1999] Journal of International Economic Law 445.

——, *Norms and Institutions in Global Competition Policy* [2000] American Journal of International Law 478.

Temple Lang John, *Two Important Merger Regulation Judgements: The Implications of Schneider-Legrand and Tetra Laval-Sidel* [2003] European Law Review 259.

The Answer to Extraterritorial Issues in Merger Review (1997–98) 7 George Mason Law Review 525.

The Doha Agenda Competition Policy Newsletter (February 2002) 27.

Thouvenin Jean Marc, *L'arrêt Airtours du 6 Juin 2002: l'Irruption du juge dans le contrôle des concentrations entre entreprises* [2002] Revue de Marche Commun et de l'Union Européenne 482.

——, *Concurrence (concentration): Après l'arrêt Airtours trois nouveaux avertissements à la Commission*, [2003] Revue de Marche Commun et de l'Union Européenne 12.

Tizzano Antonio, *Appunti sulla cooperazione internazionale in tema di concorrenza* [1999] Il Diritto dell'Unione Europea 695.

——, *Quelques observations sur la coopération international en matière de concurrence*, [2000] Il Diritto dell'Unione Europea 75.

Todino Mario, *International Competition Network. The State of the Play after Naples* [2003] World Competition 283.

——, *La riforma del controllo delle concentrazioni nel diritto comunitario* [2004] Contratto e Impresa/Europa 1068.

Todorov Francisco and Valcke Anthony, *Procedural Aspects of Judicial Review of Merger Decision* Lawyers' Europe, (Winter 2003) 7.

Torremans Paul, *Extraterritorial Application of E.C. and U.S. Competition Law* [1996] European Law Review 280.

Toth A.G., The Oxford Encyclopaedia of European community law: volume III. Competition law and policy, Oxford University Press, (2008).

Trebilcock Michael and Iacobucci Edmund, *Designing Competition Law Institutions* (2002) 25 World Competition 361.

Turner James M., *Mega Merger, Mega Problems. A Critique of the European Community's Commission on Competition's Review of the AOL/Time Warner Merger* (2002) 17 American University International Law Review 131.

Ullrich Hanns, International Harmonisation of Competition Law: Making Diversity a Workable Concept in Hanns Ullrich (ed.) Comparative Competition Law: Approaching an International System of Antitrust Law, (Nomos Verlagsgesellschaft Baden-Baden).

——, (ed.) Comparative Competition Law: Approaching an International System of Antitrust Law, (Nomos Verlagsgesellschaft Baden-Baden, 1998).

Ulrich Schawalbe, Daniel Zimmel, Law and economics in european merger control, Oxford University Press, (2009).

Valentine Debra, Building a Cooperative Framework for Oversight in Mergers-**???**

Van den Bossche A.M., *The International Dimension of EC Competition. The Case of the Europe Agreements* [1997] European Competition Law Review 24.

Van Gerven Walter *EC Jurisdiction in Antitrust Matters: The Wood Pulp Judgement* [1992] Fordham Corporate Law Institute 71.

Van Gerven Walter and Hoet Lorelien, *Gencor: Some Notes on Transnational Competition Law Issues* (2001) 28 (2) Legal Issues of European Integration 195.

Van Miert Karel, *Competition Policy in Relation to the CEEC. Achievements and Challenges*, Competition Newsletter, (June 1998) 1.

Vickers J. *Competition, economics and policy*, (2003), ECLR, 95.
Vickers John, *Competition Economics and Policy* [2003] European Competition Law Review 95.
Voelcker Sven, *Leveraging as a theory of competitive harm in EU Merger Control* [2003] Common Market Law Review 581.
Voigt Stefan, *Switching to Substantial Impediments of Competition (SIC) Can Have Substantial Cost-SIC* [2004] European Competition Law Review 584.
Von Fickenstein Konrad, *International Antitrust Policy and the International Competition Network* [2002] Fordham Corporate Law Institute 37.
Von Meibom Wolfgang and Geiger Andreas, *A World Competition Law As an Ultima Ratio* [2002] European Competition Law Review 445.
Warner Mark, *After Seattle: Is There a Future for Trade and Competition Policy Role-making?* [2000] International Trade Law and Regulation 66.
Watson Peter, Flynn Joseph and Conwell Chad, Completing the World Trading System. Proposal for a Millennium Round (Kluwer Law International, The Hague/London 1999).
Waverman Leonard et al. (eds.), Competition Policy in the Global Economy: Modalities for Cooperation, (Routledge London & New York, 1997).
Weber Waller Spencer, *An International Common Law of Antitrust* (1999–00) 34 New England Law Review 163.
——, *Public Choice Theory and the International Harmonization of Antitrust Law* [2003] The Antitrust Bulletin 427.
Weinttraub Russel, *Globalization's Effect on Antitrust Law* (1999–00) 34 New England Law Review 27.
Weitbrecht Andreas, *EU Merger Control in 2001—The Year of Controversy* [2002] European Competition Law Review 407.
Wesseling R., *The modernisation of EC antitrust law*, Hart publishing, 2000.
Whish R., *Competition law*, Lexis Nexis, 2003.
Whish Richard, Competition Law, (Oxford University Press Oxford, 2005).
Whytock Christopher, *A Rational Design Theory of Transgovernmentalism: The Case of E.U.-U.S. Merger Review Cooperation* (2005) 23 Boston University International Law Journal 1.
Wijckmans Frank, *Internationalization of Competition Policy: Observations from a European Practioner's Perspectives* (2004) 48 Antitrust Bulletin 1037.
Wilson Joseph, Globalization and the Limits of National Merger Control Laws, (Kluwer Law International, The Hague/London/New York 2003).
Wisner Robert and Gallus Nick, *The Emergence of the WTO Competition Law: The Mexico Telecommunications and Canada. Wheat and Grain Decisions* [2004] International Trade and Law Review 91.
Witterick Crystal, *Foundation for an Effective Merger Law* in Global Competition Review, The 2006 Asia-Pacific Antitrust & Trade Review, 3.
Wood Diane, *The Impossible Dream: Real International Antitrust* [1992] University Chicago Legal B.277.
——, *International Harmonization of Antitrust Law* [2002] Chicago journal of International Law 391.
——, *Soft Harmonization Among Competition Laws: Track Record and Prospects* [2003] The Antitrust Bulletin 305.
Yeo Jin Chun, *The GE/Honeywell Merger Debacle: The Enforcement of Antitrust/Competition Laws Across the Atlantic Ponds* (2002) 13 New York International Law Review 61.
Ysewyn Johan, *The New World of the Merger Task Force* [2002] European Competition Law Review 207.
Zaman Niek, Cross-border mergers in Europe, (2006), European Journal of law reform, 124.
Zarzur Christianne, Barreira Lilian, Bonini Thiago and da Rocha V., Brazil, in Maher Dabbah and Paul Lasok (eds) Merger Control Worldwide (Cambridge University Press, Cambridge 2005).
Zweifel Thomas, *Best and Worst Practices in European, US and Swiss Merger Regulation*[2003] Journal of Common Market Studies.

INDEX

Nijhoff International Trade Law Series

ISSN 1877-7392

1. Zleptnig, S. *Non-Economic Objectives in WTO Law.* Justification Provisions of GATT, GATS, SPS and TBT Agreements. 2009. ISBN 978 90 04 17860 1
2. Liakopoulos, D. and A. Marsilia, *The Regulation of Transnational Mergers in International and European Law.* 2009. ISBN 978 90 04 17771 0

www.ingramcontent.com/pod-product-compliance
Lightning Source LLC
Chambersburg PA
CBHW071437230926
51846CB00001B/267
9789004177710